BBC

DOCTOR WHO

THE TWELFTH DOCTOR

VOL 3: HYPERION

"Nothing short of extraordinary. *Doctor Who: The Twelfth Doctor* just keeps getting better."
SNAP POW

"Gets inside you and will not let you go. A feast for the eyeballs!"
WARPED FACTOR

"Fans, you'll be pleasantly surprised – and if you're new to the series, then this is the comic for you!"
FLICKERING MYTH

"I'm strapped in for the ride!"
NEEDLESS ESSENTIALS

"Exciting, fast-moving, funny, and mysterious."
GEEK MOM

"Has every trademark of a classic, Moffat-written episode."
MIND OF THE GEEK

"Highly recommended!"
COMIC OF THE DAY

"One of the finest introductions to everything Doctor Who."
KABOOOOM

"So reminiscent of the TV show, you'll be reading it from behind the sofa!"
POP CULTURE BANDIT

"`A wonderful spot for a new reader to jump in."
THE GEEK GIRL PROJECT

"A dazzling and delightful adventure."
BLOGTOR WHO

"Good, old-fashioned scary *Who!*"
NEWSARAMA

"Feels like an episode of the series!"
HOW TO LOVE COMICS

"Feels exactly like the best-written episodes of the eighth season!"
WHATCHA READING

TITAN COMICS

EDITOR
Andrew James

ASSISTANT EDITORS
Gabriela Houston
& Jessica Burton

COLLECTION DESIGNER
Rob Farmer

SENIOR EDITOR
Steve White

TITAN COMICS EDITORIAL
Lizzie Kaye, Tom Williams

PRODUCTION SUPERVISORS
Maria Pearson, Jackie Flook

PRODUCTION CONTROLLER
Obi Onuora

STUDIO MANAGER
Selina Juneja

SENIOR SALES MANAGER
Steve Tothill

SENIOR MARKETING & PRESS OFFICER
Owen Johnson

DIRECT SALES & MARKETING MANAGER
Ricky Claydon

COMMERCIAL MANAGER
Michelle Fairlamb

PUBLISHING MANAGER
Darryl Tothill

PUBLISHING DIRECTOR
Chris Teather

OPERATIONS DIRECTOR
Leigh Baulch

EXECUTIVE DIRECTOR
Vivian Cheung

PUBLISHER
Nick Landau

Special thanks to
Steven Moffat, Brian Minchin, Mandy Thwaites, Matt Nicholls, James Dudley, Edward Russell, De Ritchie, Scott Handcock, Kirsty Mullan, Kate Bush, J Nocciolino, and Ed Casey for their invaluable assist

BBC WORLDWIDE

DIRECTOR OF EDITORIAL GOVERNANCE
Nicolas Brett

DIRECTOR OF CONSUMERPRODUCTS AND PUBLISHING
Andrew Moultrie

HEAD OF UK PUBLISHING
Chris Kerwin

PUBLISHER
Mandy Thwaites

PUBLISHING CO-ORDINATOR
Eva Abramik

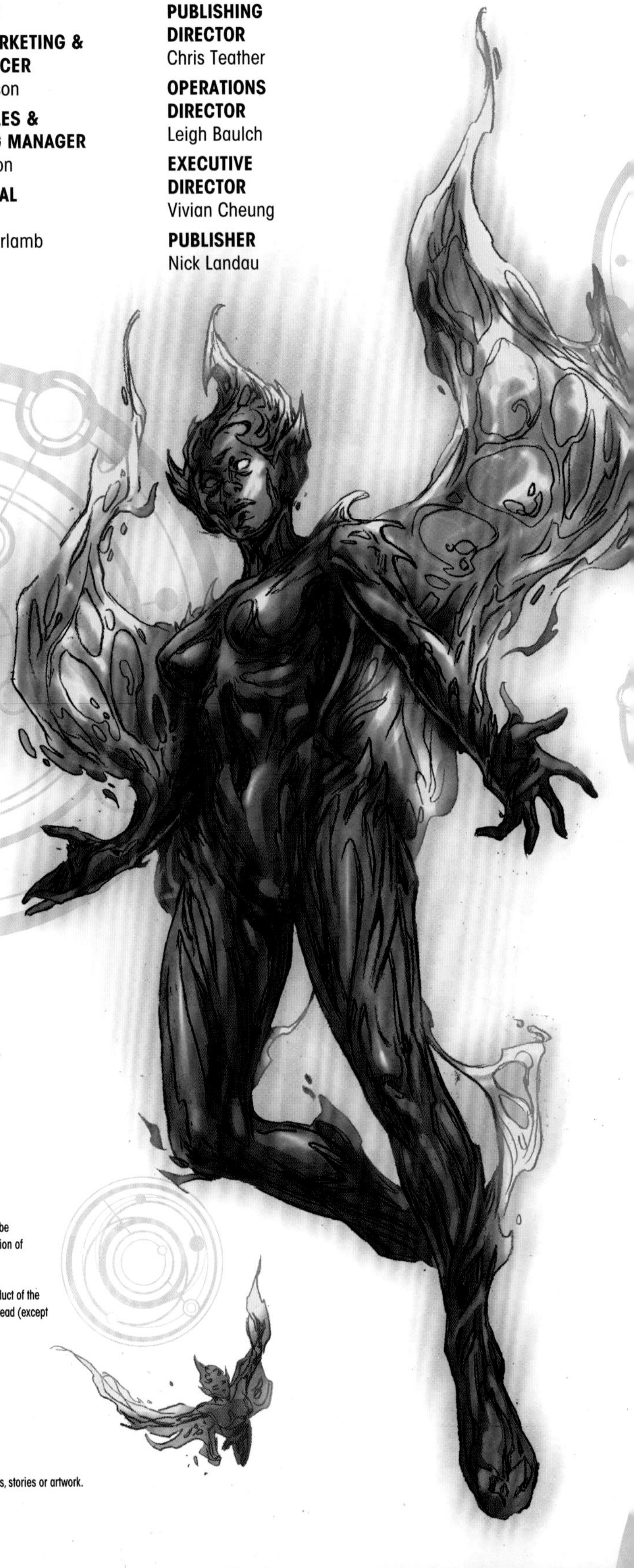

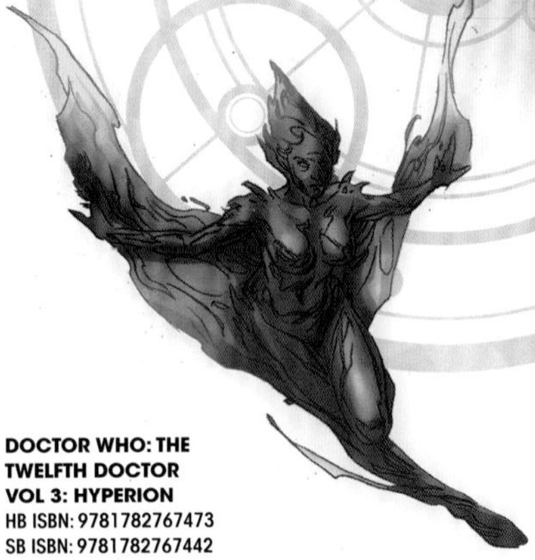

DOCTOR WHO: THE TWELFTH DOCTOR VOL 3: HYPERION
HB ISBN: 9781782767473
SB ISBN: 9781782767442

Published by Titan Comics, a division of Titan Publishing Group, Ltd. 144 Southwark Street, London, SE1 0UP.

A CIP catalogue record for this title is available from the British Library.
First edition: April 2016

10 9 8 7 6 5 4 3 2 1

Printed in China. TC0930.

DOCTOR WHO

THE TWELFTH DOCTOR

VOL 3: HYPERION

WRITERS: ROBBIE MORRISON, GEORGE MANN

ARTISTS: DANIEL INDRO, MARIANO LACLAUSTRA, RONILSON FREIRE

COLORISTS: SLAMET MUJIONO, LUIS GUERRERO

LETTERS: RICHARD STARKINGS AND COMICRAFT'S JIMMY BETANCOURT

www.titan-comics.c•••

BBC

DOCTOR WHO

THE TWELFTH DOCTOR

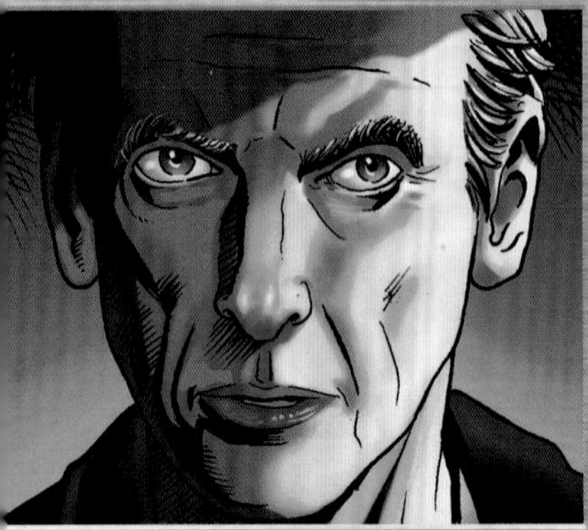

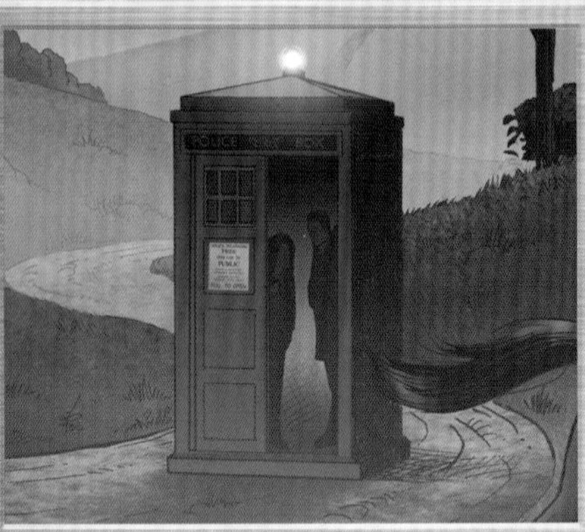

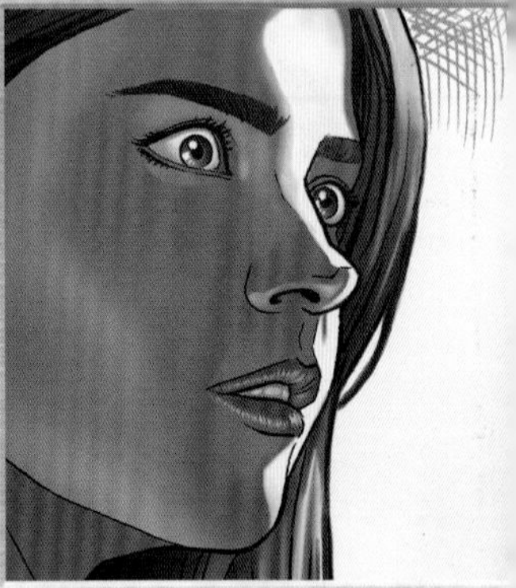

THE DOCTOR

An alien who walks like a man. Last of the Time Lords of Gallifrey. Never cruel or cowardly, he champions the oppressed across time and space. Forever traveling, the Doctor lives to see the universe anew through the eyes of his human companions!

THE TARDIS

'Time and Relative Dimension in Space'. Bigger on the inside, this unassuming blue box is your ticket to unforgettable adventure!

The Doctor likes to think he's in control, but more often than not, the TARDIS takes him where and when he needs to be...

CLARA OSWALD

Clara Oswald has stuck with the Doc through thick and thin, witnessing all manner of strange, wonderful an terrifying things in his company!

Now a teacher at Coal Hill School she juggles her 'real life' on Earth with her secret adventures aboard the TARDIS!

PREVIOUSLY...

When Clara and the Doctor landed in 1960s Las Vegas for rest and relaxation, their luck quickly ran out! A group of intergalactic high-stakes marauders, known as the Cybock Imperium, crashed the party, intent on world domination – and on erasing all who stood against them with the help of a stolen Time Lord weapon!

Now, having saved existence from the tyrannical tentacles of the Cybocks, the Doctor and Clara set off in search of a new adventure, further into the past...

When you've finished reading the collection, please email your thoughts to doctorwhocomic@titanemail.com

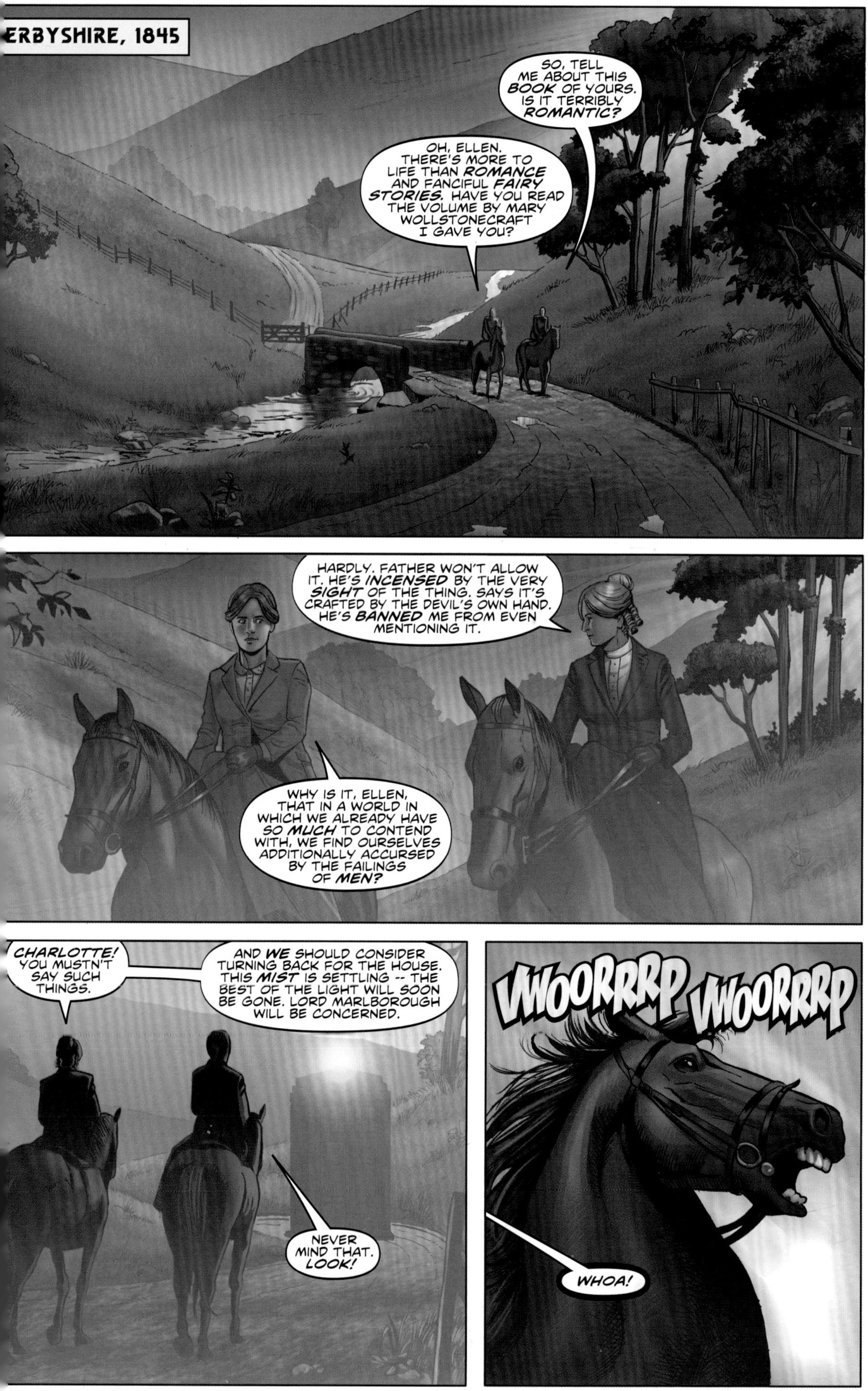
ERBYSHIRE, 1845
SO, TELL ME ABOUT THIS BOOK OF YOURS. IS IT TERRIBLY ROMANTIC?
OH, ELLEN. THERE'S MORE TO LIFE THAN ROMANCE AND FANCIFUL FAIRY STORIES. HAVE YOU READ THE VOLUME BY MARY WOLLSTONECRAFT I GAVE YOU?
HARDLY. FATHER WON'T ALLOW IT. HE'S INCENSED BY THE VERY SIGHT OF THE THING. SAYS IT'S CRAFTED BY THE DEVIL'S OWN HAND. HE'S BANNED ME FROM EVEN MENTIONING IT.
WHY IS IT, ELLEN, THAT IN A WORLD IN WHICH WE ALREADY HAVE SO MUCH TO CONTEND WITH, WE FIND OURSELVES ADDITIONALLY ACCURSED BY THE FAILINGS OF MEN?
CHARLOTTE! YOU MUSTN'T SAY SUCH THINGS.
AND WE SHOULD CONSIDER TURNING BACK FOR THE HOUSE. THIS MIST IS SETTLING -- THE BEST OF THE LIGHT WILL SOON BE GONE. LORD MARLBOROUGH WILL BE CONCERNED.
NEVER MIND THAT. LOOK!
VWOORRRP VWOORRRP
WHOA!

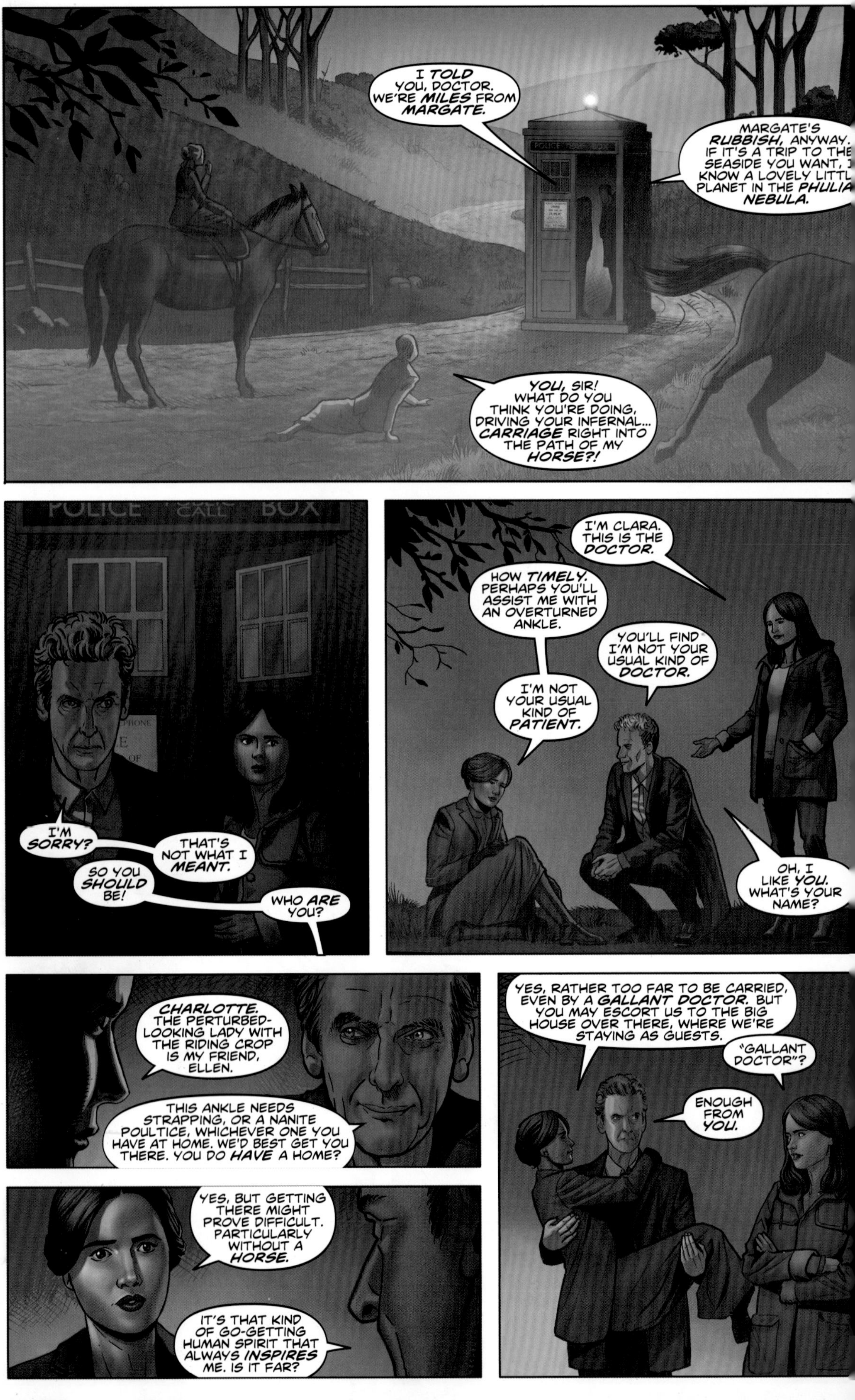
I TOLD YOU, DOCTOR. WE'RE MILES FROM MARGATE.
MARGATE'S RUBBISH, ANYWAY. IF IT'S A TRIP TO THE SEASIDE YOU WANT, I KNOW A LOVELY LITTL PLANET IN THE PHULIA NEBULA.
YOU, SIR! WHAT DO YOU THINK YOU'RE DOING, DRIVING YOUR INFERNAL... CARRIAGE RIGHT INTO THE PATH OF MY HORSE?!
I'M SORRY?
THAT'S NOT WHAT I MEANT.
SO YOU SHOULD BE!
WHO ARE YOU?
I'M CLARA. THIS IS THE DOCTOR.
HOW TIMELY. PERHAPS YOU'LL ASSIST ME WITH AN OVERTURNED ANKLE.
YOU'LL FIND I'M NOT YOUR USUAL KIND OF DOCTOR.
I'M NOT YOUR USUAL KIND OF PATIENT.
OH, I LIKE YOU. WHAT'S YOUR NAME?
CHARLOTTE. THE PERTURBED-LOOKING LADY WITH THE RIDING CROP IS MY FRIEND, ELLEN.
THIS ANKLE NEEDS STRAPPING, OR A NANITE POULTICE, WHICHEVER ONE YOU HAVE AT HOME. WE'D BEST GET YOU THERE. YOU DO HAVE A HOME?
YES, BUT GETTING THERE MIGHT PROVE DIFFICULT. PARTICULARLY WITHOUT A HORSE.
IT'S THAT KIND OF GO-GETTING HUMAN SPIRIT THAT ALWAYS INSPIRES ME. IS IT FAR?
YES, RATHER TOO FAR TO BE CARRIED, EVEN BY A GALLANT DOCTOR. BUT YOU MAY ESCORT US TO THE BIG HOUSE OVER THERE, WHERE WE'RE STAYING AS GUESTS.
"GALLANT DOCTOR"?
ENOUGH FROM YOU.

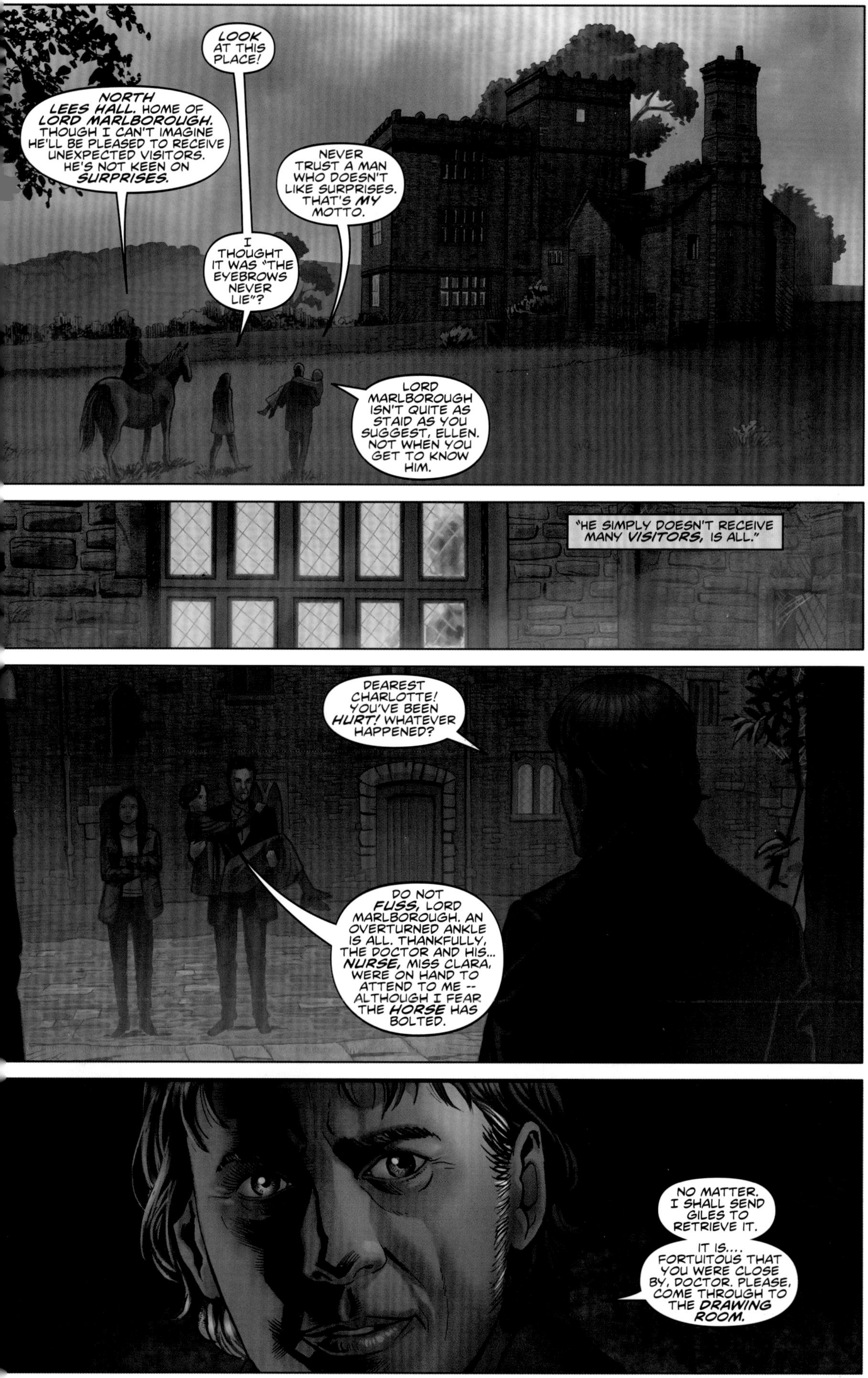
NORTH LEES HALL. HOME OF LORD MARLBOROUGH. THOUGH I CAN'T IMAGINE HE'LL BE PLEASED TO RECEIVE UNEXPECTED VISITORS. HE'S NOT KEEN ON SURPRISES.
LOOK AT THIS PLACE!
NEVER TRUST A MAN WHO DOESN'T LIKE SURPRISES. THAT'S MY MOTTO.
I THOUGHT IT WAS "THE EYEBROWS NEVER LIE"?
LORD MARLBOROUGH ISN'T QUITE AS STAID AS YOU SUGGEST, ELLEN. NOT WHEN YOU GET TO KNOW HIM.
"HE SIMPLY DOESN'T RECEIVE MANY VISITORS, IS ALL."
DEAREST CHARLOTTE! YOU'VE BEEN HURT! WHATEVER HAPPENED?
DO NOT FUSS, LORD MARLBOROUGH. AN OVERTURNED ANKLE IS ALL. THANKFULLY, THE DOCTOR AND HIS... NURSE, MISS CLARA, WERE ON HAND TO ATTEND TO ME -- ALTHOUGH I FEAR THE HORSE HAS BOLTED.
NO MATTER. I SHALL SEND GILES TO RETRIEVE IT.
IT IS.... FORTUITOUS THAT YOU WERE CLOSE BY, DOCTOR. PLEASE, COME THROUGH TO THE DRAWING ROOM.

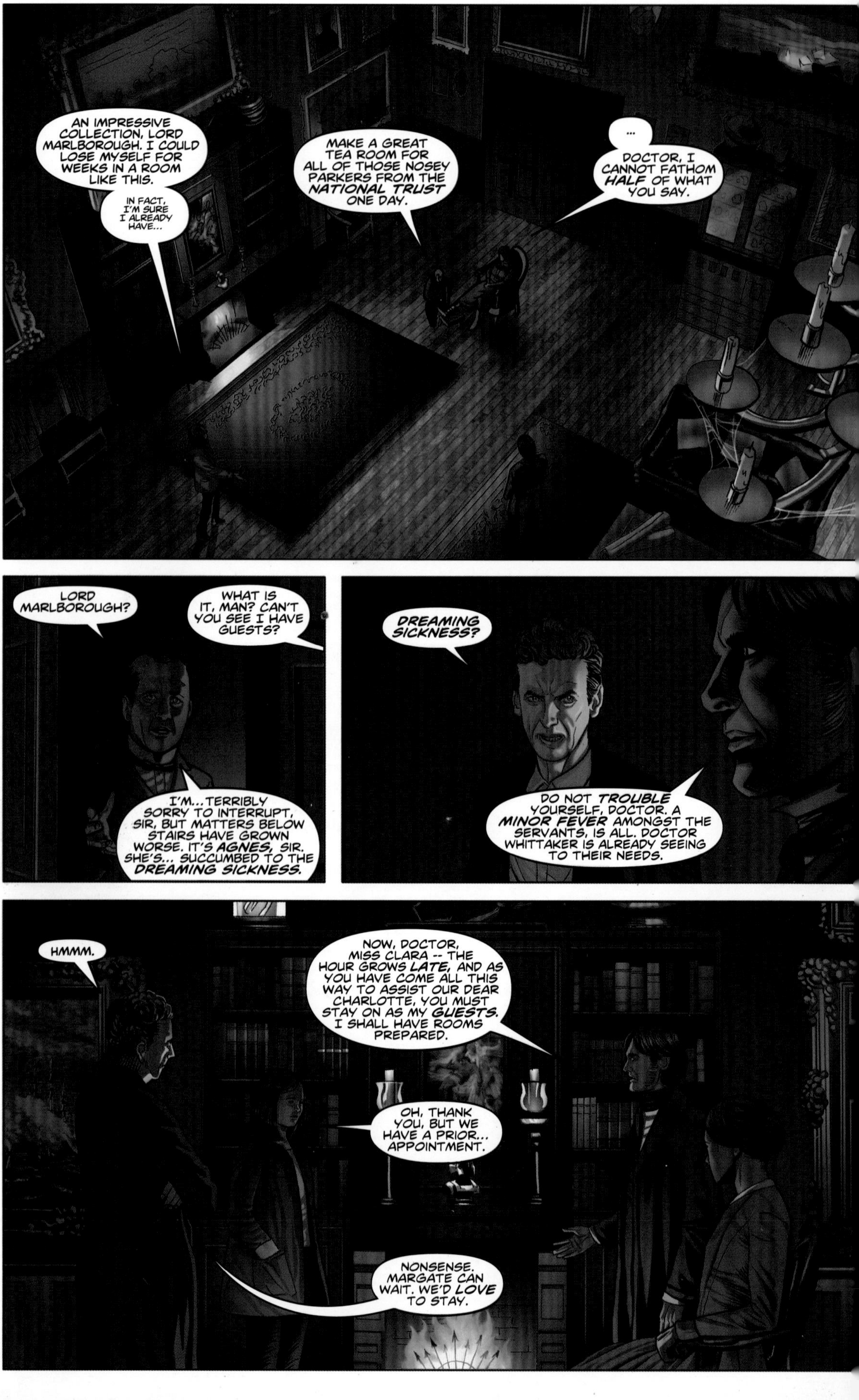
AN IMPRESSIVE COLLECTION, LORD MARLBOROUGH. I COULD LOSE MYSELF FOR WEEKS IN A ROOM LIKE THIS.
IN FACT, I'M SURE I ALREADY HAVE...
MAKE A GREAT TEA ROOM FOR ALL OF THOSE NOSEY PARKERS FROM THE NATIONAL TRUST ONE DAY.
...
DOCTOR, I CANNOT FATHOM HALF OF WHAT YOU SAY.
LORD MARLBOROUGH?
WHAT IS IT, MAN? CAN'T YOU SEE I HAVE GUESTS?
I'M... TERRIBLY SORRY TO INTERRUPT, SIR, BUT MATTERS BELOW STAIRS HAVE GROWN WORSE. IT'S AGNES, SIR. SHE'S... SUCCUMBED TO THE DREAMING SICKNESS.
DREAMING SICKNESS?
DO NOT TROUBLE YOURSELF, DOCTOR. A MINOR FEVER AMONGST THE SERVANTS, IS ALL. DOCTOR WHITTAKER IS ALREADY SEEING TO THEIR NEEDS.
HMMM.
NOW, DOCTOR, MISS CLARA -- THE HOUR GROWS LATE, AND AS YOU HAVE COME ALL THIS WAY TO ASSIST OUR DEAR CHARLOTTE, YOU MUST STAY ON AS MY GUESTS. I SHALL HAVE ROOMS PREPARED.
OH, THANK YOU, BUT WE HAVE A PRIOR... APPOINTMENT.
NONSENSE. MARGATE CAN WAIT. WE'D LOVE TO STAY.

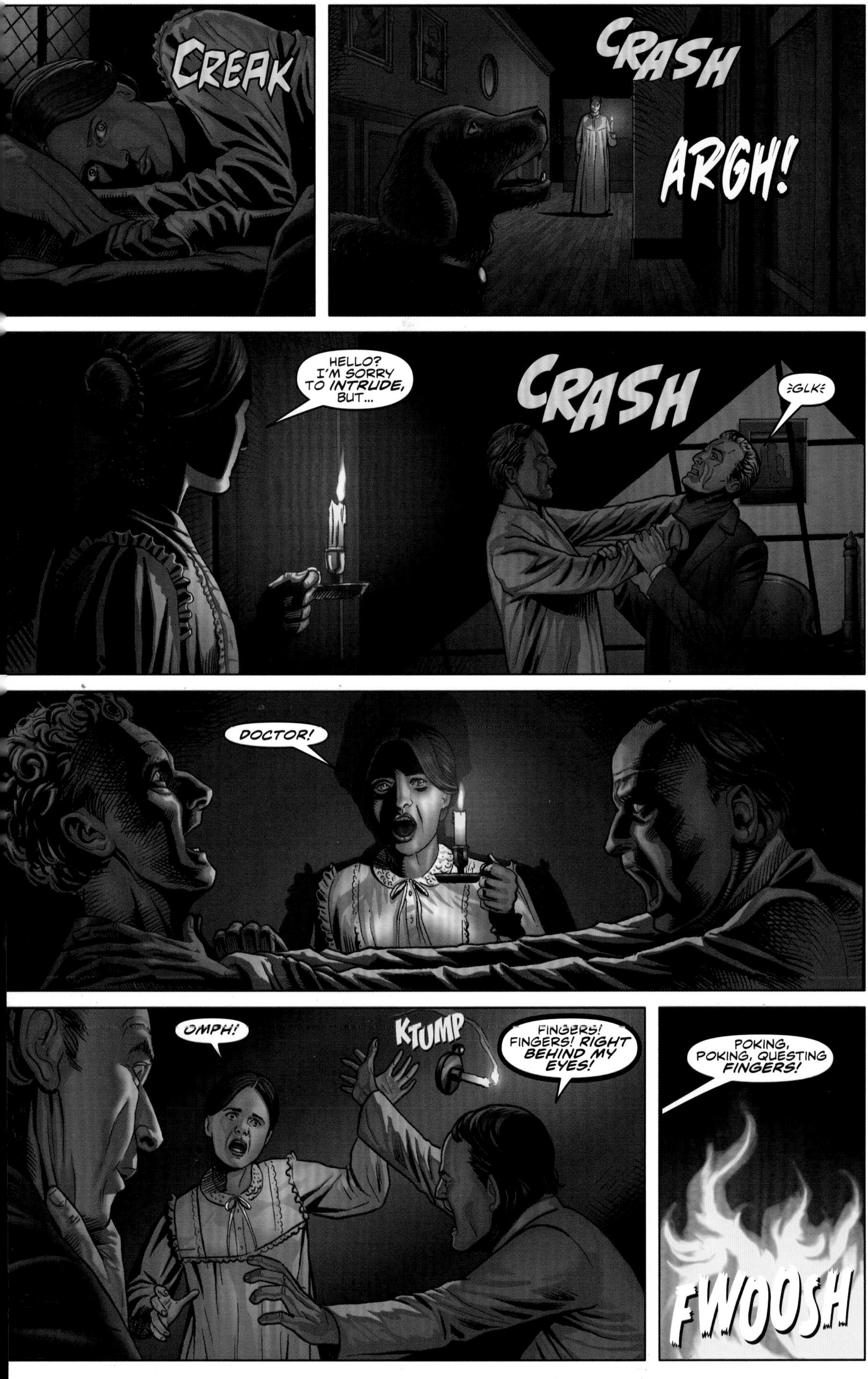
CREAK
CRASH
ARGH!
HELLO? I'M SORRY TO INTRUDE, BUT...
CRASH
GLK
DOCTOR!
OMPH!
KTUMP
FINGERS! FINGERS! RIGHT BEHIND MY EYES!
POKING, POKING, QUESTING FINGERS!
FWOOSH

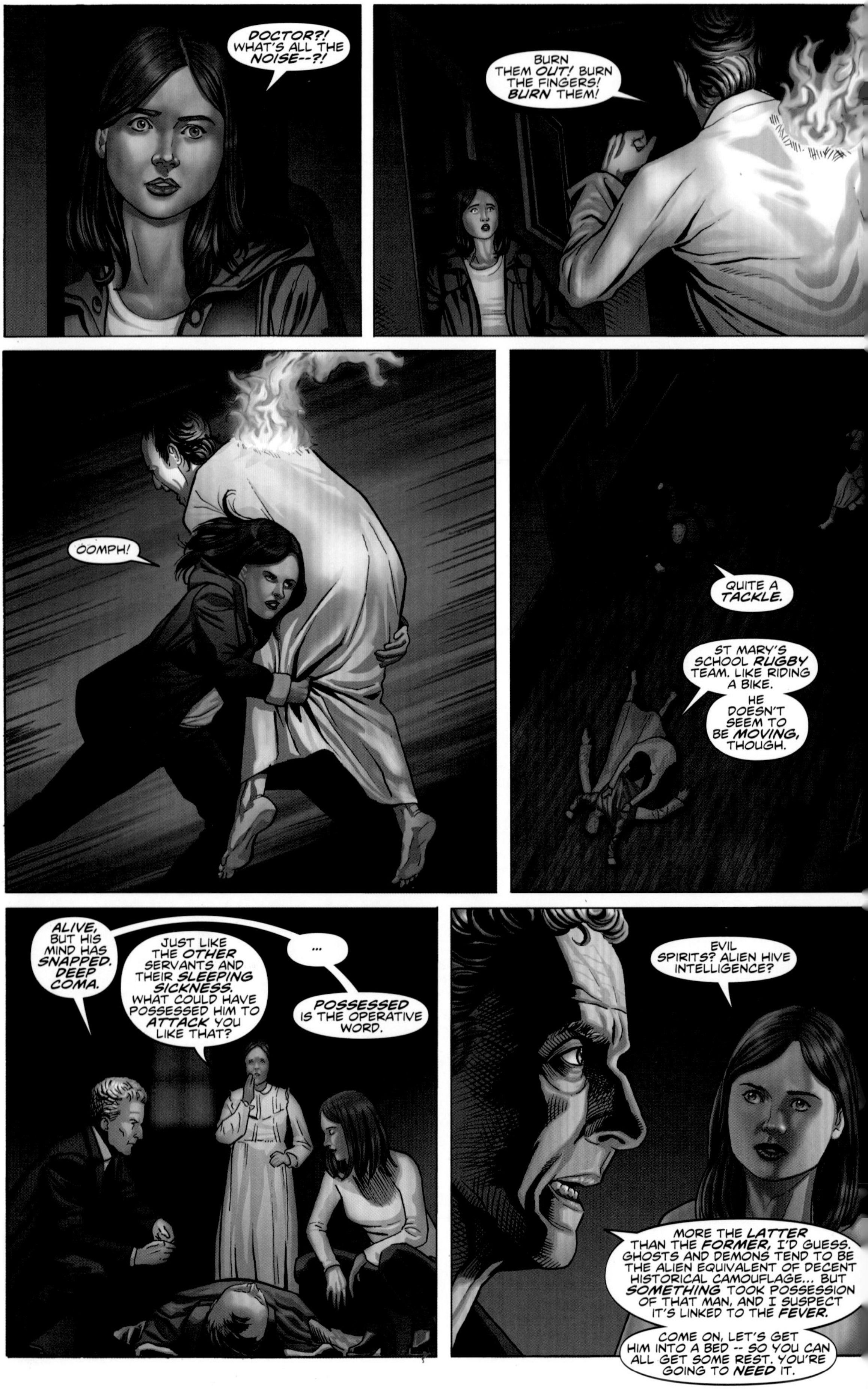
DOCTOR?! WHAT'S ALL THE NOISE--?!
BURN THEM OUT! BURN THE FINGERS! BURN THEM!
OOMPH!
QUITE A TACKLE.
ST MARY'S SCHOOL RUGBY TEAM. LIKE RIDING A BIKE.
HE DOESN'T SEEM TO BE MOVING, THOUGH.
ALIVE, BUT HIS MIND HAS SNAPPED. DEEP COMA.
JUST LIKE THE OTHER SERVANTS AND THEIR SLEEPING SICKNESS. WHAT COULD HAVE POSSESSED HIM TO ATTACK YOU LIKE THAT?
...
POSSESSED IS THE OPERATIVE WORD.
EVIL SPIRITS? ALIEN HIVE INTELLIGENCE?
MORE THE LATTER THAN THE FORMER, I'D GUESS. GHOSTS AND DEMONS TEND TO BE THE ALIEN EQUIVALENT OF DECENT HISTORICAL CAMOUFLAGE... BUT SOMETHING TOOK POSSESSION OF THAT MAN, AND I SUSPECT IT'S LINKED TO THE FEVER.
COME ON, LET'S GET HIM INTO A BED -- SO YOU CAN ALL GET SOME REST. YOU'RE GOING TO NEED IT.

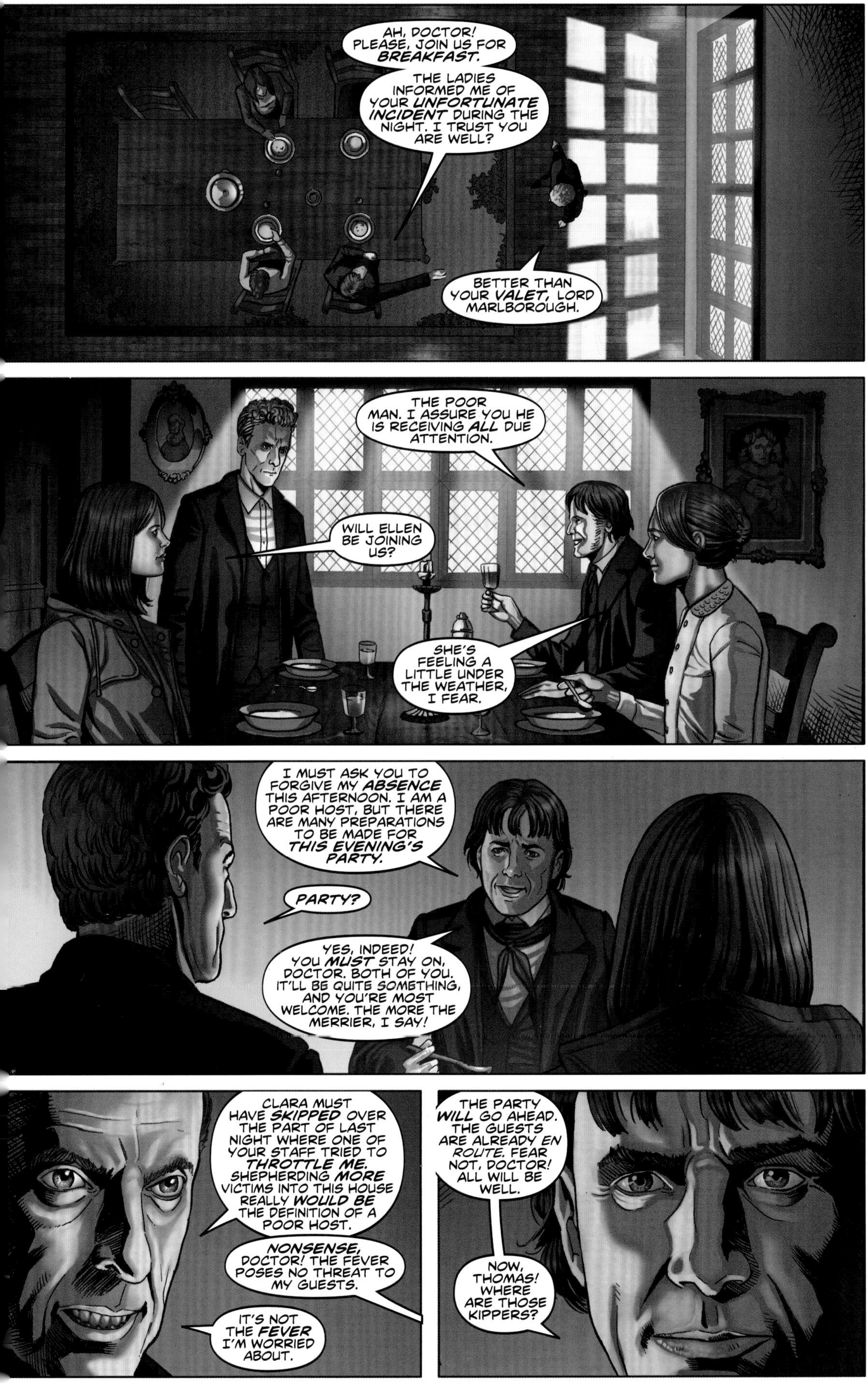

AH, DOCTOR! PLEASE, JOIN US FOR BREAKFAST.
THE LADIES INFORMED ME OF YOUR UNFORTUNATE INCIDENT DURING THE NIGHT. I TRUST YOU ARE WELL?
BETTER THAN YOUR VALET, LORD MARLBOROUGH.
THE POOR MAN. I ASSURE YOU HE IS RECEIVING ALL DUE ATTENTION.
WILL ELLEN BE JOINING US?
SHE'S FEELING A LITTLE UNDER THE WEATHER, I FEAR.
I MUST ASK YOU TO FORGIVE MY ABSENCE THIS AFTERNOON. I AM A POOR HOST, BUT THERE ARE MANY PREPARATIONS TO BE MADE FOR THIS EVENING'S PARTY.
PARTY?
YES, INDEED! YOU MUST STAY ON, DOCTOR. BOTH OF YOU. IT'LL BE QUITE SOMETHING, AND YOU'RE MOST WELCOME. THE MORE THE MERRIER, I SAY!
CLARA MUST HAVE SKIPPED OVER THE PART OF LAST NIGHT WHERE ONE OF YOUR STAFF TRIED TO THROTTLE ME. SHEPHERDING MORE VICTIMS INTO THIS HOUSE REALLY WOULD BE THE DEFINITION OF A POOR HOST.
NONSENSE, DOCTOR! THE FEVER POSES NO THREAT TO MY GUESTS.
IT'S NOT THE FEVER I'M WORRIED ABOUT.
THE PARTY WILL GO AHEAD. THE GUESTS ARE ALREADY EN ROUTE. FEAR NOT, DOCTOR! ALL WILL BE WELL.
NOW, THOMAS! WHERE ARE THOSE KIPPERS?

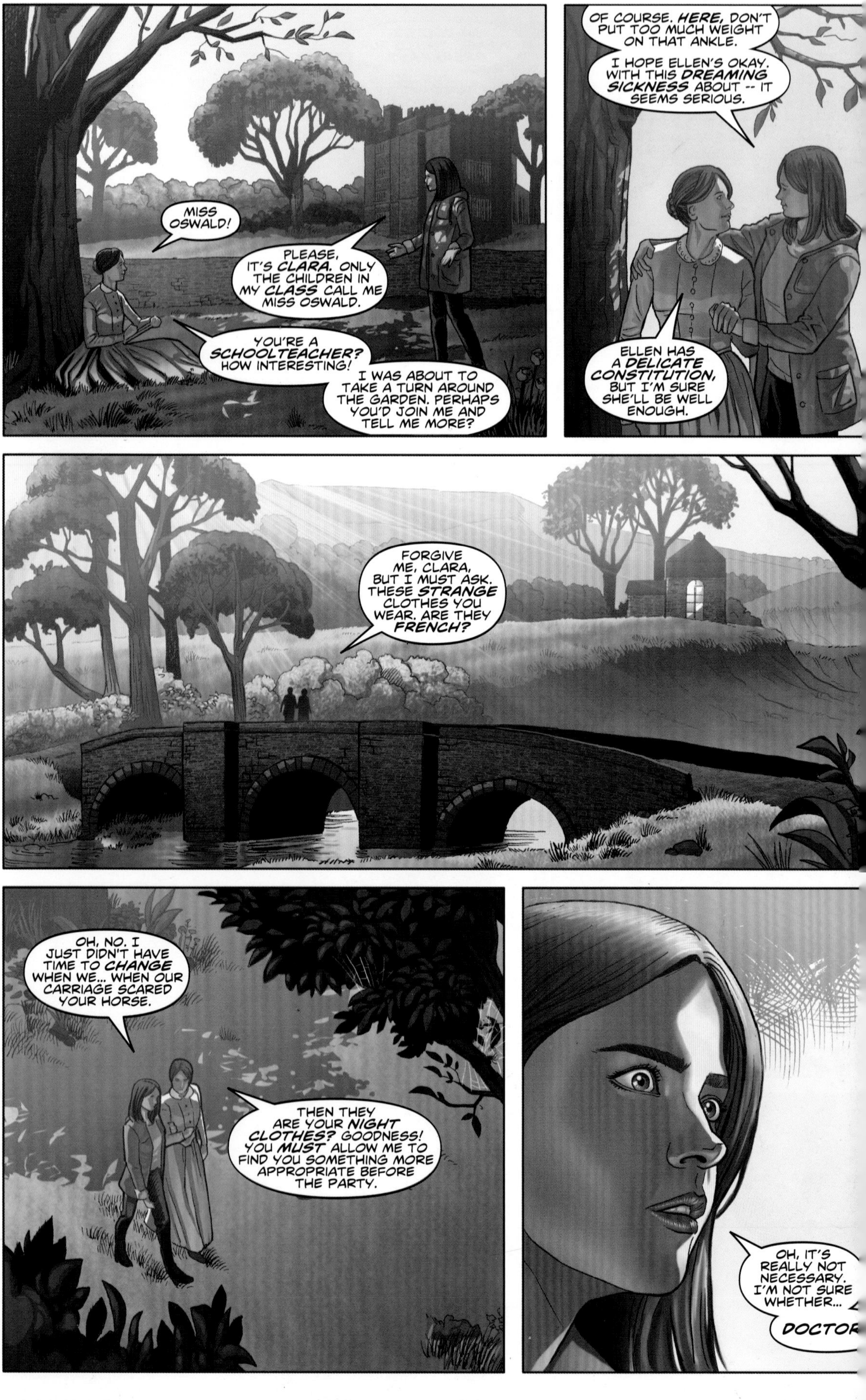
MISS OSWALD!
PLEASE, IT'S CLARA. ONLY THE CHILDREN IN MY CLASS CALL ME MISS OSWALD.
YOU'RE A SCHOOLTEACHER? HOW INTERESTING!
I WAS ABOUT TO TAKE A TURN AROUND THE GARDEN. PERHAPS YOU'D JOIN ME AND TELL ME MORE?
OF COURSE. HERE, DON'T PUT TOO MUCH WEIGHT ON THAT ANKLE.
I HOPE ELLEN'S OKAY. WITH THIS DREAMING SICKNESS ABOUT -- IT SEEMS SERIOUS.
ELLEN HAS A DELICATE CONSTITUTION, BUT I'M SURE SHE'LL BE WELL ENOUGH.
FORGIVE ME, CLARA, BUT I MUST ASK. THESE STRANGE CLOTHES YOU WEAR. ARE THEY FRENCH?
OH, NO. I JUST DIDN'T HAVE TIME TO CHANGE WHEN WE... WHEN OUR CARRIAGE SCARED YOUR HORSE.
THEN THEY ARE YOUR NIGHT CLOTHES? GOODNESS! YOU MUST ALLOW ME TO FIND YOU SOMETHING MORE APPROPRIATE BEFORE THE PARTY.
OH, IT'S REALLY NOT NECESSARY. I'M NOT SURE WHETHER...

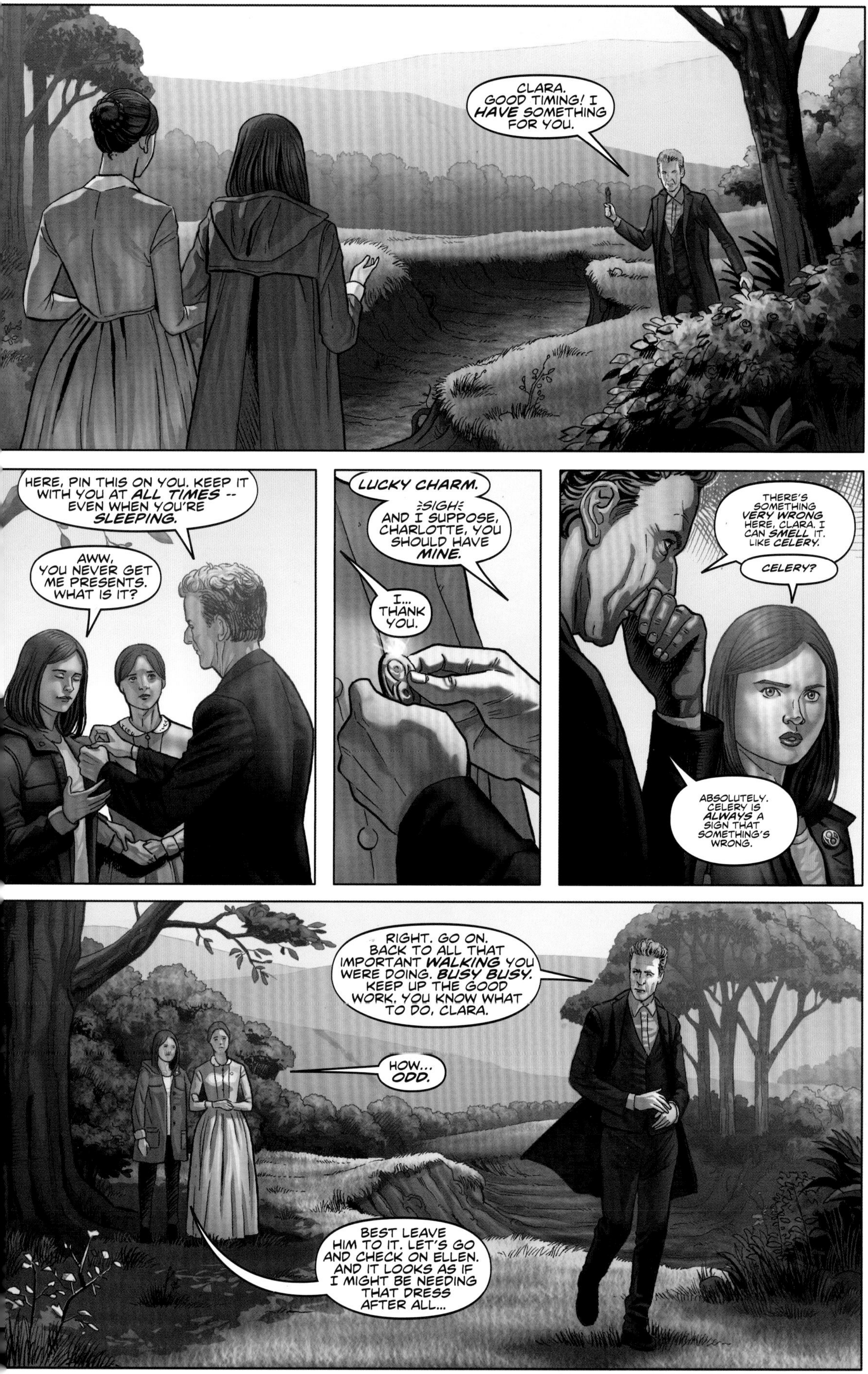
CLARA. GOOD TIMING! I HAVE SOMETHING FOR YOU.
HERE, PIN THIS ON YOU. KEEP IT WITH YOU AT ALL TIMES -- EVEN WHEN YOU'RE SLEEPING.
AWW, YOU NEVER GET ME PRESENTS. WHAT IS IT?
LUCKY CHARM.
SIGH AND I SUPPOSE, CHARLOTTE, YOU SHOULD HAVE MINE.
I... THANK YOU.
THERE'S SOMETHING VERY WRONG HERE, CLARA. I CAN SMELL IT. LIKE CELERY.
CELERY?
ABSOLUTELY. CELERY IS ALWAYS A SIGN THAT SOMETHING'S WRONG.
RIGHT. GO ON. BACK TO ALL THAT IMPORTANT WALKING YOU WERE DOING. BUSY BUSY. KEEP UP THE GOOD WORK. YOU KNOW WHAT TO DO, CLARA.
HOW... ODD.
BEST LEAVE HIM TO IT. LET'S GO AND CHECK ON ELLEN. AND IT LOOKS AS IF I MIGHT BE NEEDING THAT DRESS AFTER ALL...

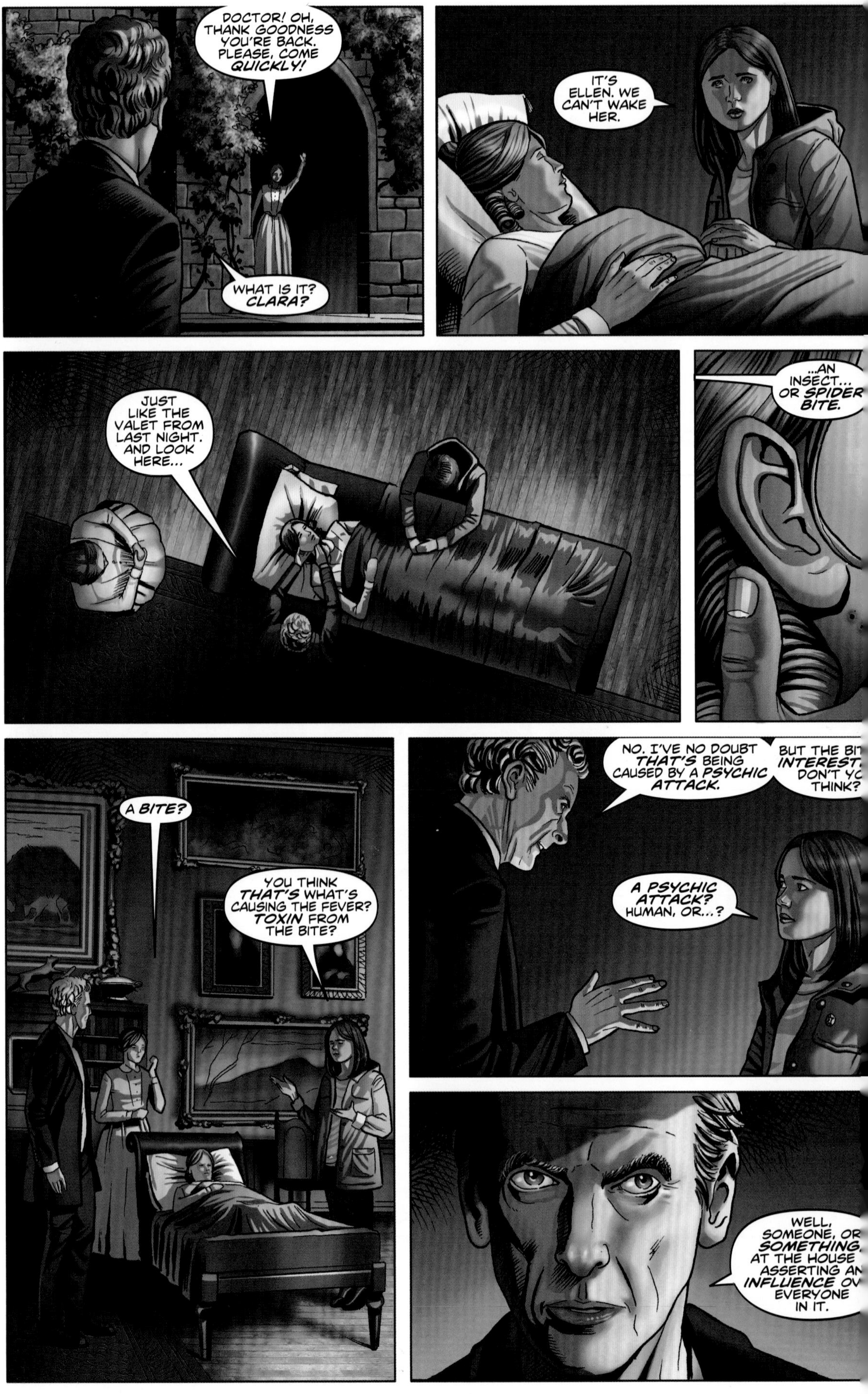
DOCTOR! OH, THANK GOODNESS YOU'RE BACK. PLEASE, COME QUICKLY!
WHAT IS IT? CLARA?
IT'S ELLEN. WE CAN'T WAKE HER.
JUST LIKE THE VALET FROM LAST NIGHT. AND LOOK HERE...
...AN INSECT... OR SPIDER BITE.
A BITE?
YOU THINK THAT'S WHAT'S CAUSING THE FEVER? TOXIN FROM THE BITE?
NO. I'VE NO DOUBT THAT'S BEING CAUSED BY A PSYCHIC ATTACK.
BUT THE BIT INTEREST DON'T YO THINK?
A PSYCHIC ATTACK? HUMAN, OR...?
WELL, SOMEONE, OR SOMETHING, AT THE HOUSE ASSERTING AN INFLUENCE OV EVERYONE IN IT.

THEN WHY AREN'T *WE*--?

THE *BROOCHES.* THEY'RE NEGATING THE EFFECT, CREATING A *PROTECTIVE FIELD* AROUND YOU.

WHAT ABOUT *YOU?* YOU GAVE YOUR BROOCH TO CHARLOTTE.

WHATEVER IT IS, IT WASN'T EXPECTING *MY* BRAIN. I CAN HOLD OUT... FOR A WHILE, AT LEAST.

AND ELLEN?

DOCTOR, IF YOU KNOW WHAT'S GOING ON...

SOME. NOT ENOUGH. I'D TELL YOU IF I DID. ALL I KNOW IS IT'S *NOT GOOD.*

STAY HERE, KEEP AN EYE ON ELLEN. AND *MARLBOROUGH.*

WHERE ARE *YOU* GOING?

CHARLOTTE'S GOING TO SHOW ME THE *STABLE BLOCK.* I'VE A FEELING I'LL FIND SOME ANSWERS THERE.

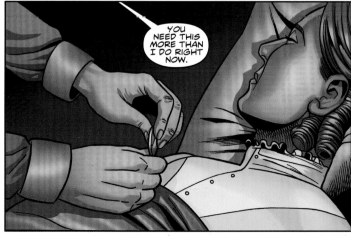

YOU NEED THIS MORE THAN I DO RIGHT NOW.

THERE'S *HIDDEN TECHNOLOGY* AROUND HERE, CHARLOTTE. SOMETHING THAT SHOULDN'T EXIST IN THIS *CENTURY.* SOMETHING THAT SHOULDN'T EXIST ON THIS *PLANET.*

BREEE

IN THERE...

... AND SUDDENLY THINGS START TO MAKE A LOT MORE *SENSE.*

NOT TO *ME!* WHAT IS THAT THING?

A *SALVAGED* SPACE VESSEL. IT LOOKS AS IF SOMEONE IS ATTEMPTING TO *REPAIR* IT.

YOU CAN'T BE *SERIOUS!*

OH, I'M *VERY* SERIOUS. SOMETHING *CRASHED* -- FURROWS IN THE FLOWERBEDS. LIKELY THE *SAME* SOMETHING THAT'S BEEN *POKING AROUND* IN THE *MINDS* OF THE PEOPLE HERE.

LORD MARLBOROUGH HAS AN *UNWANTED* VISITOR... AND I'M NOT TALKING ABOUT *CLARA.*

WHAT ARE WE GOING TO DO?

WE'RE GOING BACK TO THE HOUSE TO *RUIN* LORD MARLBOROUGH'S PARTY.

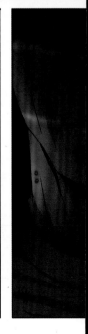

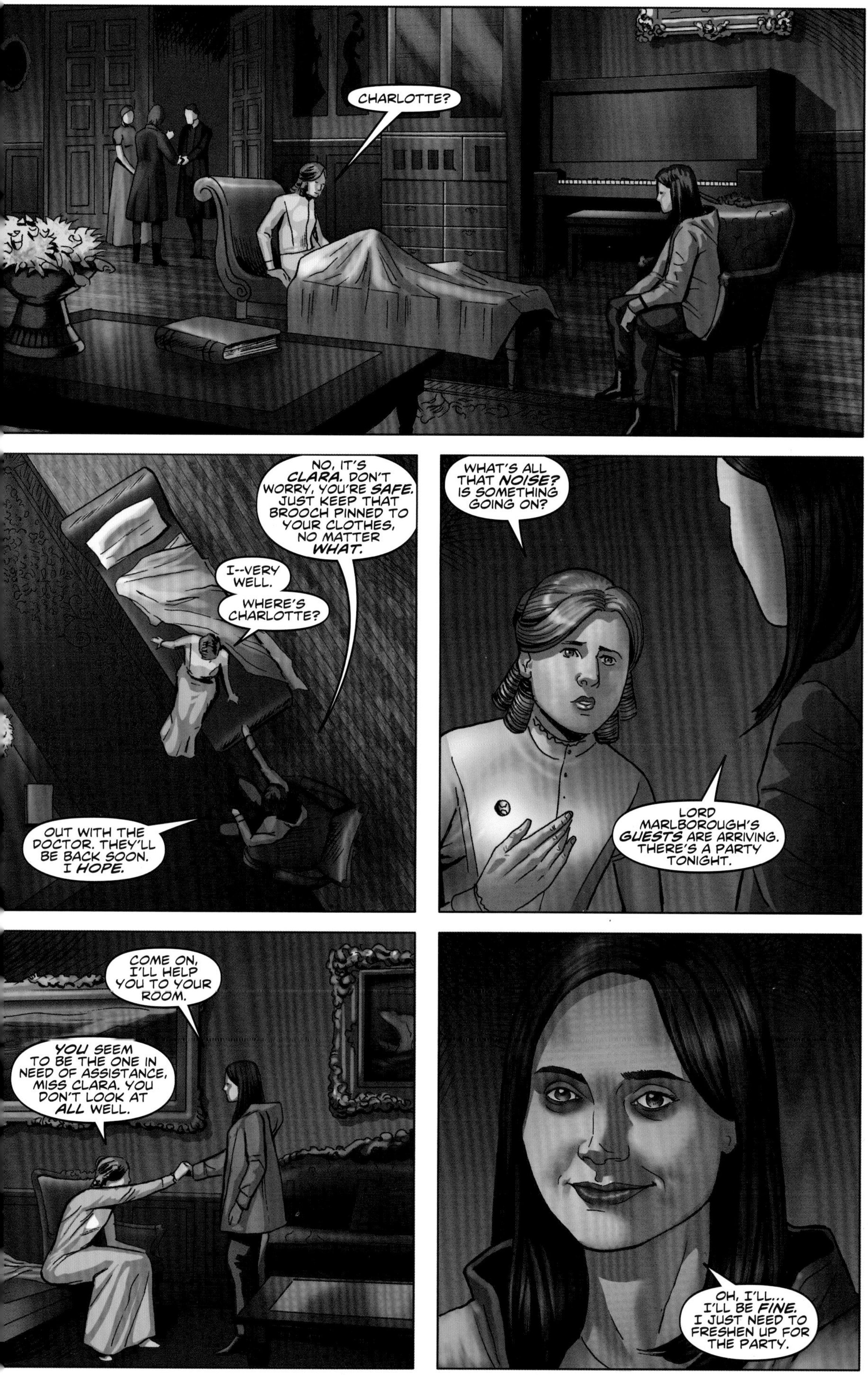
CHARLOTTE?
NO, IT'S CLARA. DON'T WORRY, YOU'RE SAFE. JUST KEEP THAT BROOCH PINNED TO YOUR CLOTHES, NO MATTER WHAT.
I--VERY WELL.
WHERE'S CHARLOTTE?
OUT WITH THE DOCTOR. THEY'LL BE BACK SOON. I HOPE.
WHAT'S ALL THAT NOISE? IS SOMETHING GOING ON?
LORD MARLBOROUGH'S GUESTS ARE ARRIVING. THERE'S A PARTY TONIGHT.
COME ON, I'LL HELP YOU TO YOUR ROOM.
YOU SEEM TO BE THE ONE IN NEED OF ASSISTANCE, MISS CLARA. YOU DON'T LOOK AT ALL WELL.
OH, I'LL... I'LL BE FINE. I JUST NEED TO FRESHEN UP FOR THE PARTY.

WHATEVER *HAS* HAPPENED TO CHARLOTTE AND THE DOCTOR?

THEY WENT FOR A WALK IN THE GROUNDS... AND MUST HAVE BEEN *WAYLAID.* I'M... SURE THEY'LL BE ALONG SHORTLY.

SKKTTRR

SKKTTRR

SKKTTRR

WHAT A SHAME! THEY'RE GOING TO MISS ALL OF THE *FUN.*

SKKTTRR

SKKTTRR

SKKTTR

SKKTTR

OWWW!

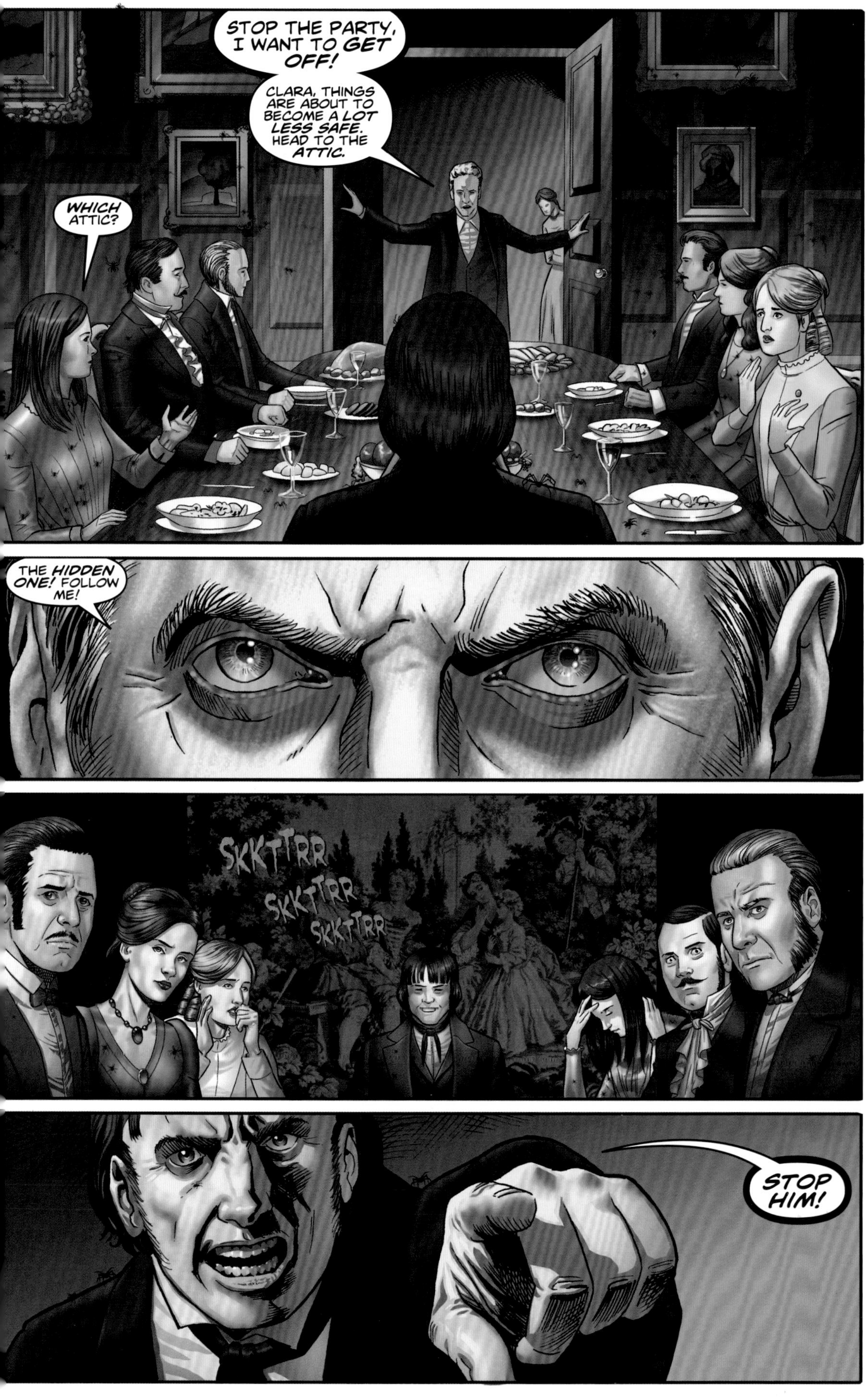
STOP THE PARTY, I WANT TO GET OFF!
CLARA, THINGS ARE ABOUT TO BECOME A LOT LESS SAFE. HEAD TO THE ATTIC.
WHICH ATTIC?
THE HIDDEN ONE! FOLLOW ME!
SKKTTRR
SKKTTRR
SKKTTRR
STOP HIM!

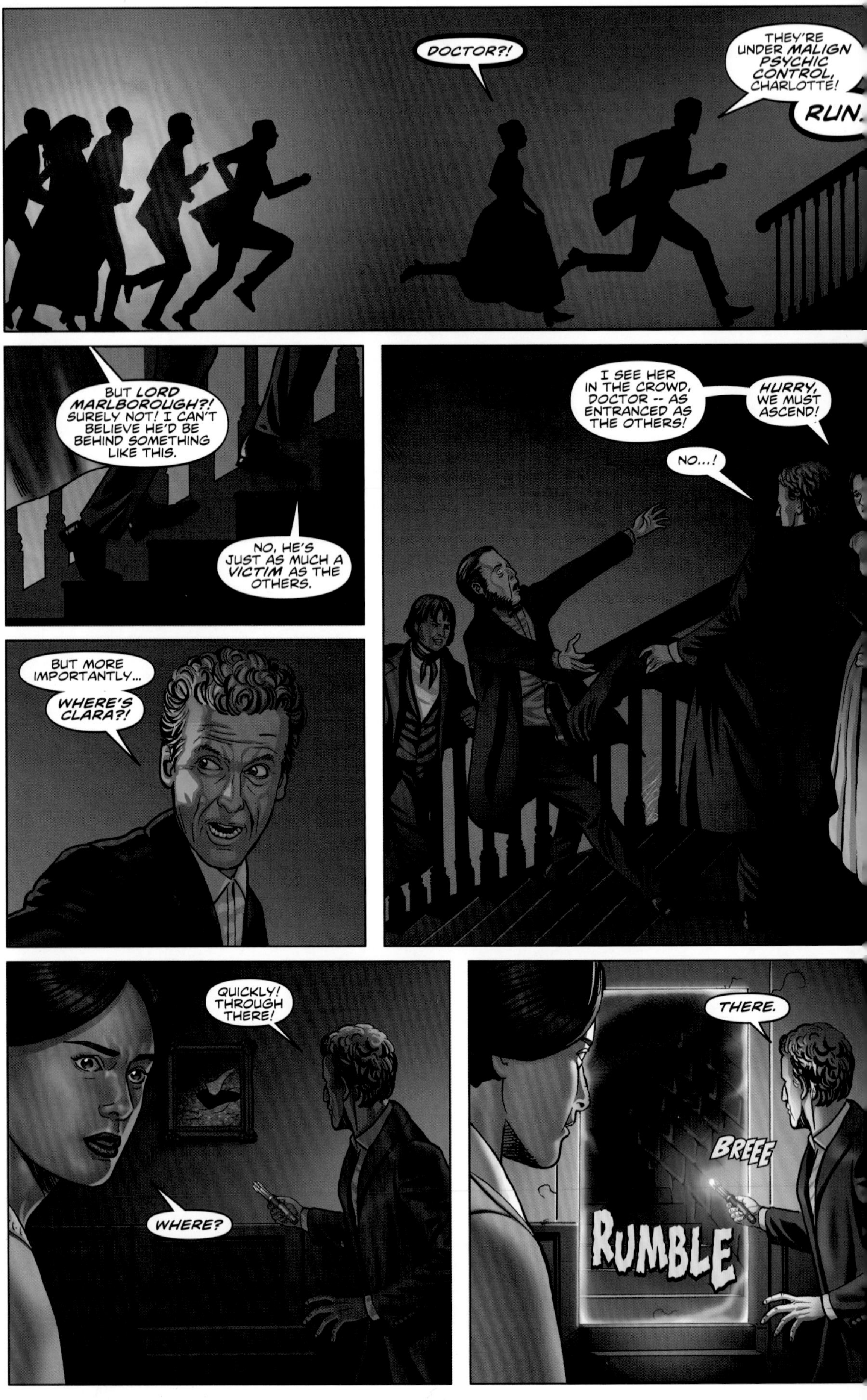
DOCTOR?!
THEY'RE UNDER MALIGN PSYCHIC CONTROL, CHARLOTTE!
RUN.
BUT LORD MARLBOROUGH?! SURELY NOT! I CAN'T BELIEVE HE'D BE BEHIND SOMETHING LIKE THIS.
NO, HE'S JUST AS MUCH A VICTIM AS THE OTHERS.
BUT MORE IMPORTANTLY...
WHERE'S CLARA?!
I SEE HER IN THE CROWD, DOCTOR -- AS ENTRANCED AS THE OTHERS!
HURRY, WE MUST ASCEND!
NO...!
QUICKLY! THROUGH THERE!
WHERE?
THERE.
BREEE
RUMBLE

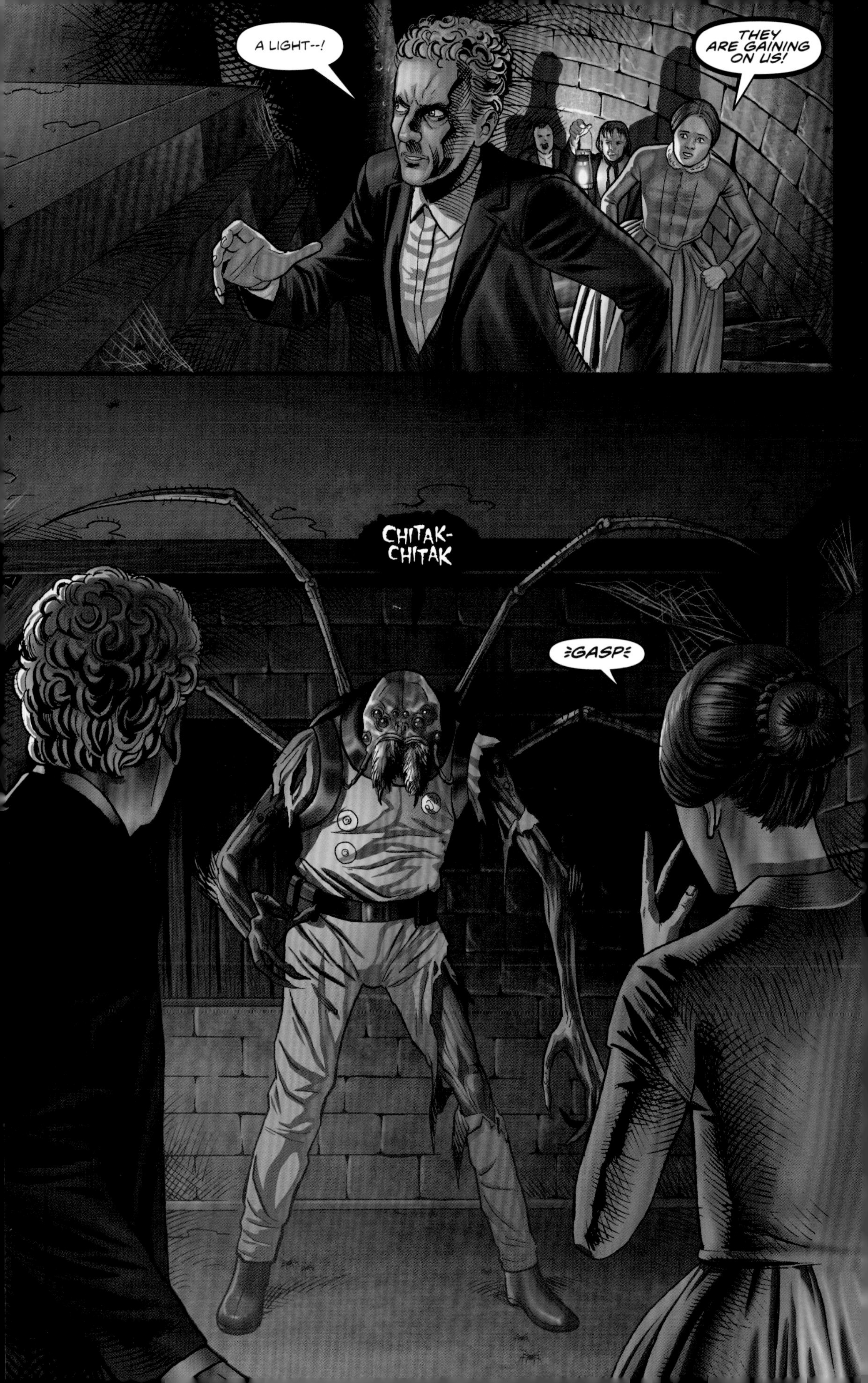
A LIGHT--!
THEY ARE GAINING ON US!
CHITAK-CHITAK
GASP

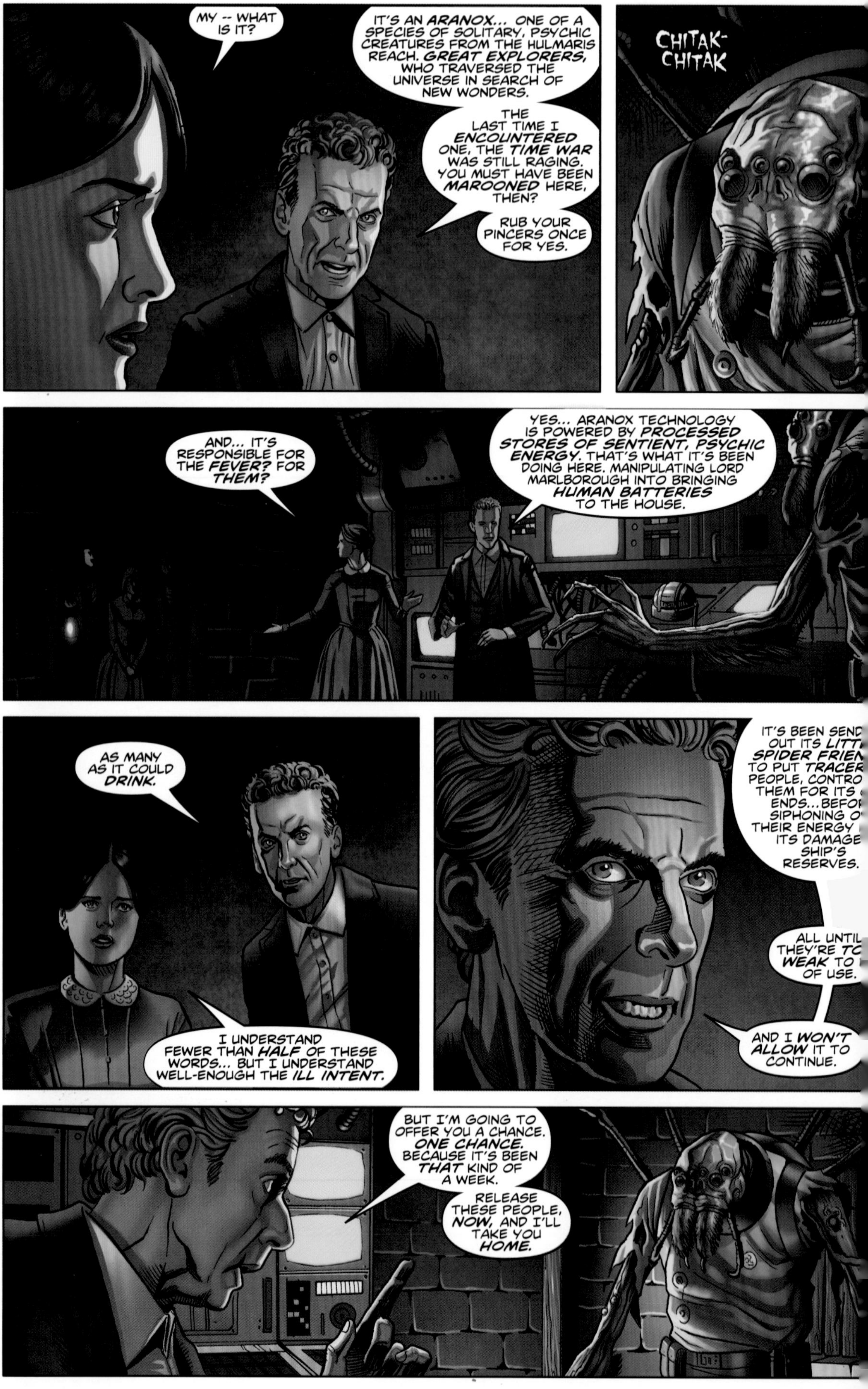
MY -- WHAT IS IT?
IT'S AN ARANOX... ONE OF A SPECIES OF SOLITARY, PSYCHIC CREATURES FROM THE HULMARIS REACH. GREAT EXPLORERS, WHO TRAVERSED THE UNIVERSE IN SEARCH OF NEW WONDERS.
THE LAST TIME I ENCOUNTERED ONE, THE TIME WAR WAS STILL RAGING. YOU MUST HAVE BEEN MAROONED HERE, THEN?
RUB YOUR PINCERS ONCE FOR YES.
CHITAK-CHITAK
AND... IT'S RESPONSIBLE FOR THE FEVER? FOR THEM?
YES... ARANOX TECHNOLOGY IS POWERED BY PROCESSED STORES OF SENTIENT, PSYCHIC ENERGY. THAT'S WHAT IT'S BEEN DOING HERE. MANIPULATING LORD MARLBOROUGH INTO BRINGING HUMAN BATTERIES TO THE HOUSE.
AS MANY AS IT COULD DRINK.
I UNDERSTAND FEWER THAN HALF OF THESE WORDS... BUT I UNDERSTAND WELL-ENOUGH THE ILL INTENT.
IT'S BEEN SEND OUT ITS LITT SPIDER FRIEN TO PUT TRACER PEOPLE, CONTRO THEM FOR ITS ENDS... BEFO SIPHONING O THEIR ENERGY ITS DAMAGE SHIP'S RESERVES.
ALL UNTIL THEY'RE TO WEAK TO OF USE.
AND I WON'T ALLOW IT TO CONTINUE.
BUT I'M GOING TO OFFER YOU A CHANCE. ONE CHANCE. BECAUSE IT'S BEEN THAT KIND OF A WEEK.
RELEASE THESE PEOPLE, NOW, AND I'LL TAKE YOU HOME.

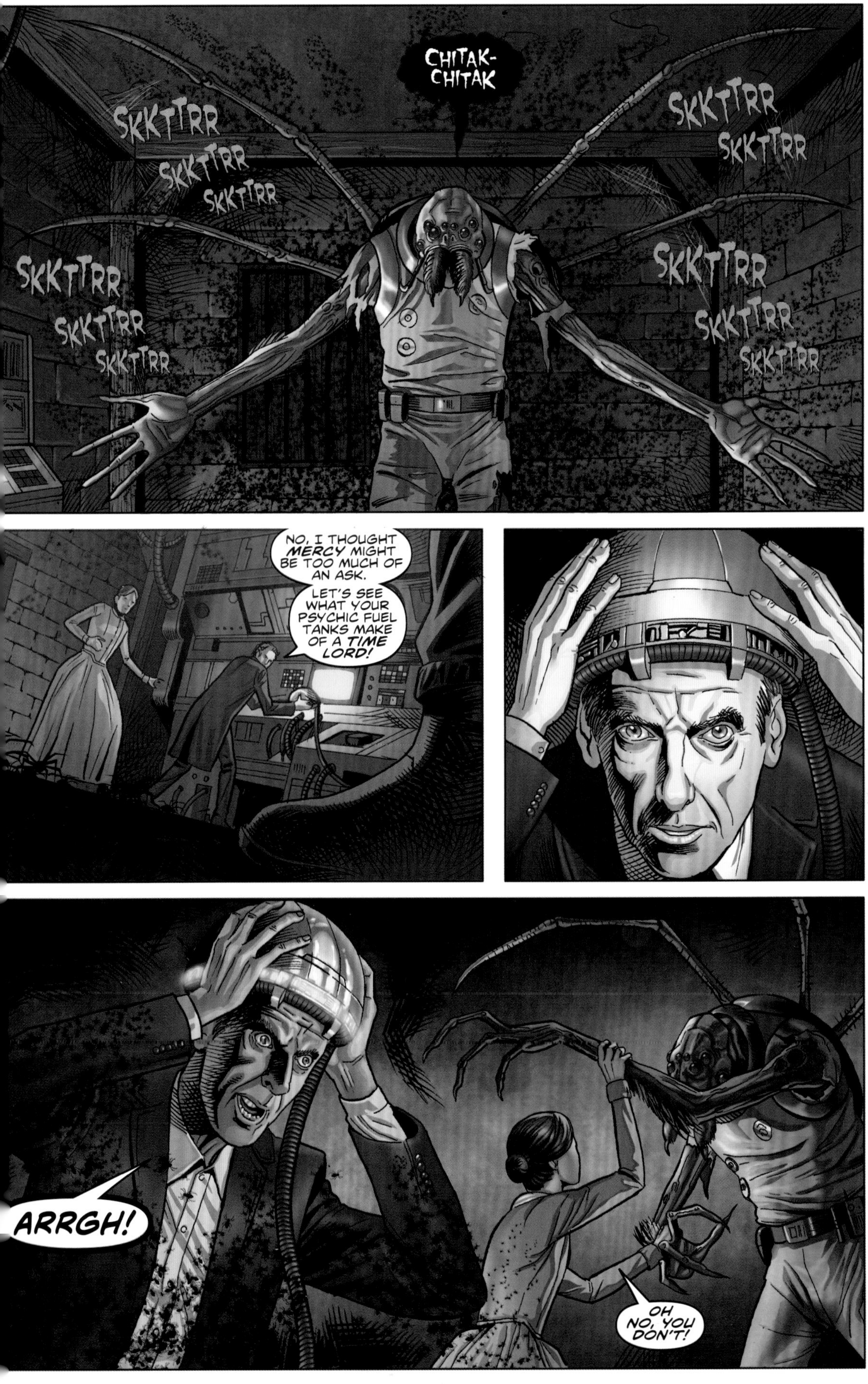
CHITAK-CHITAK
SKKTTRR SKKTTRR SKKTTRR
SKKTTRR SKKTTRR
SKKTTRR SKKTTRR SKKTTRR
SKKTTRR SKKTTRR SKKTTRR
NO, I THOUGHT MERCY MIGHT BE TOO MUCH OF AN ASK.
LET'S SEE WHAT YOUR PSYCHIC FUEL TANKS MAKE OF A TIME LORD!
ARRGH!
OH NO, YOU DON'T!

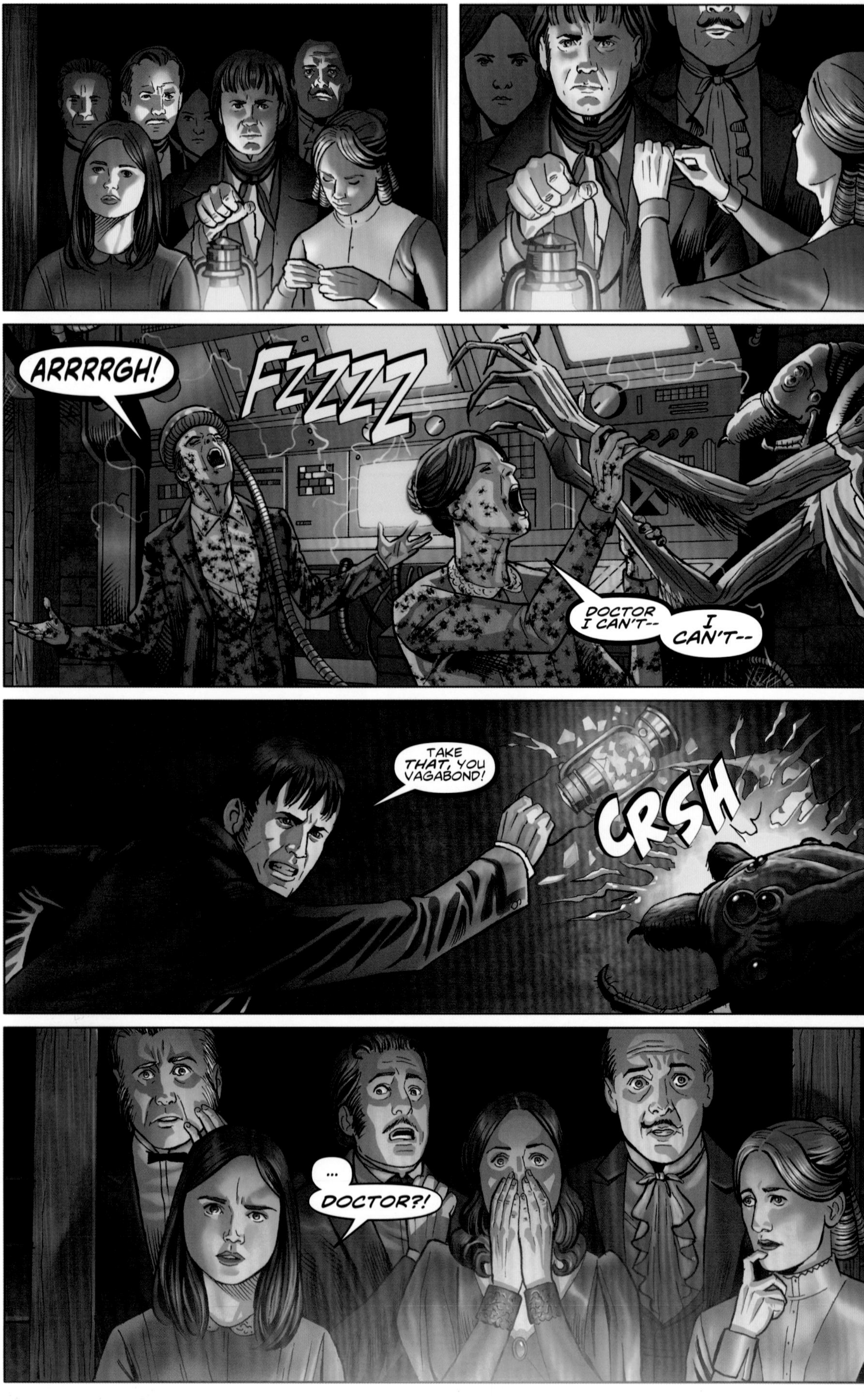
ARRRRGH!
FZZZZ
DOCTOR I CAN'T--
I CAN'T--
TAKE THAT, YOU VAGABOND!
CRSH
... DOCTOR?!

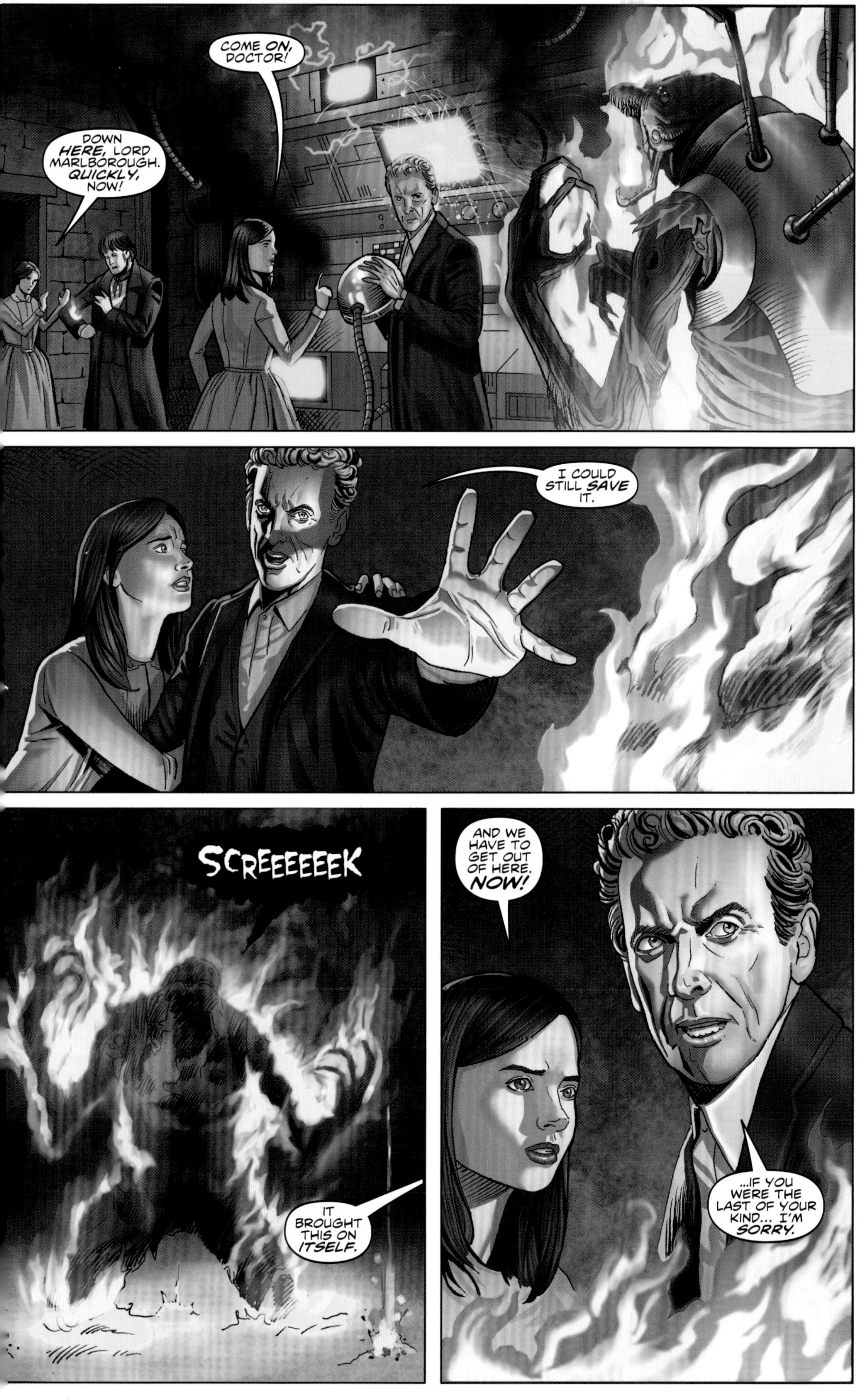
COME ON, DOCTOR!
DOWN HERE, LORD MARLBOROUGH. QUICKLY, NOW!
I COULD STILL SAVE IT.
SCREEEEEEK
IT BROUGHT THIS ON ITSELF.
AND WE HAVE TO GET OUT OF HERE. NOW!
...IF YOU WERE THE LAST OF YOUR KIND... I'M SORRY.

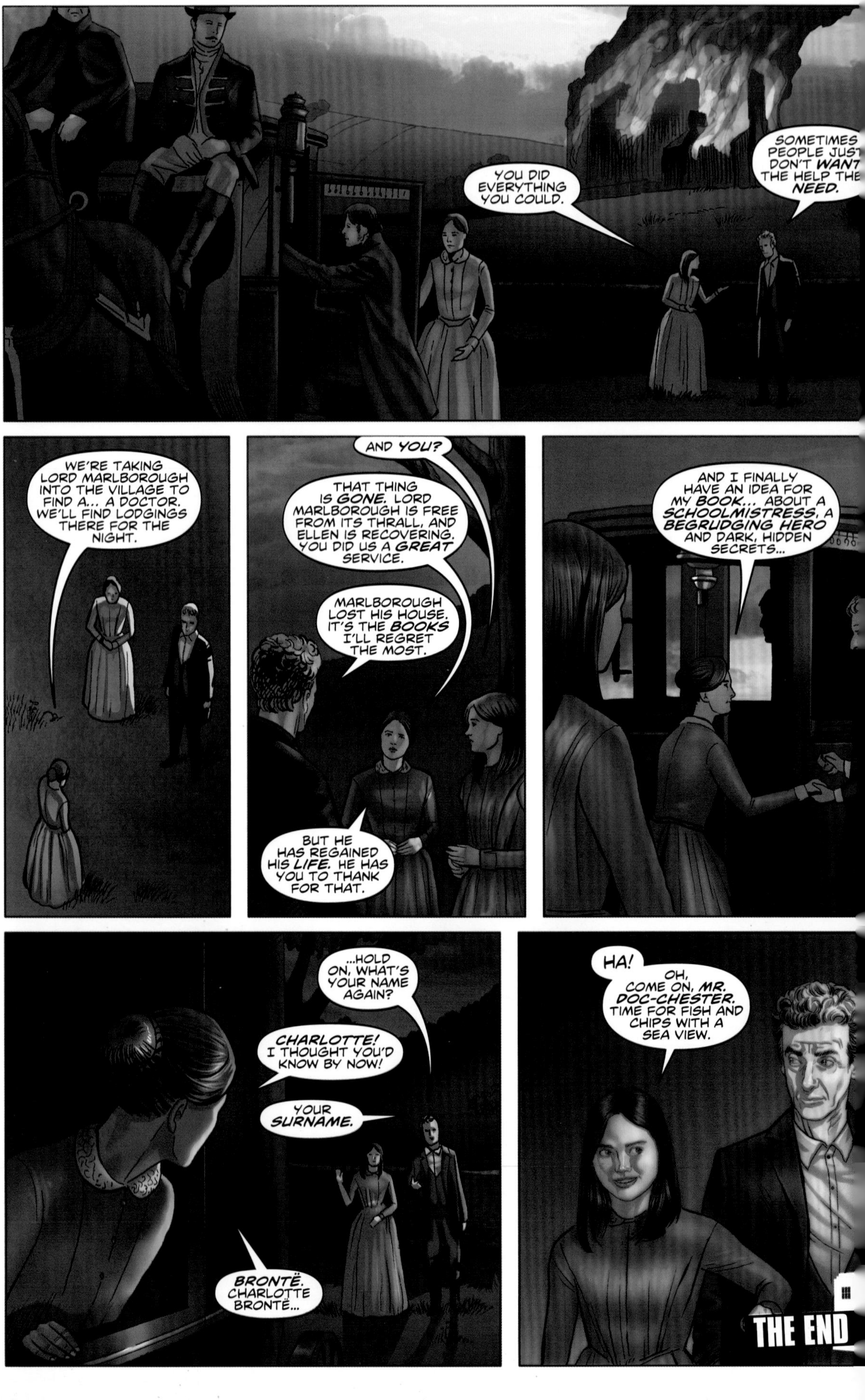
YOU DID EVERYTHING YOU COULD.
SOMETIMES PEOPLE JUST DON'T WANT THE HELP THE NEED.
WE'RE TAKING LORD MARLBOROUGH INTO THE VILLAGE TO FIND A... A DOCTOR. WE'LL FIND LODGINGS THERE FOR THE NIGHT.
AND YOU?
THAT THING IS GONE. LORD MARLBOROUGH IS FREE FROM ITS THRALL, AND ELLEN IS RECOVERING. YOU DID US A GREAT SERVICE.
MARLBOROUGH LOST HIS HOUSE. IT'S THE BOOKS I'LL REGRET THE MOST.
BUT HE HAS REGAINED HIS LIFE. HE HAS YOU TO THANK FOR THAT.
AND I FINALLY HAVE AN IDEA FOR MY BOOK... ABOUT A SCHOOLMISTRESS, A BEGRUDGING HERO AND DARK, HIDDEN SECRETS...
...HOLD ON, WHAT'S YOUR NAME AGAIN?
CHARLOTTE! I THOUGHT YOU'D KNOW BY NOW!
YOUR SURNAME.
BRONTË. CHARLOTTE BRONTË...
HA!
OH, COME ON, MR. DOC-CHESTER. TIME FOR FISH AND CHIPS WITH A SEA VIEW.
THE END

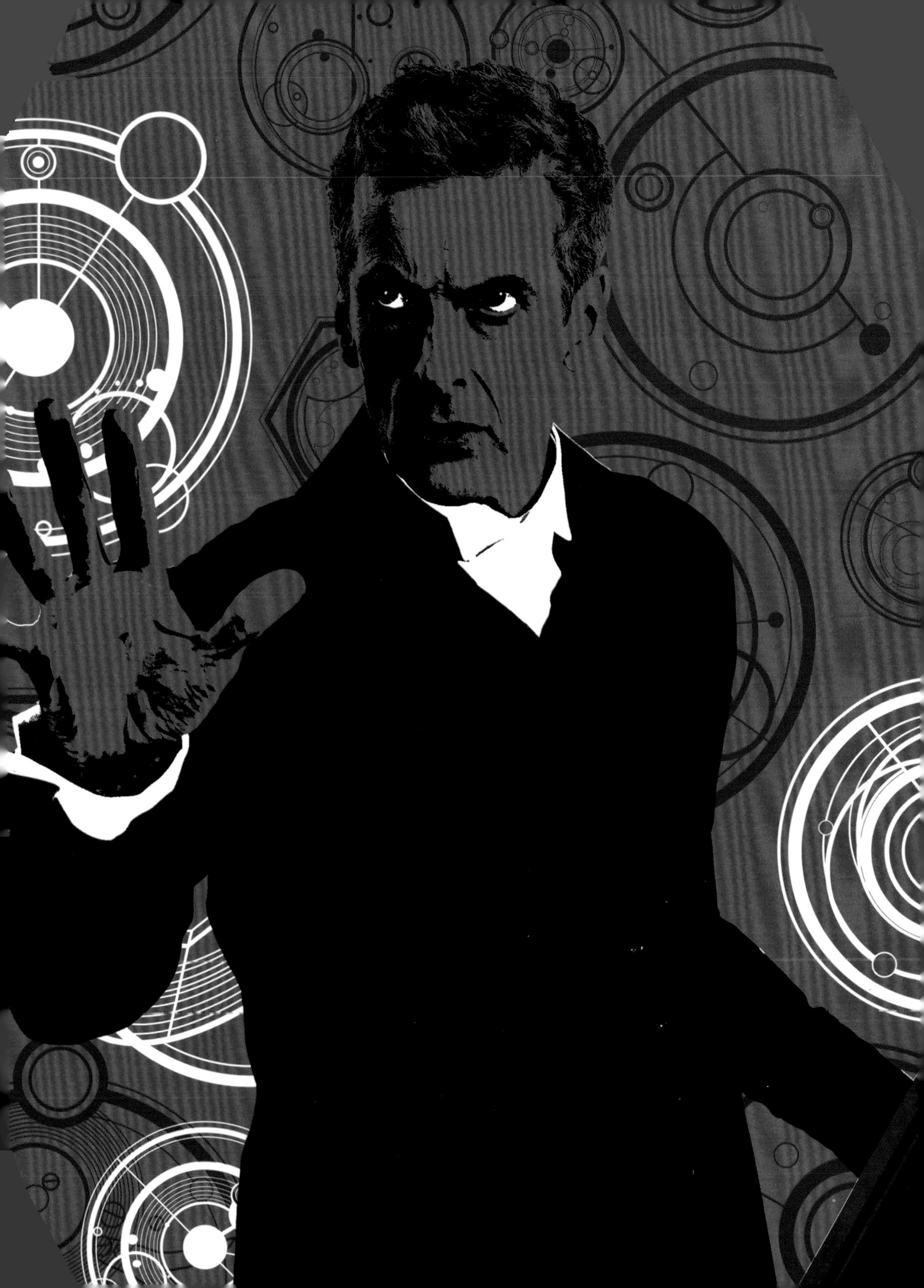

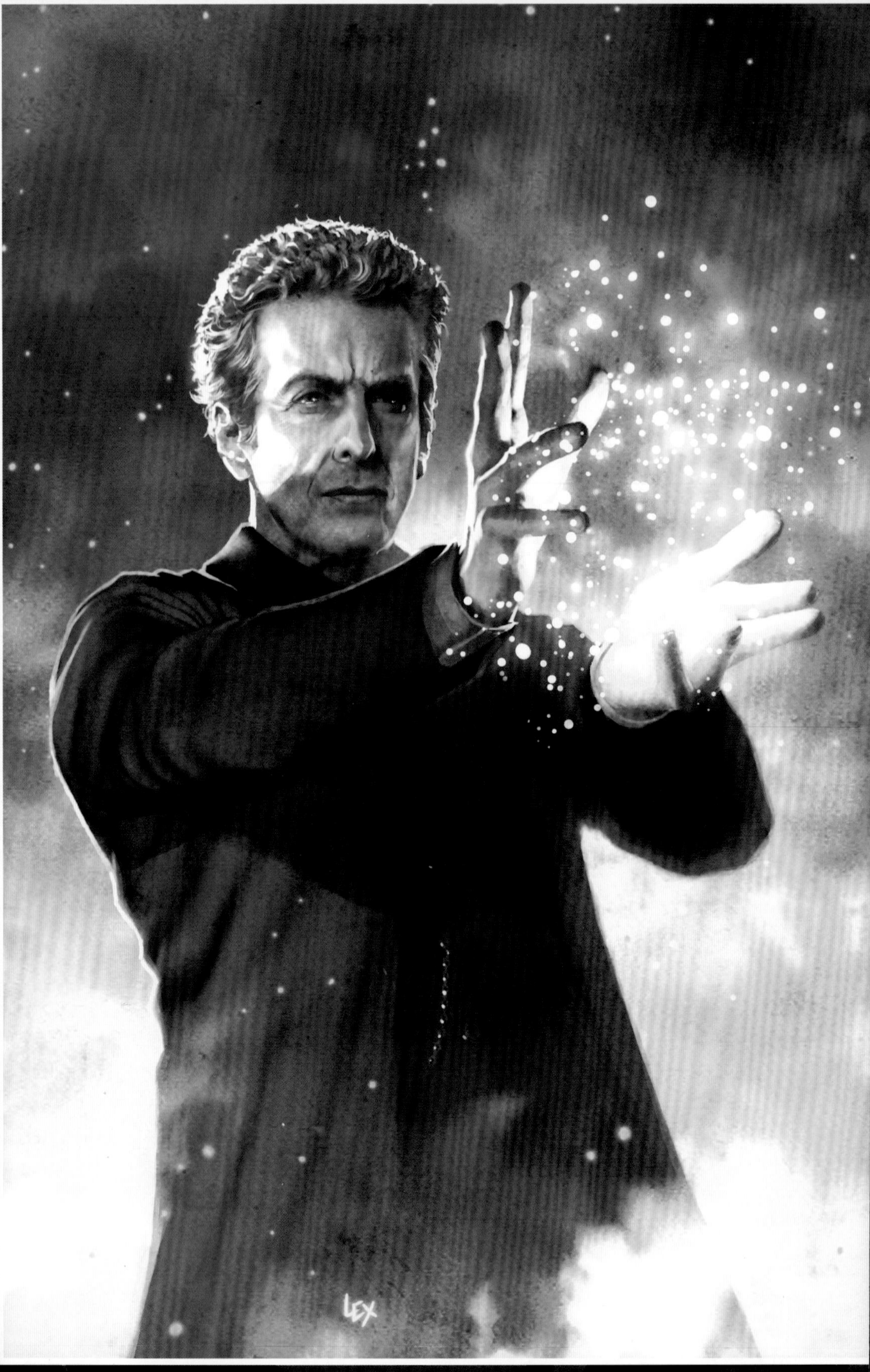
LEX

THE HYPERION EMPIRE Cover: ALEX RONALD

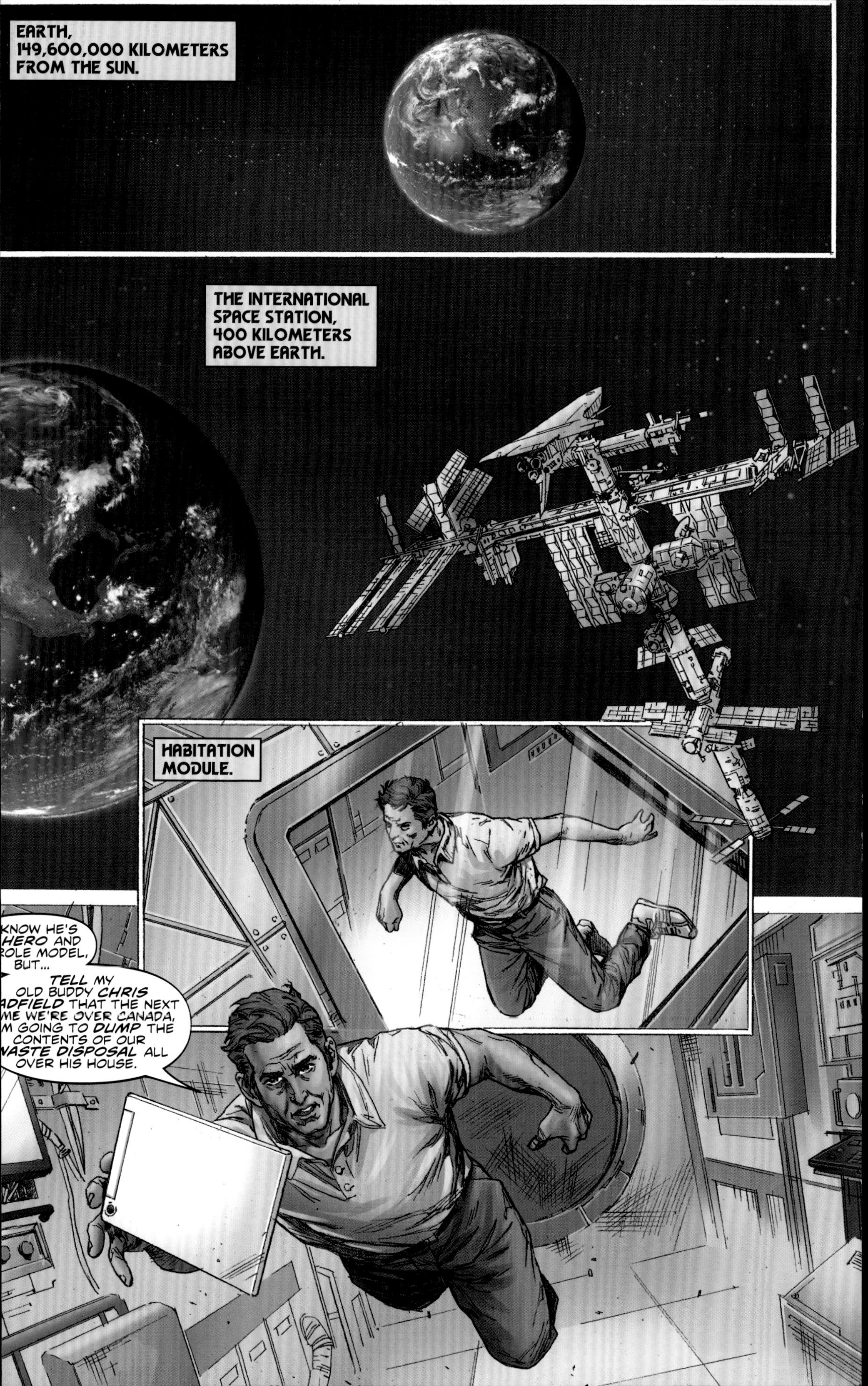
EARTH, 149,600,000 KILOMETERS FROM THE SUN.
THE INTERNATIONAL SPACE STATION, 400 KILOMETERS ABOVE EARTH.
HABITATION MODULE.
KNOW HE'S HERO AND ROLE MODEL, BUT...
TELL MY OLD BUDDY CHRIS ADFIELD THAT THE NEXT ME WE'RE OVER CANADA, M GOING TO DUMP THE CONTENTS OF OUR WASTE DISPOSAL ALL OVER HIS HOUSE.

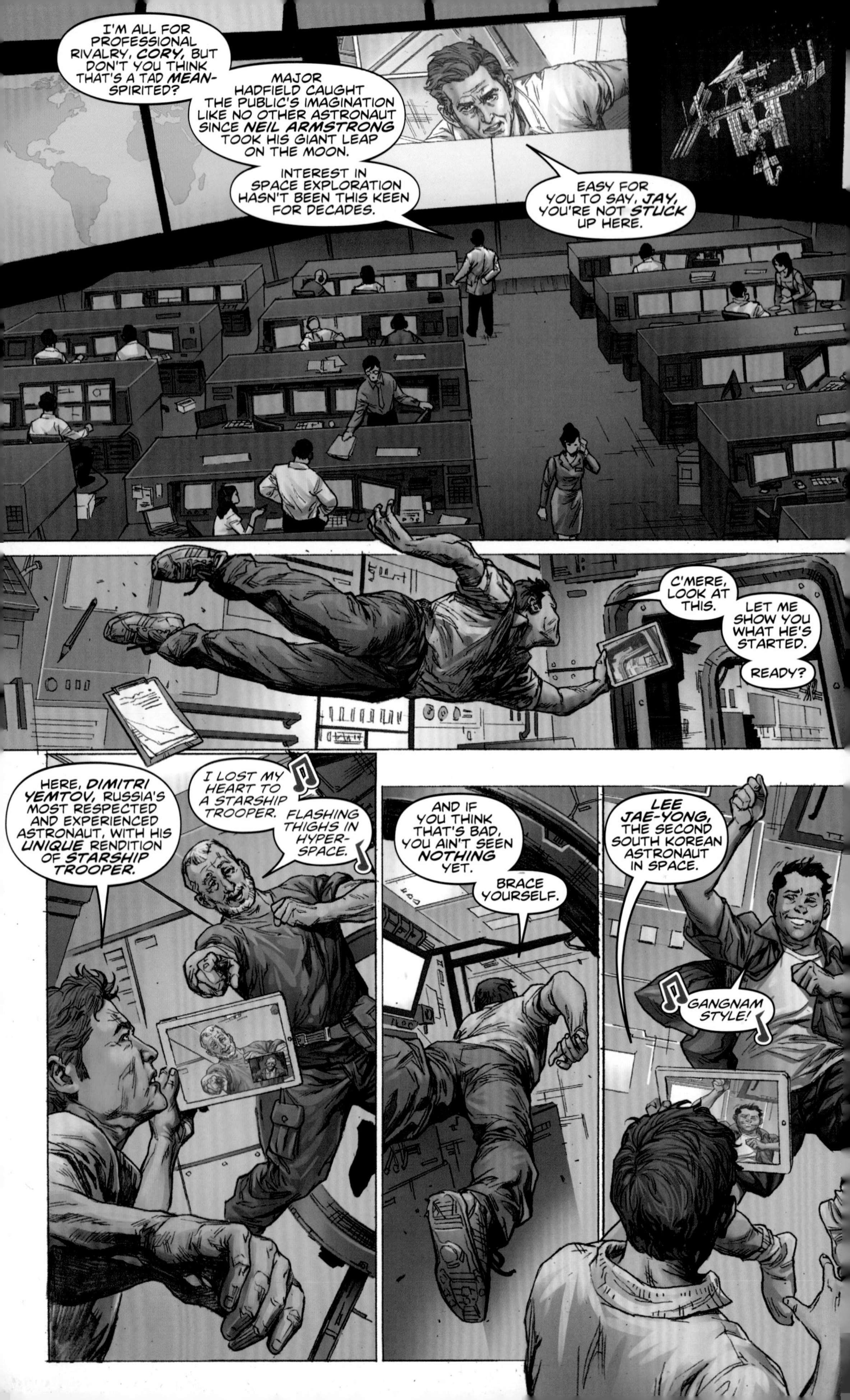
I'M ALL FOR PROFESSIONAL RIVALRY, CORY, BUT DON'T YOU THINK THAT'S A TAD MEAN-SPIRITED?
MAJOR HADFIELD CAUGHT THE PUBLIC'S IMAGINATION LIKE NO OTHER ASTRONAUT SINCE NEIL ARMSTRONG TOOK HIS GIANT LEAP ON THE MOON.
INTEREST IN SPACE EXPLORATION HASN'T BEEN THIS KEEN FOR DECADES.
EASY FOR YOU TO SAY, JAY, YOU'RE NOT STUCK UP HERE.
C'MERE, LOOK AT THIS.
LET ME SHOW YOU WHAT HE'S STARTED.
READY?
HERE, DIMITRI YEMTOV, RUSSIA'S MOST RESPECTED AND EXPERIENCED ASTRONAUT, WITH HIS UNIQUE RENDITION OF STARSHIP TROOPER.
I LOST MY HEART TO A STARSHIP TROOPER.
FLASHING THIGHS IN HYPER-SPACE.
AND IF YOU THINK THAT'S BAD, YOU AIN'T SEEN NOTHING YET.
BRACE YOURSELF.
LEE JAE-YONG, THE SECOND SOUTH KOREAN ASTRONAUT IN SPACE.
GANGNAM STYLE!

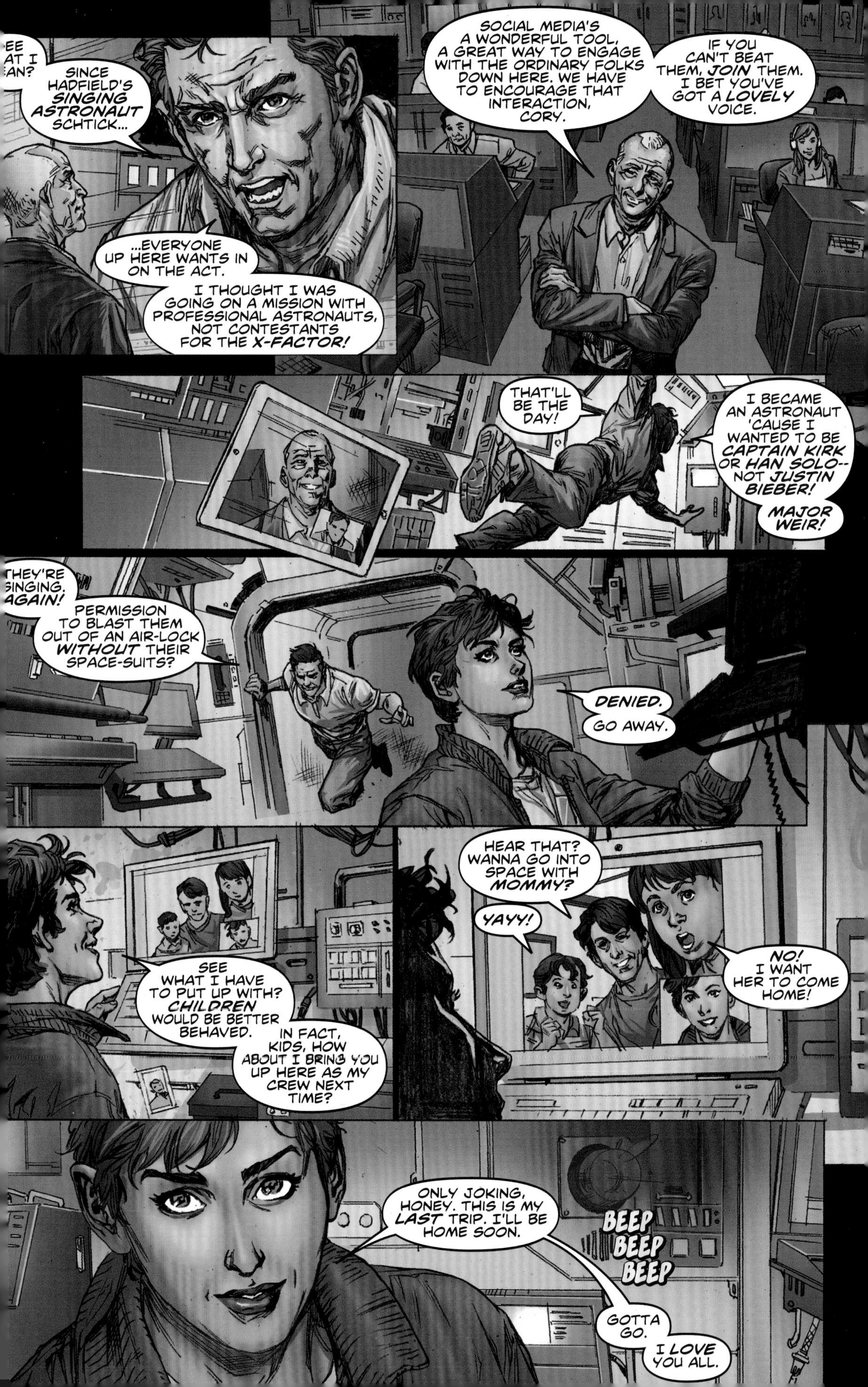

EE AT I EAN?
SINCE HADFIELD'S SINGING ASTRONAUT SCHTICK...
...EVERYONE UP HERE WANTS IN ON THE ACT.
I THOUGHT I WAS GOING ON A MISSION WITH PROFESSIONAL ASTRONAUTS, NOT CONTESTANTS FOR THE X-FACTOR!
SOCIAL MEDIA'S A WONDERFUL TOOL, A GREAT WAY TO ENGAGE WITH THE ORDINARY FOLKS DOWN HERE. WE HAVE TO ENCOURAGE THAT INTERACTION, CORY.
IF YOU CAN'T BEAT THEM, JOIN THEM. I BET YOU'VE GOT A LOVELY VOICE.
THAT'LL BE THE DAY!
I BECAME AN ASTRONAUT 'CAUSE I WANTED TO BE CAPTAIN KIRK OR HAN SOLO-- NOT JUSTIN BIEBER!
MAJOR WEIR!
THEY'RE SINGING. AGAIN!
PERMISSION TO BLAST THEM OUT OF AN AIR-LOCK WITHOUT THEIR SPACE-SUITS?
DENIED.
GO AWAY.
SEE WHAT I HAVE TO PUT UP WITH? CHILDREN WOULD BE BETTER BEHAVED.
IN FACT, KIDS, HOW ABOUT I BRING YOU UP HERE AS MY CREW NEXT TIME?
HEAR THAT? WANNA GO INTO SPACE WITH MOMMY?
YAYY!
NO! I WANT HER TO COME HOME!
ONLY JOKING, HONEY. THIS IS MY LAST TRIP. I'LL BE HOME SOON.
BEEP BEEP BEEP
GOTTA GO.
I LOVE YOU ALL.

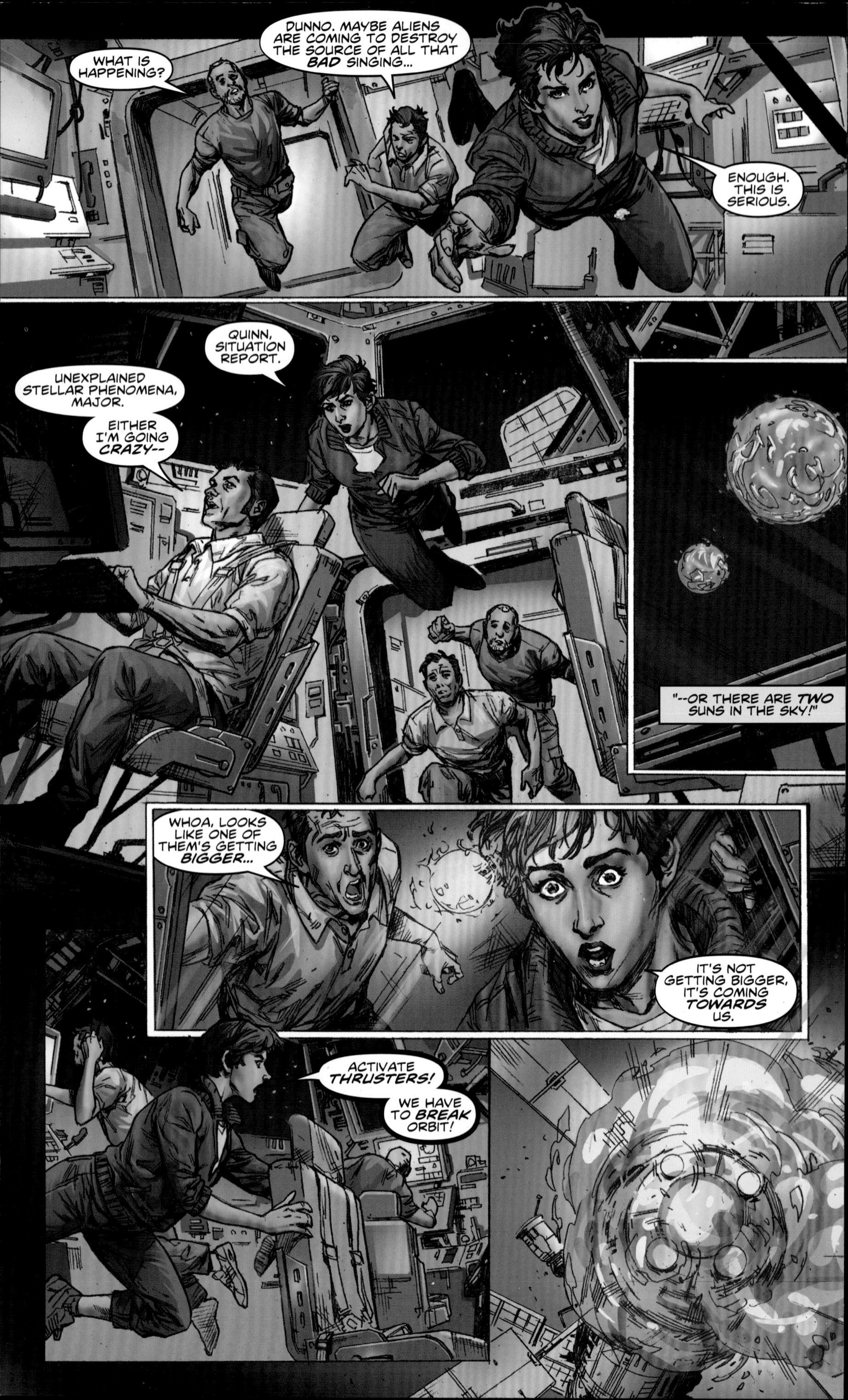
WHAT IS HAPPENING?
DUNNO. MAYBE ALIENS ARE COMING TO DESTROY THE SOURCE OF ALL THAT BAD SINGING...
ENOUGH. THIS IS SERIOUS.
QUINN, SITUATION REPORT.
UNEXPLAINED STELLAR PHENOMENA, MAJOR.
EITHER I'M GOING CRAZY--
"--OR THERE ARE TWO SUNS IN THE SKY!"
WHOA, LOOKS LIKE ONE OF THEM'S GETTING BIGGER...
IT'S NOT GETTING BIGGER, IT'S COMING TOWARDS US.
ACTIVATE THRUSTERS!
WE HAVE TO BREAK ORBIT!

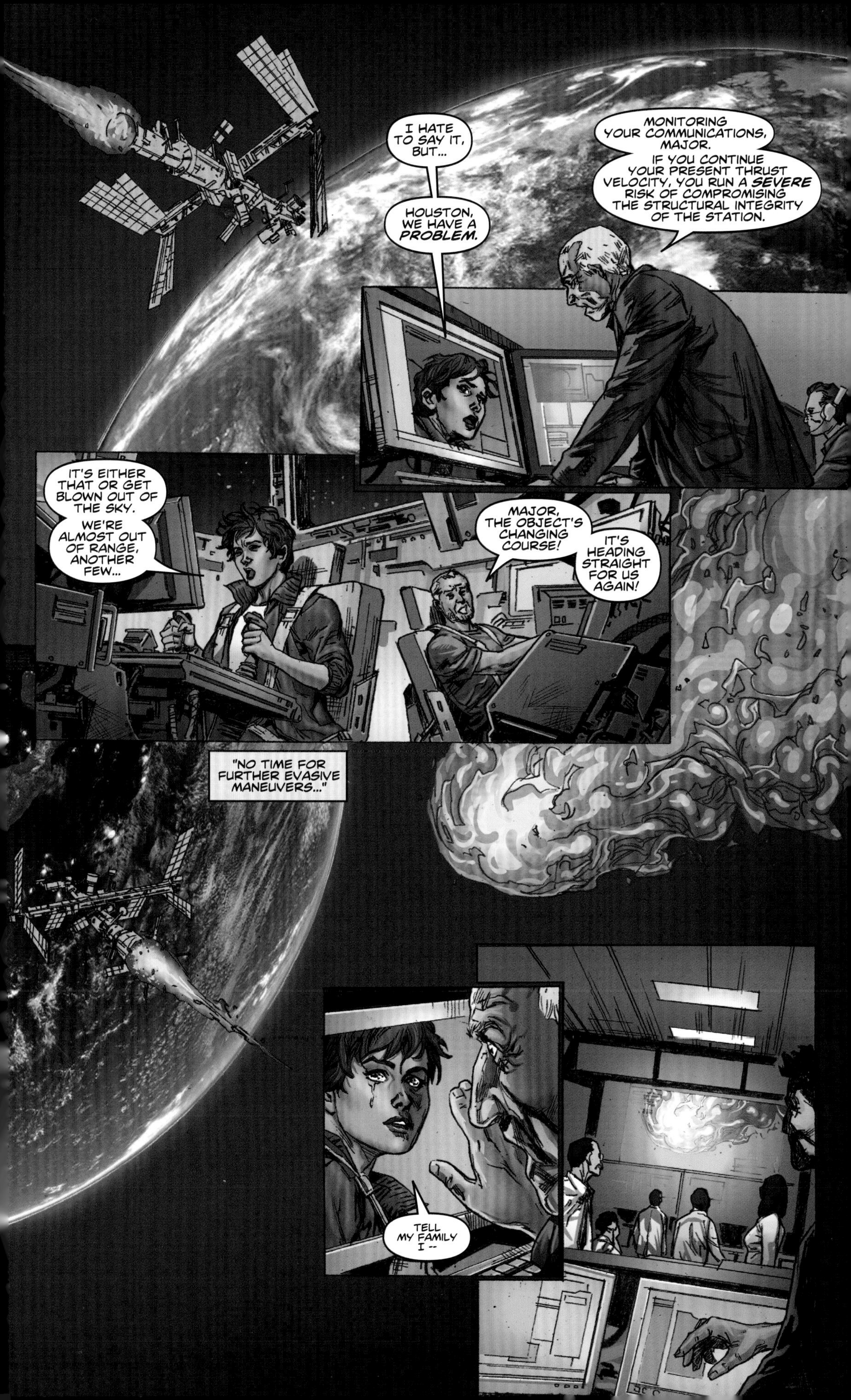
I HATE TO SAY IT, BUT...
HOUSTON, WE HAVE A PROBLEM.
MONITORING YOUR COMMUNICATIONS, MAJOR.
IF YOU CONTINUE YOUR PRESENT THRUST VELOCITY, YOU RUN A SEVERE RISK OF COMPROMISING THE STRUCTURAL INTEGRITY OF THE STATION.
IT'S EITHER THAT OR GET BLOWN OUT OF THE SKY.
WE'RE ALMOST OUT OF RANGE, ANOTHER FEW...
MAJOR, THE OBJECT'S CHANGING COURSE!
IT'S HEADING STRAIGHT FOR US AGAIN!
"NO TIME FOR FURTHER EVASIVE MANEUVERS..."
TELL MY FAMILY I --

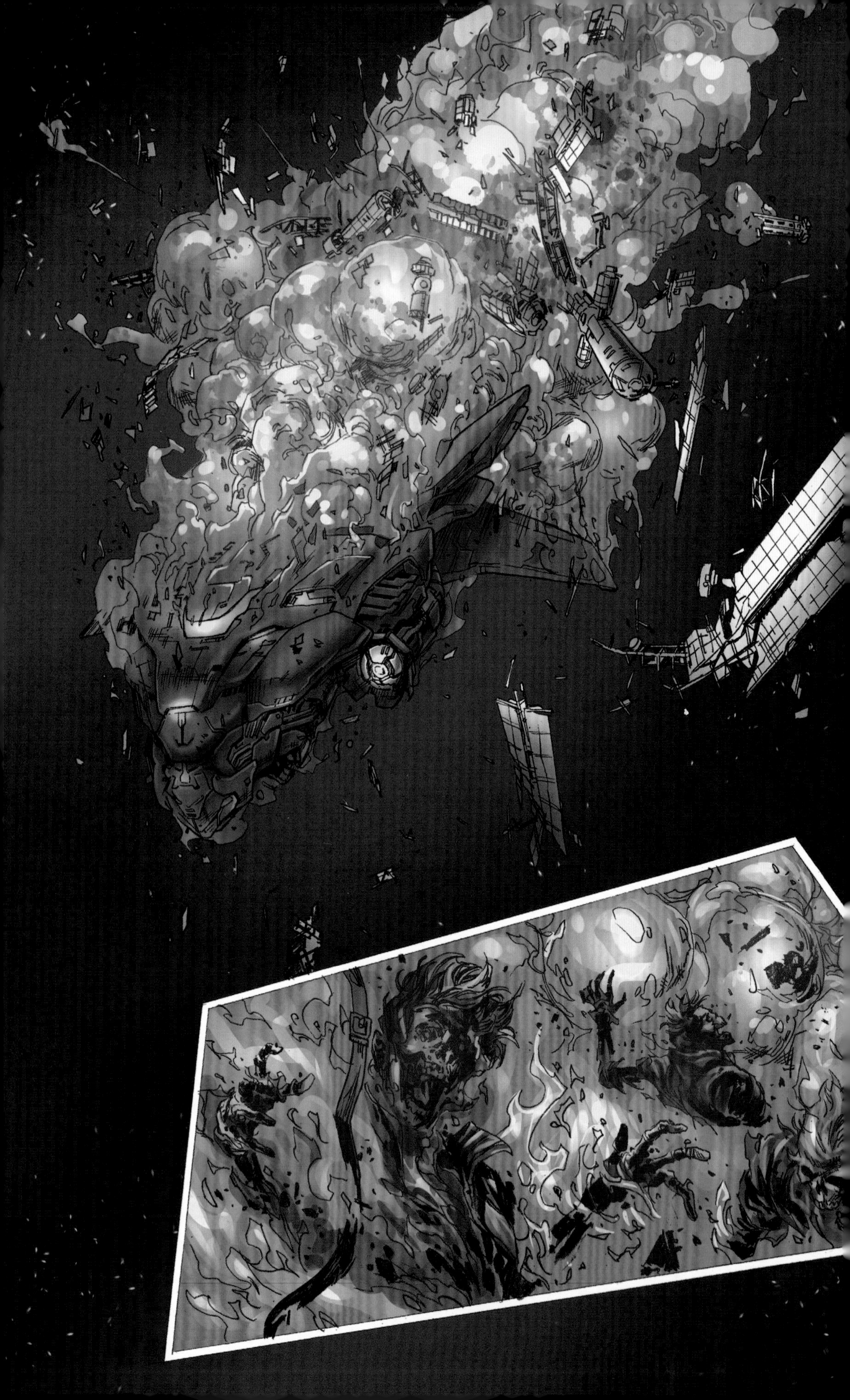

THE HYPERION EMPIRE

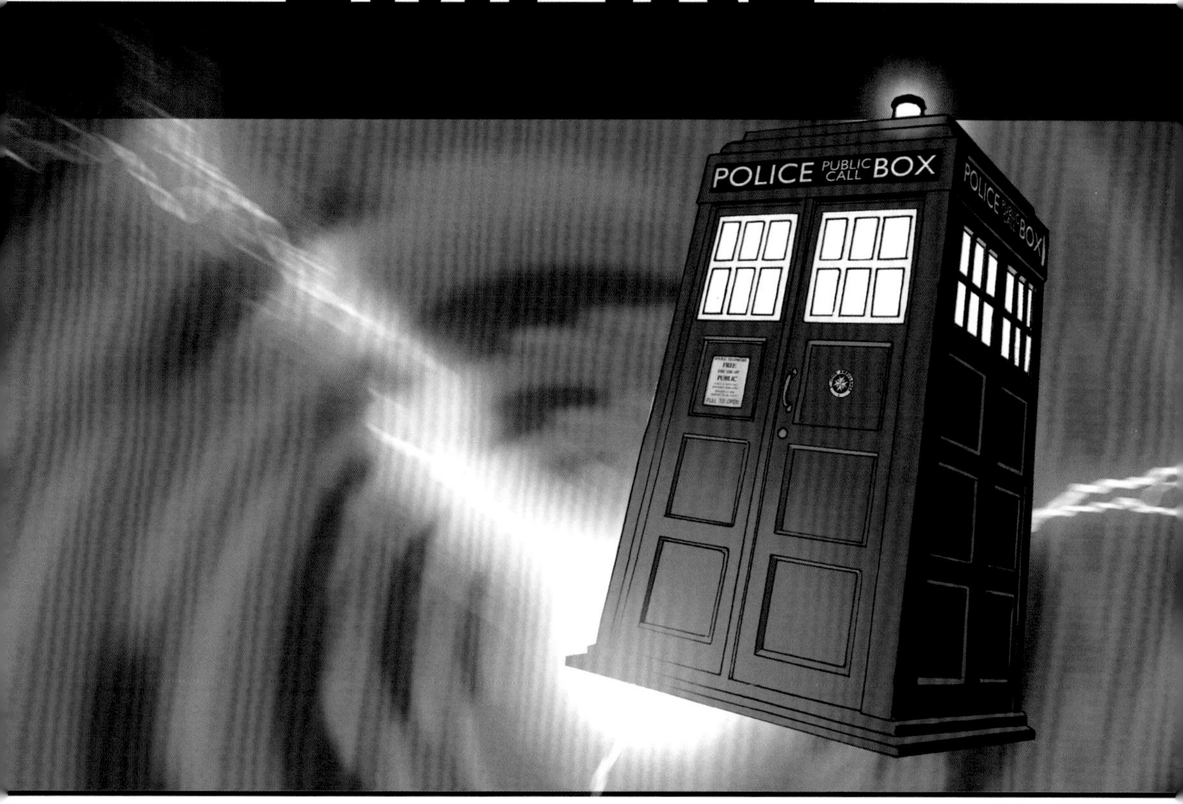
POLICE PUBLIC CALL BOX

WRITER
ROBBIE MORRISON

ARTIST
DANIEL INDRO

COLORIST
SLAMET MUJIONO

LETTERER
RICHARD STARKINGS AND COMICRAFT'S JIMMY BETANCOURT

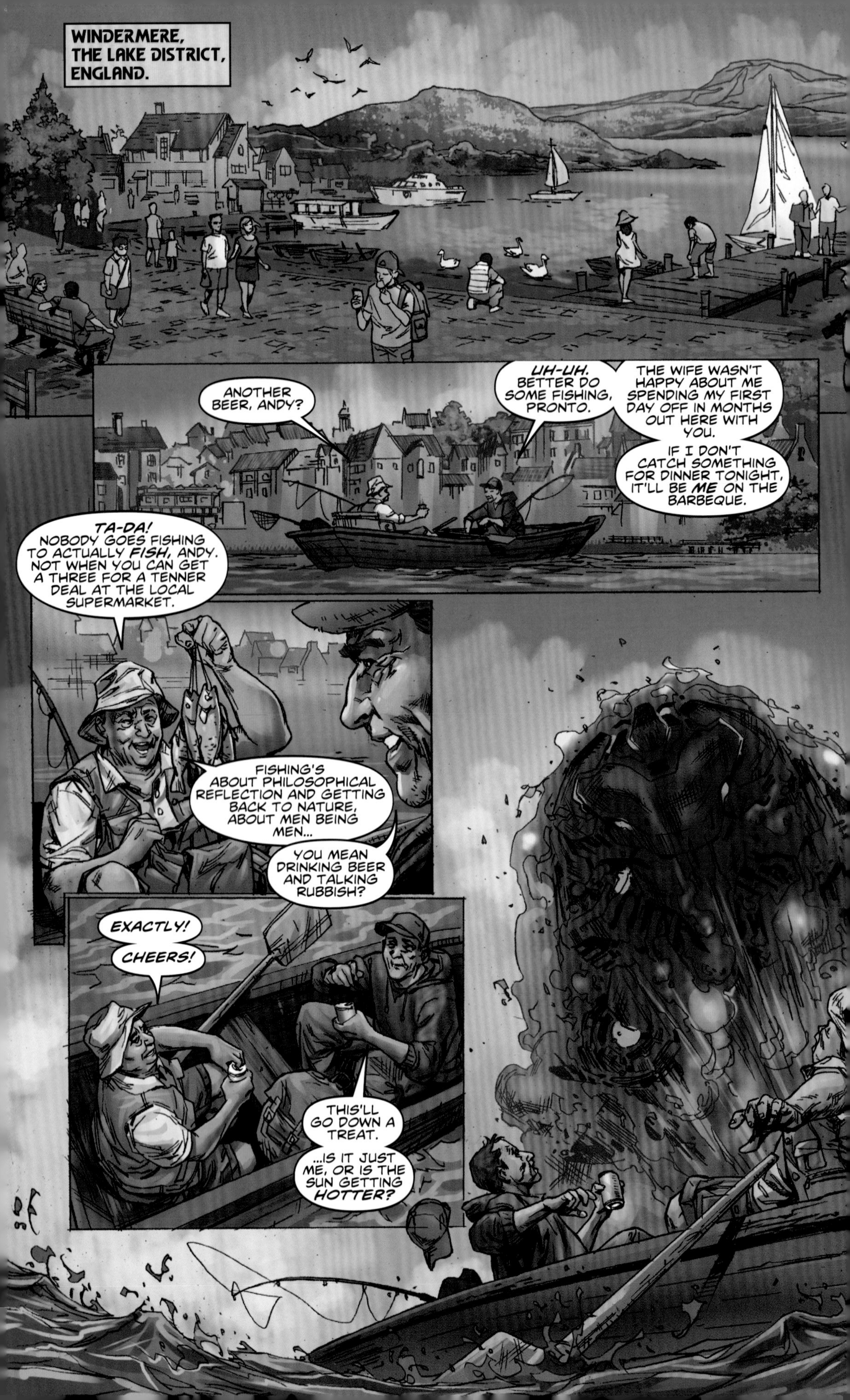
WINDERMERE, THE LAKE DISTRICT, ENGLAND.
ANOTHER BEER, ANDY?
UH-UH. BETTER DO SOME FISHING, PRONTO.
THE WIFE WASN'T HAPPY ABOUT ME SPENDING MY FIRST DAY OFF IN MONTHS OUT HERE WITH YOU.
IF I DON'T CATCH SOMETHING FOR DINNER TONIGHT, IT'LL BE ME ON THE BARBEQUE.
TA-DA! NOBODY GOES FISHING TO ACTUALLY FISH, ANDY. NOT WHEN YOU CAN GET A THREE FOR A TENNER DEAL AT THE LOCAL SUPERMARKET.
FISHING'S ABOUT PHILOSOPHICAL REFLECTION AND GETTING BACK TO NATURE, ABOUT MEN BEING MEN...
YOU MEAN DRINKING BEER AND TALKING RUBBISH?
EXACTLY!
CHEERS!
THIS'LL GO DOWN A TREAT.
...IS IT JUST ME, OR IS THE SUN GETTING HOTTER?

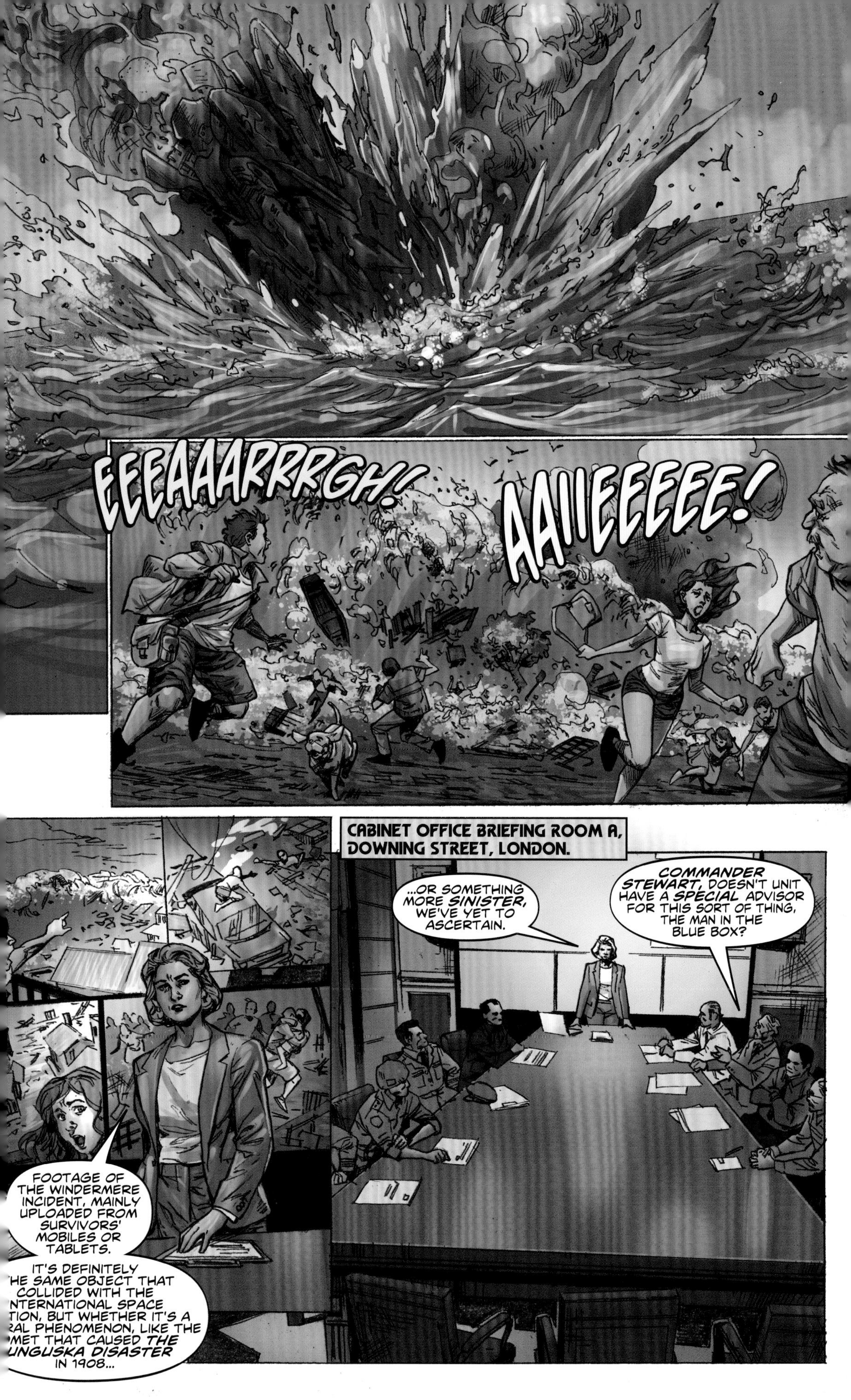
EEEAAARRRGH!!
AAIIEEEEE!
CABINET OFFICE BRIEFING ROOM A, DOWNING STREET, LONDON.
FOOTAGE OF THE WINDERMERE INCIDENT, MAINLY UPLOADED FROM SURVIVORS' MOBILES OR TABLETS.
IT'S DEFINITELY HE SAME OBJECT THAT COLLIDED WITH THE NTERNATIONAL SPACE TION, BUT WHETHER IT'S A RAL PHENOMENON, LIKE THE MET THAT CAUSED THE UNGUSKA DISASTER IN 1908...
...OR SOMETHING MORE SINISTER, WE'VE YET TO ASCERTAIN.
COMMANDER STEWART, DOESN'T UNIT HAVE A SPECIAL ADVISOR FOR THIS SORT OF THING, THE MAN IN THE BLUE BOX?

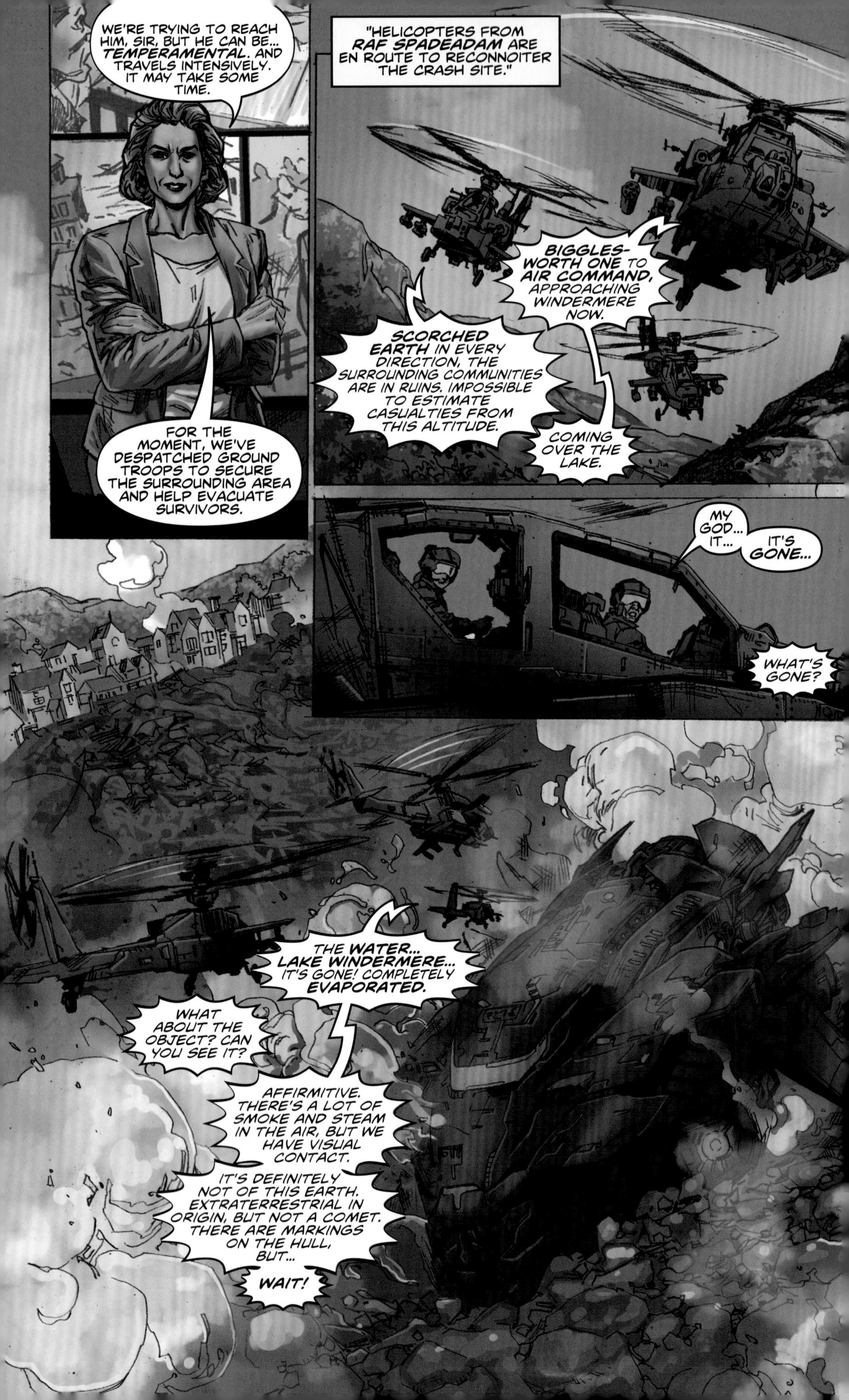
WE'RE TRYING TO REACH HIM, SIR, BUT HE CAN BE... TEMPERAMENTAL. AND TRAVELS INTENSIVELY. IT MAY TAKE SOME TIME.
FOR THE MOMENT, WE'VE DESPATCHED GROUND TROOPS TO SECURE THE SURROUNDING AREA AND HELP EVACUATE SURVIVORS.
"HELICOPTERS FROM RAF SPADEADAM ARE EN ROUTE TO RECONNOITER THE CRASH SITE."
BIGGLES-WORTH ONE TO AIR COMMAND, APPROACHING WINDERMERE NOW.
SCORCHED EARTH IN EVERY DIRECTION, THE SURROUNDING COMMUNITIES ARE IN RUINS. IMPOSSIBLE TO ESTIMATE CASUALTIES FROM THIS ALTITUDE.
COMING OVER THE LAKE.
MY GOD... IT...
IT'S GONE...
WHAT'S GONE?
THE WATER... LAKE WINDERMERE... IT'S GONE! COMPLETELY EVAPORATED.
WHAT ABOUT THE OBJECT? CAN YOU SEE IT?
AFFIRMITIVE. THERE'S A LOT OF SMOKE AND STEAM IN THE AIR, BUT WE HAVE VISUAL CONTACT.
IT'S DEFINITELY NOT OF THIS EARTH. EXTRATERRESTRIAL IN ORIGIN, BUT NOT A COMET. THERE ARE MARKINGS ON THE HULL, BUT...
WAIT!

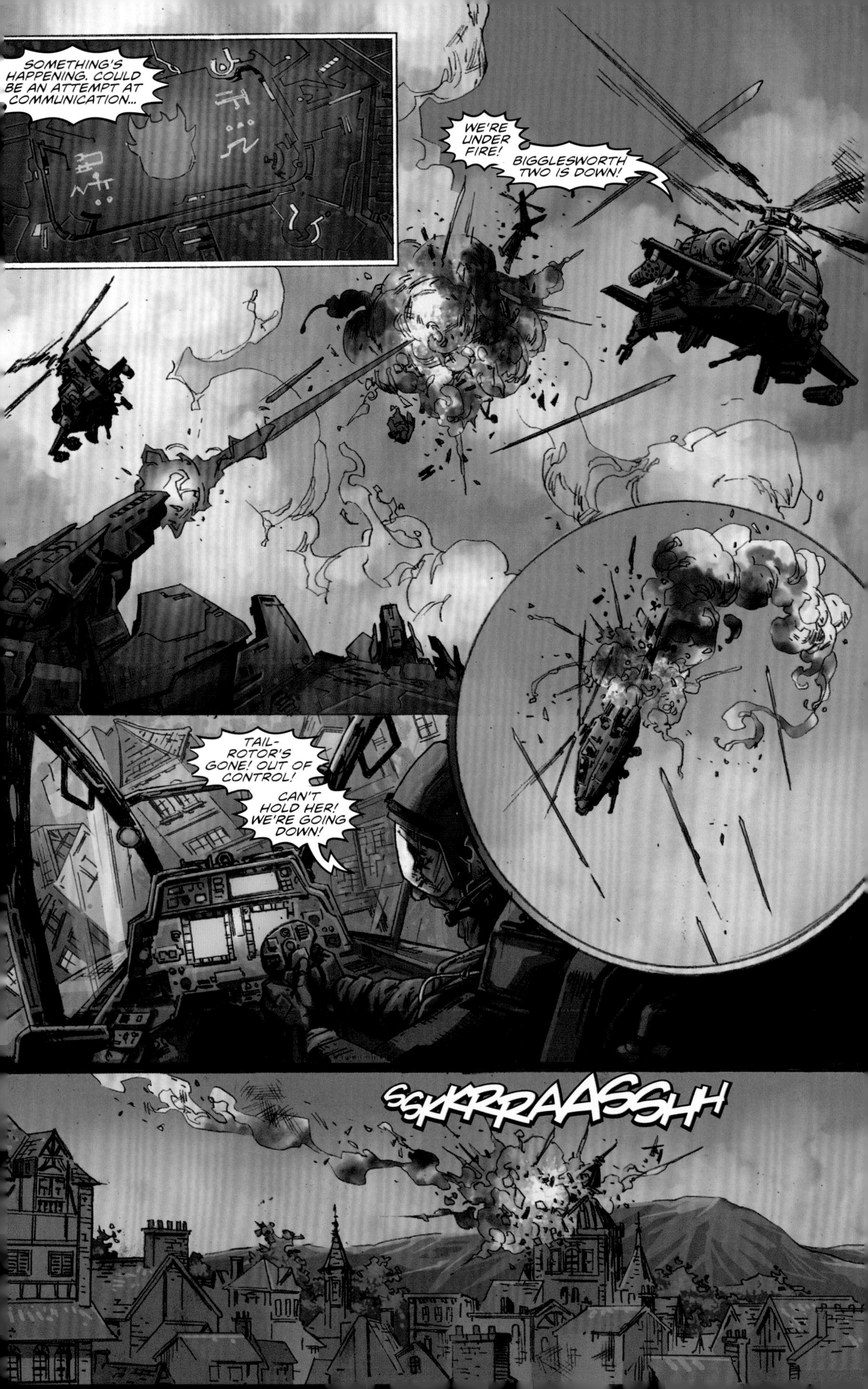
SOMETHING'S HAPPENING. COULD BE AN ATTEMPT AT COMMUNICATION...
WE'RE UNDER FIRE!
BIGGLESWORTH TWO IS DOWN!
TAIL-ROTOR'S GONE! OUT OF CONTROL!
CAN'T HOLD HER! WE'RE GOING DOWN!
SSKKRRAASSHH

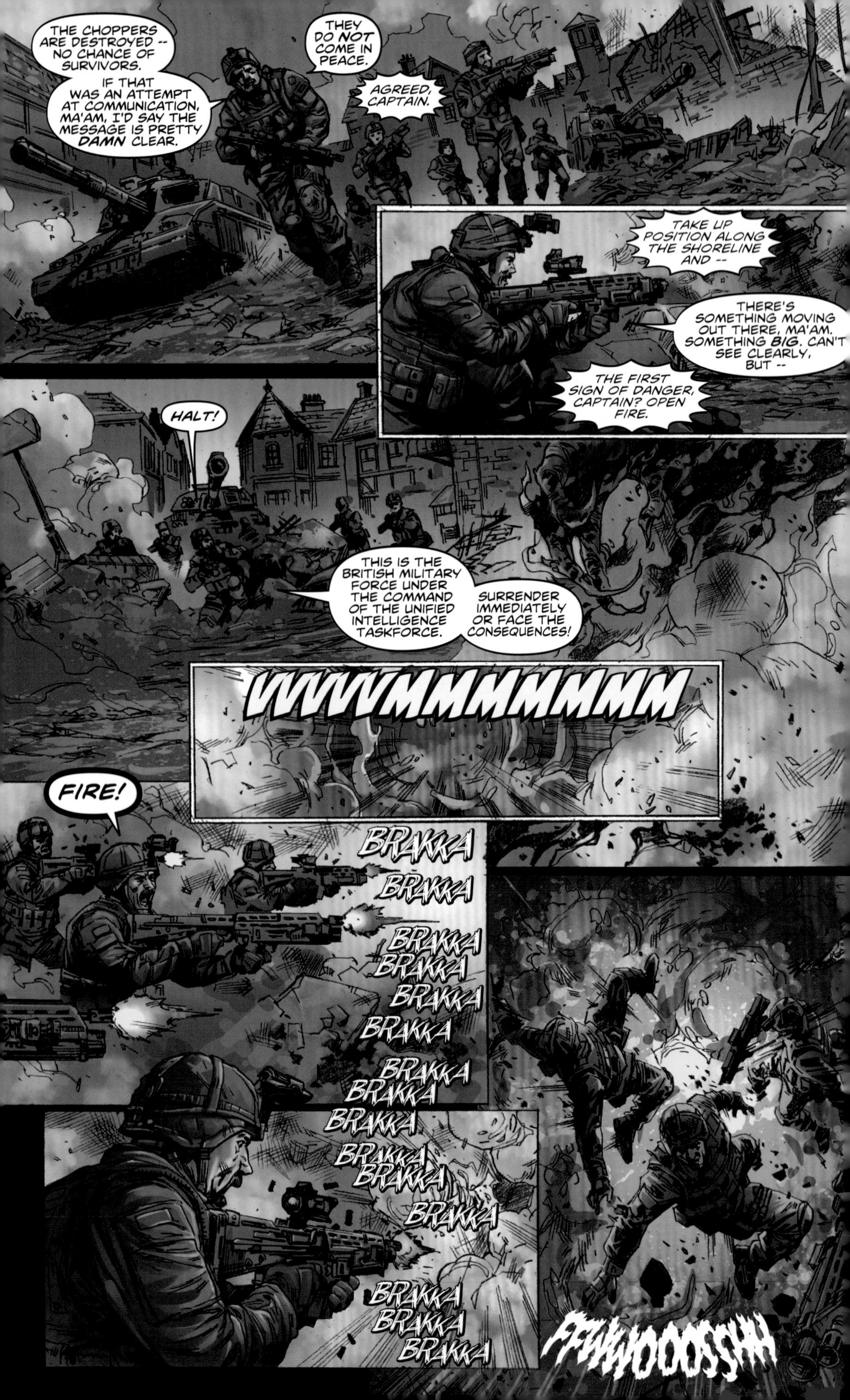
THE CHOPPERS ARE DESTROYED -- NO CHANCE OF SURVIVORS.
IF THAT WAS AN ATTEMPT AT COMMUNICATION, MA'AM, I'D SAY THE MESSAGE IS PRETTY DAMN CLEAR.
THEY DO NOT COME IN PEACE.
AGREED, CAPTAIN.
TAKE UP POSITION ALONG THE SHORELINE AND --
THERE'S SOMETHING MOVING OUT THERE, MA'AM. SOMETHING BIG. CAN'T SEE CLEARLY, BUT --
THE FIRST SIGN OF DANGER, CAPTAIN? OPEN FIRE.
HALT!
THIS IS THE BRITISH MILITARY FORCE UNDER THE COMMAND OF THE UNIFIED INTELLIGENCE TASKFORCE.
SURRENDER IMMEDIATELY OR FACE THE CONSEQUENCES!
VVVVVMMMMMMMM
FIRE!
BRAKKA
BRAKKA
BRAKKA
BRAKKA
BRAKKA
BRAKKA
BRAKKA
BRAKKA
BRAKKA
BRAKKA
BRAKKA
BRAKKA
BRAKKA
BRAKKA
BRAKKA
FFWWOOOSSHH

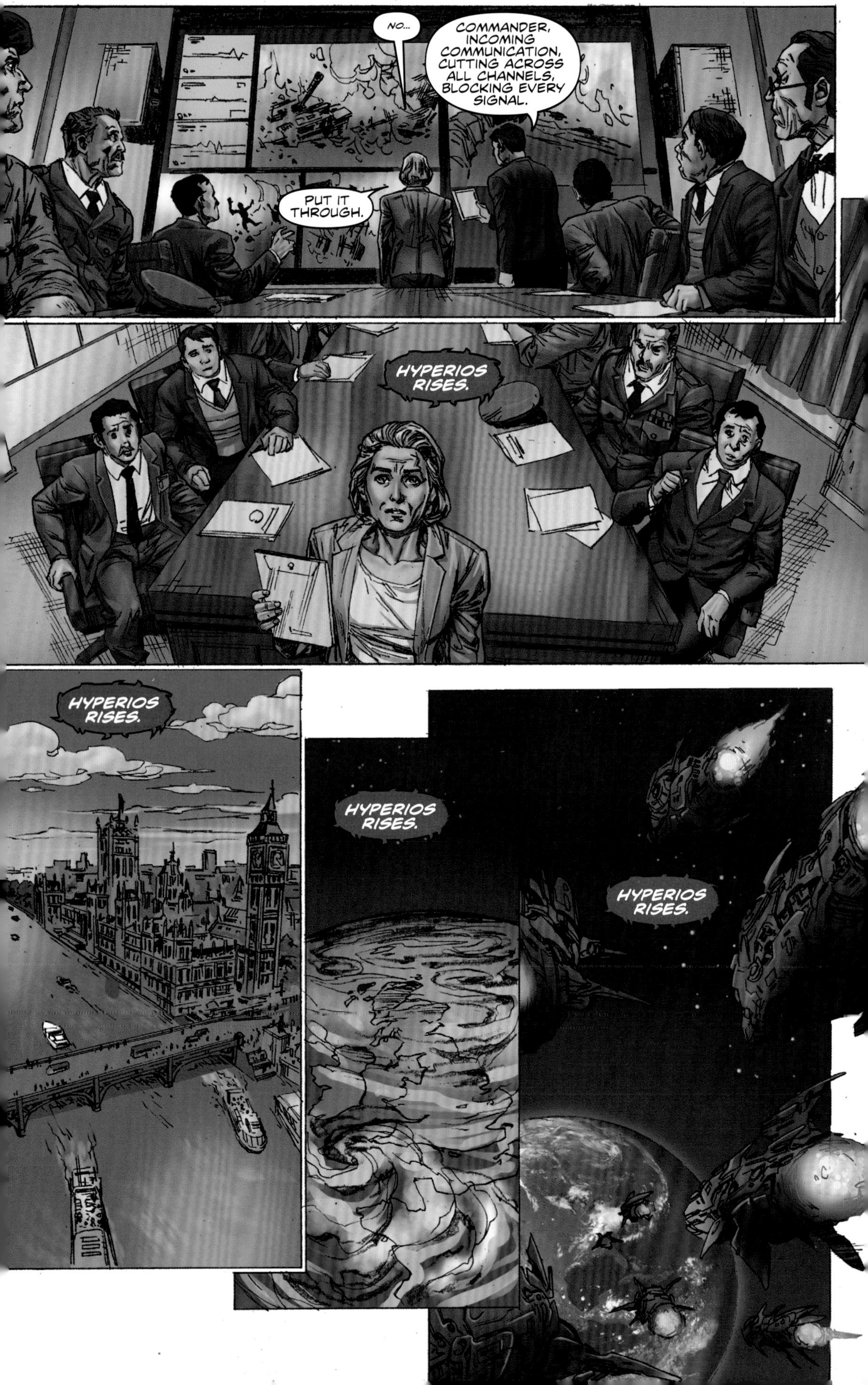
NO...
COMMANDER, INCOMING COMMUNICATION, CUTTING ACROSS ALL CHANNELS, BLOCKING EVERY SIGNAL.
PUT IT THROUGH.
HYPERIOS RISES.
HYPERIOS RISES.
HYPERIOS RISES.
HYPERIOS RISES.

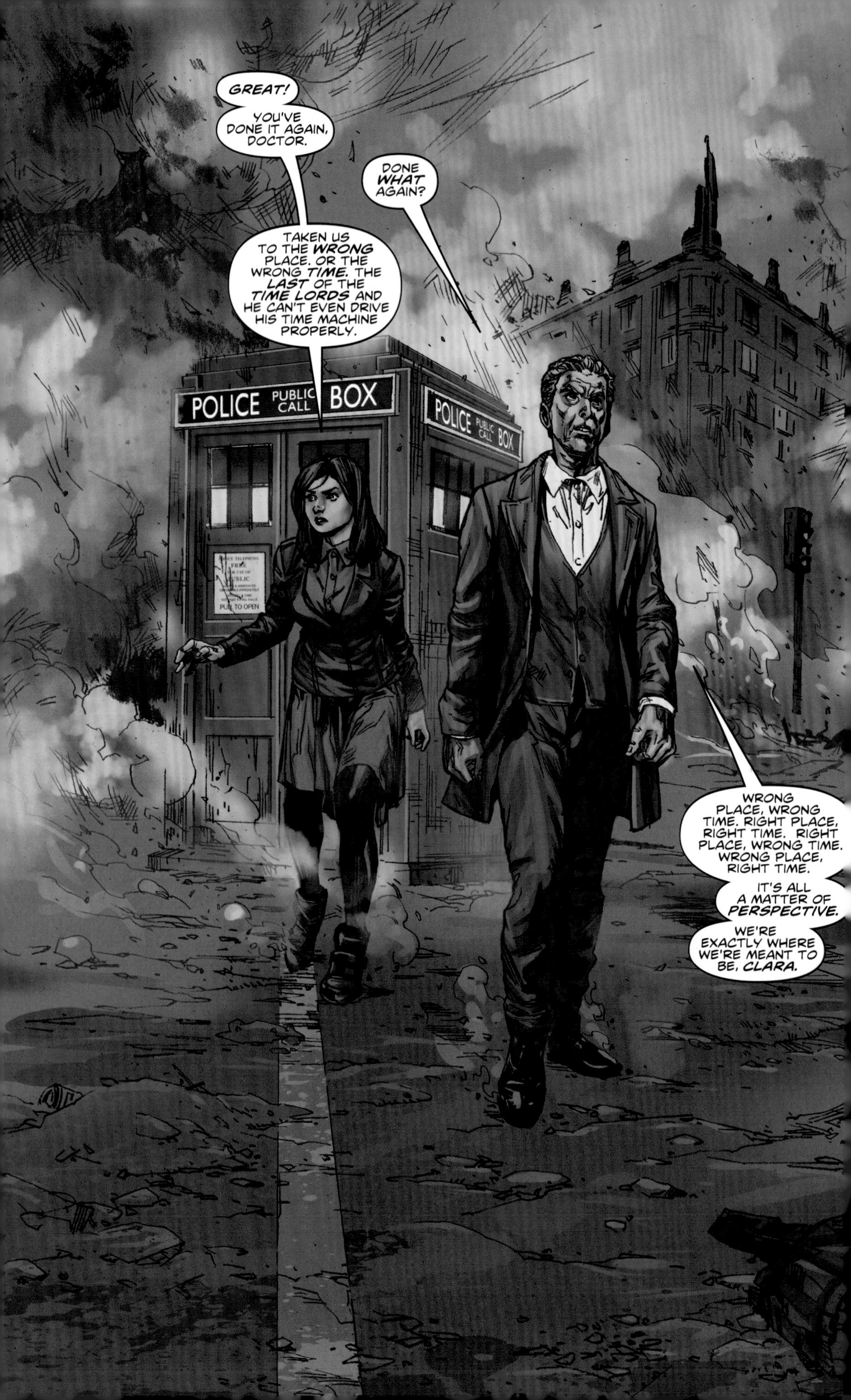
GREAT!
YOU'VE DONE IT AGAIN, DOCTOR.
TAKEN US TO THE WRONG PLACE. OR THE WRONG TIME. THE LAST OF THE TIME LORDS AND HE CAN'T EVEN DRIVE HIS TIME MACHINE PROPERLY.
DONE WHAT AGAIN?
POLICE PUBLIC CALL BOX
POLICE PUBLIC CALL BOX
PULL TO OPEN
WRONG PLACE, WRONG TIME. RIGHT PLACE, RIGHT TIME. RIGHT PLACE, WRONG TIME. WRONG PLACE, RIGHT TIME.
IT'S ALL A MATTER OF PERSPECTIVE.
WE'RE EXACTLY WHERE WE'RE MEANT TO BE, CLARA.

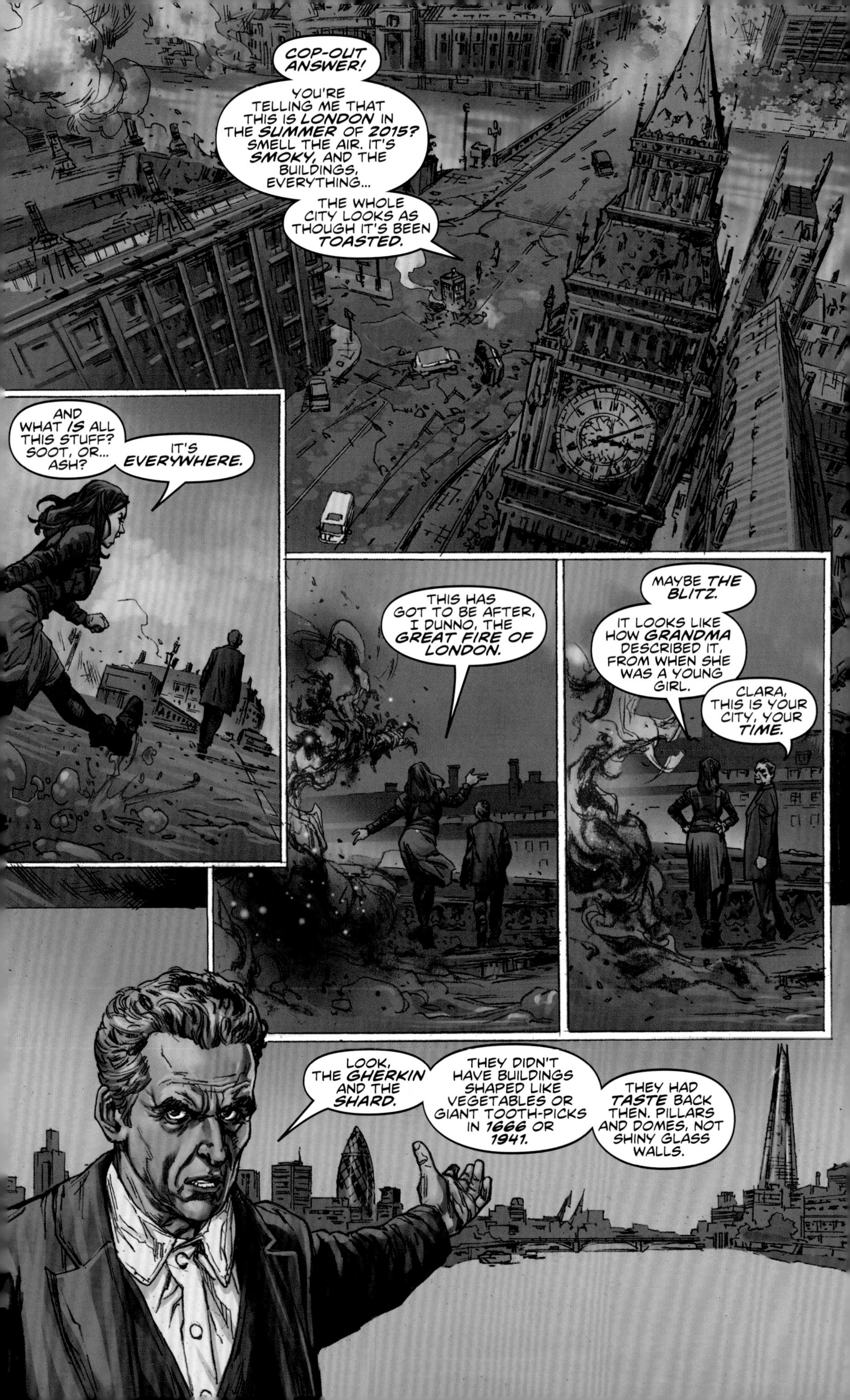
COP-OUT ANSWER!
YOU'RE TELLING ME THAT THIS IS LONDON IN THE SUMMER OF 2015? SMELL THE AIR. IT'S SMOKY, AND THE BUILDINGS, EVERYTHING...
THE WHOLE CITY LOOKS AS THOUGH IT'S BEEN TOASTED.
AND WHAT IS ALL THIS STUFF? SOOT, OR... ASH?
IT'S EVERYWHERE.
THIS HAS GOT TO BE AFTER, I DUNNO, THE GREAT FIRE OF LONDON.
MAYBE THE BLITZ.
IT LOOKS LIKE HOW GRANDMA DESCRIBED IT, FROM WHEN SHE WAS A YOUNG GIRL.
CLARA, THIS IS YOUR CITY, YOUR TIME.
LOOK, THE GHERKIN AND THE SHARD.
THEY DIDN'T HAVE BUILDINGS SHAPED LIKE VEGETABLES OR GIANT TOOTH-PICKS IN 1666 OR 1941.
THEY HAD TASTE BACK THEN. PILLARS AND DOMES, NOT SHINY GLASS WALLS.

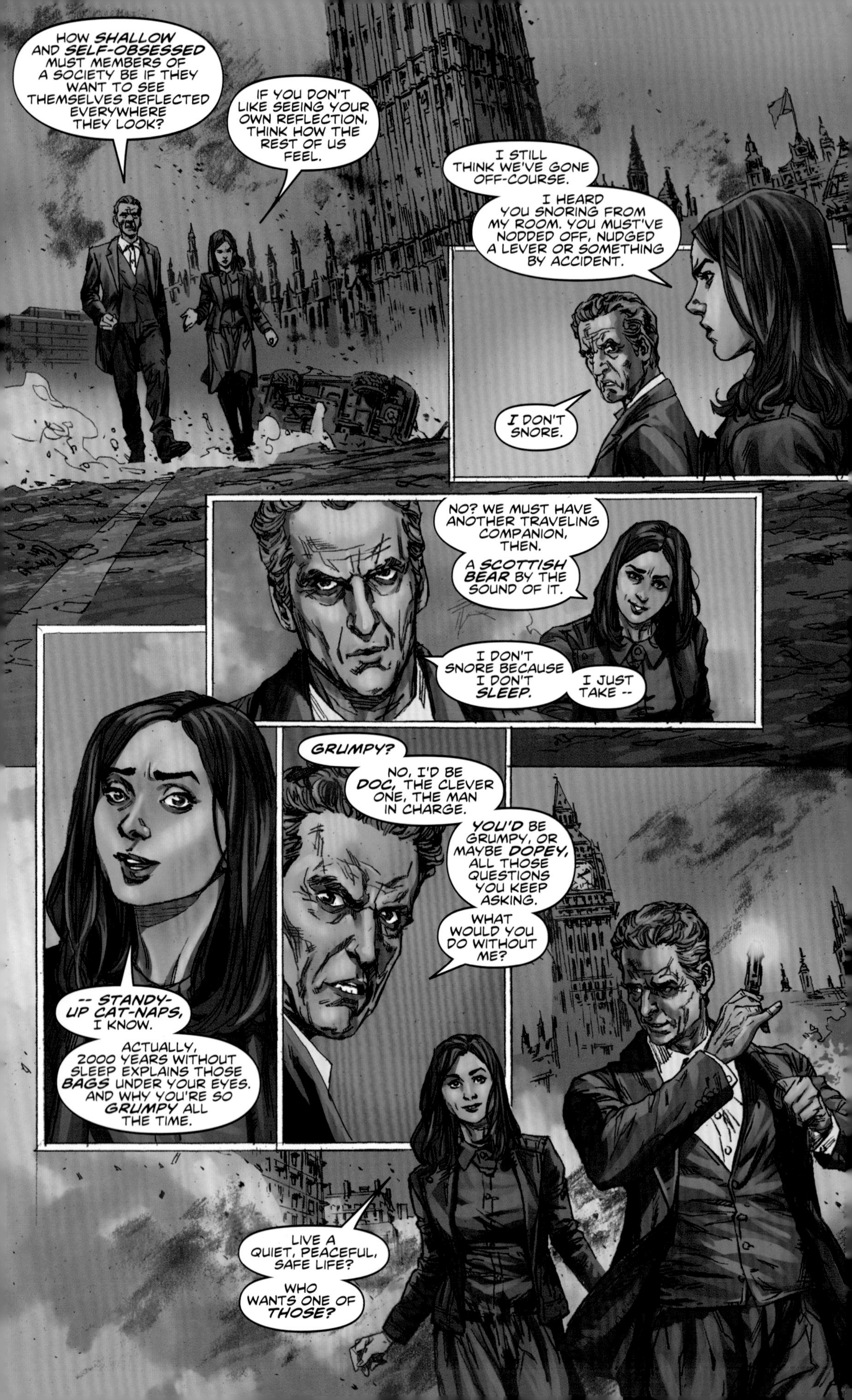
HOW SHALLOW AND SELF-OBSESSED MUST MEMBERS OF A SOCIETY BE IF THEY WANT TO SEE THEMSELVES REFLECTED EVERYWHERE THEY LOOK?
IF YOU DON'T LIKE SEEING YOUR OWN REFLECTION, THINK HOW THE REST OF US FEEL.
I STILL THINK WE'VE GONE OFF-COURSE.
I HEARD YOU SNORING FROM MY ROOM. YOU MUST'VE NODDED OFF, NUDGED A LEVER OR SOMETHING BY ACCIDENT.
I DON'T SNORE.
NO? WE MUST HAVE ANOTHER TRAVELING COMPANION, THEN.
A SCOTTISH BEAR BY THE SOUND OF IT.
I DON'T SNORE BECAUSE I DON'T SLEEP.
I JUST TAKE --
-- STANDY-UP CAT-NAPS, I KNOW.
ACTUALLY, 2000 YEARS WITHOUT SLEEP EXPLAINS THOSE BAGS UNDER YOUR EYES. AND WHY YOU'RE SO GRUMPY ALL THE TIME.
GRUMPY?
NO, I'D BE DOC, THE CLEVER ONE, THE MAN IN CHARGE.
YOU'D BE GRUMPY, OR MAYBE DOPEY, ALL THOSE QUESTIONS YOU KEEP ASKING.
WHAT WOULD YOU DO WITHOUT ME?
LIVE A QUIET, PEACEFUL, SAFE LIFE?
WHO WANTS ONE OF THOSE?

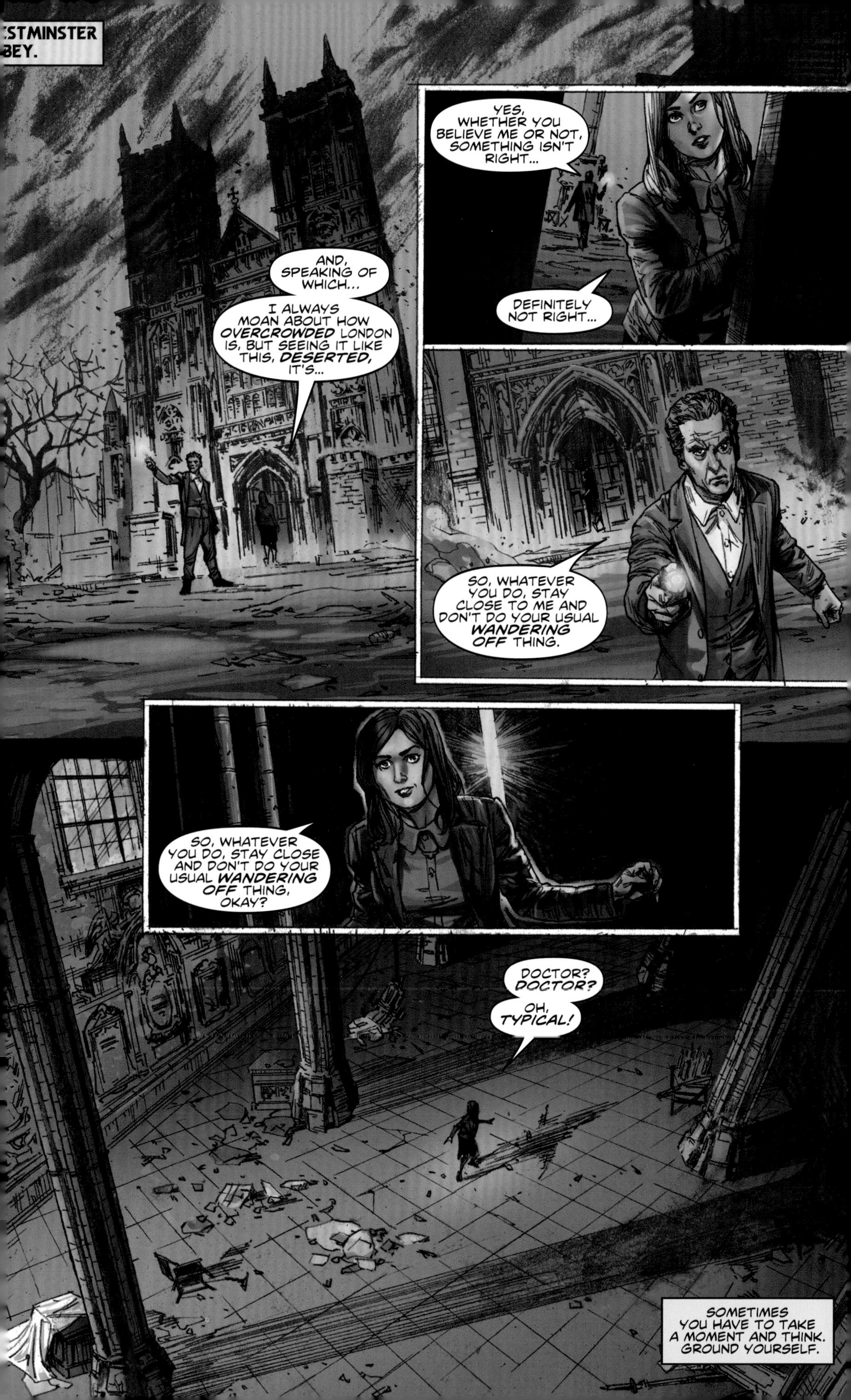
ESTMINSTER
BEY.
AND, SPEAKING OF WHICH...
I ALWAYS MOAN ABOUT HOW OVERCROWDED LONDON IS, BUT SEEING IT LIKE THIS, DESERTED, IT'S...
YES, WHETHER YOU BELIEVE ME OR NOT, SOMETHING ISN'T RIGHT...
DEFINITELY NOT RIGHT...
SO, WHATEVER YOU DO, STAY CLOSE TO ME AND DON'T DO YOUR USUAL WANDERING OFF THING.
SO, WHATEVER YOU DO, STAY CLOSE AND DON'T DO YOUR USUAL WANDERING OFF THING, OKAY?
DOCTOR? DOCTOR?
OH, TYPICAL!
SOMETIMES YOU HAVE TO TAKE A MOMENT AND THINK. GROUND YOURSELF.

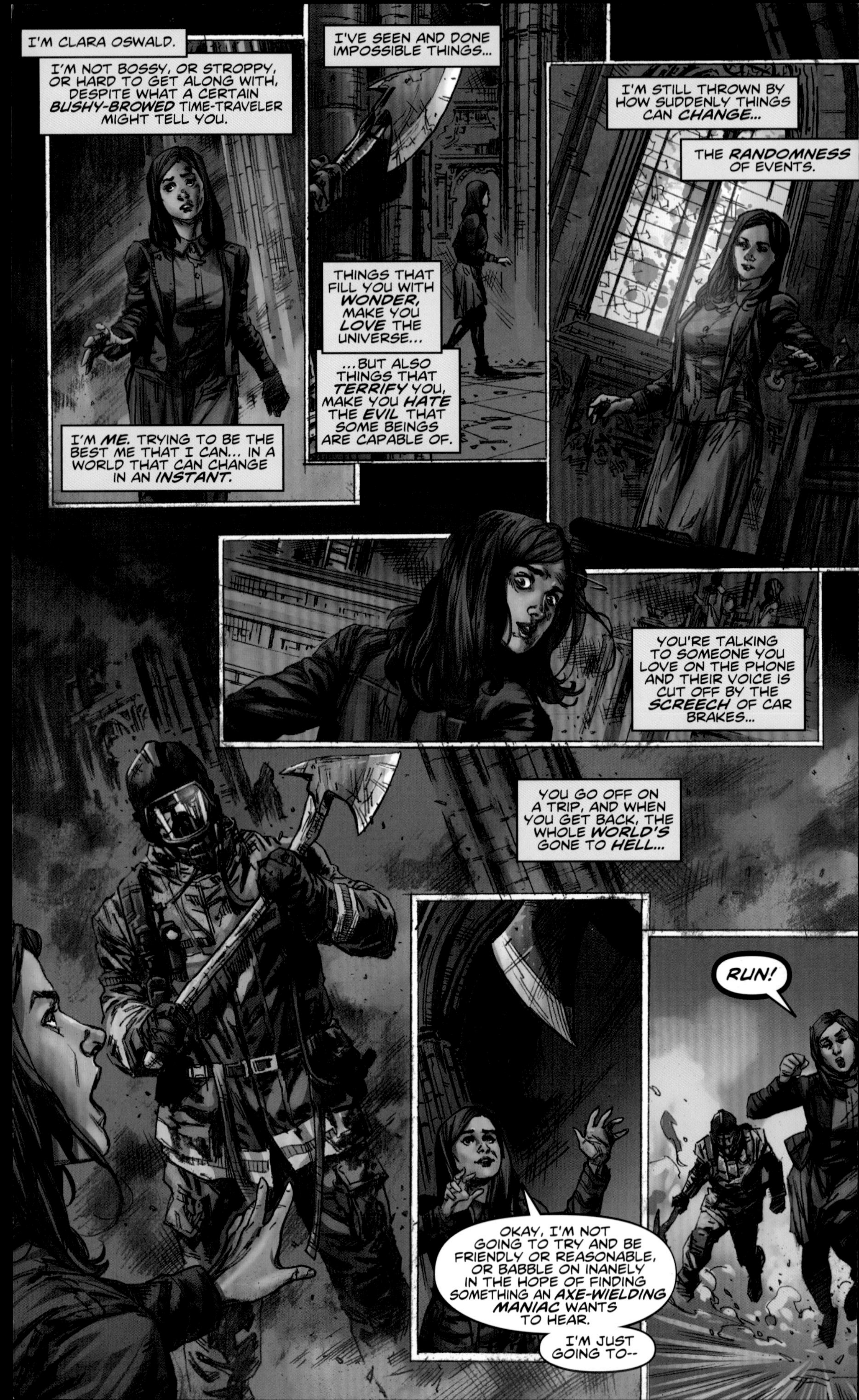
I'M CLARA OSWALD.
I'M NOT BOSSY, OR STROPPY, OR HARD TO GET ALONG WITH, DESPITE WHAT A CERTAIN BUSHY-BROWED TIME-TRAVELER MIGHT TELL YOU.
I'M ME. TRYING TO BE THE BEST ME THAT I CAN... IN A WORLD THAT CAN CHANGE IN AN INSTANT.
I'VE SEEN AND DONE IMPOSSIBLE THINGS...
THINGS THAT FILL YOU WITH WONDER, MAKE YOU LOVE THE UNIVERSE...
...BUT ALSO THINGS THAT TERRIFY YOU, MAKE YOU HATE THE EVIL THAT SOME BEINGS ARE CAPABLE OF.
I'M STILL THROWN BY HOW SUDDENLY THINGS CAN CHANGE...
THE RANDOMNESS OF EVENTS.
YOU'RE TALKING TO SOMEONE YOU LOVE ON THE PHONE AND THEIR VOICE IS CUT OFF BY THE SCREECH OF CAR BRAKES...
YOU GO OFF ON A TRIP, AND WHEN YOU GET BACK, THE WHOLE WORLD'S GONE TO HELL...
OKAY, I'M NOT GOING TO TRY AND BE FRIENDLY OR REASONABLE, OR BABBLE ON INANELY IN THE HOPE OF FINDING SOMETHING AN AXE-WIELDING MANIAC WANTS TO HEAR.
I'M JUST GOING TO--
RUN!

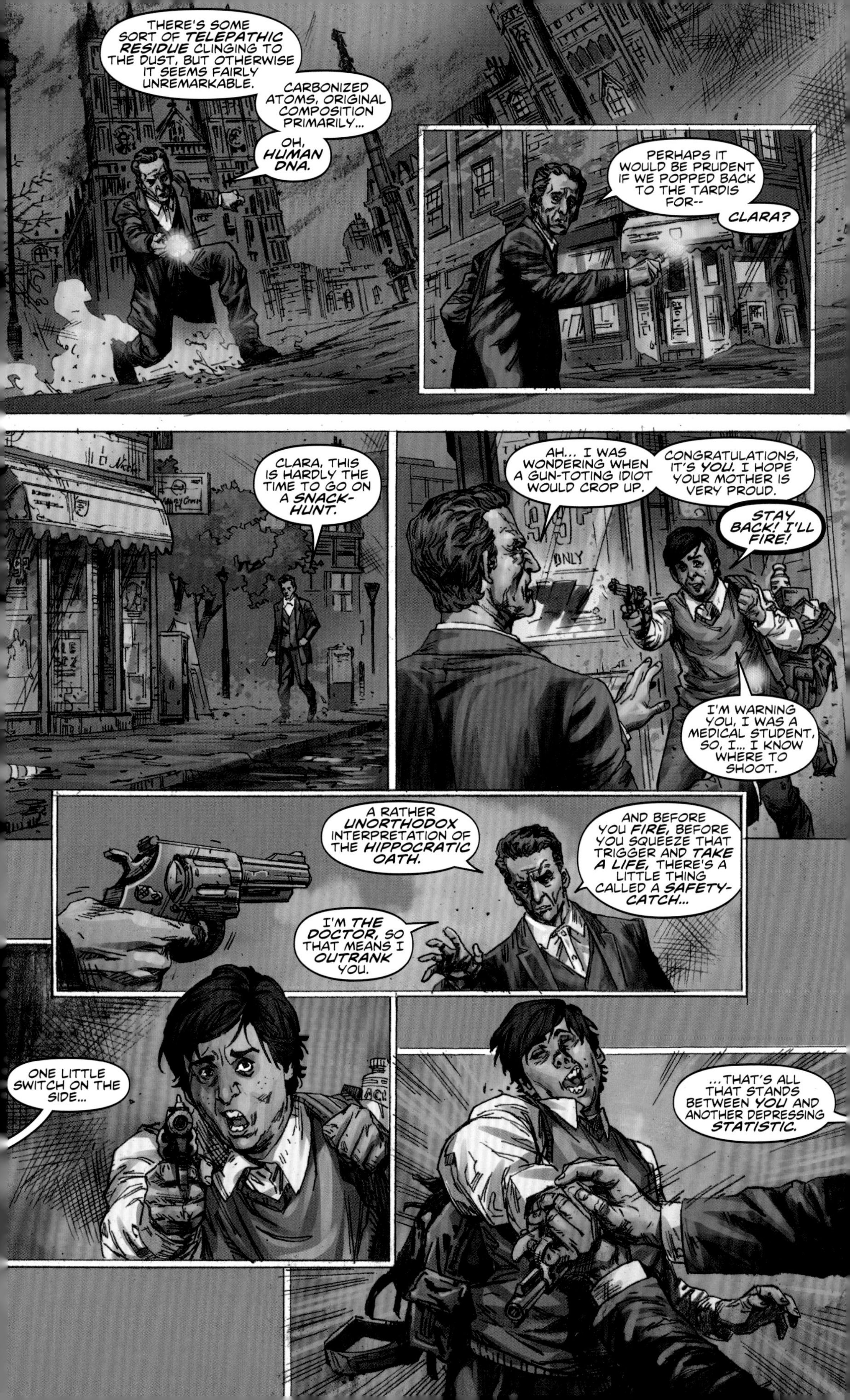
THERE'S SOME SORT OF TELEPATHIC RESIDUE CLINGING TO THE DUST, BUT OTHERWISE IT SEEMS FAIRLY UNREMARKABLE.
CARBONIZED ATOMS, ORIGINAL COMPOSITION PRIMARILY...
OH, HUMAN DNA.
PERHAPS IT WOULD BE PRUDENT IF WE POPPED BACK TO THE TARDIS FOR--
CLARA?
CLARA, THIS IS HARDLY THE TIME TO GO ON A SNACK-HUNT.
AH... I WAS WONDERING WHEN A GUN-TOTING IDIOT WOULD CROP UP.
CONGRATULATIONS, IT'S YOU. I HOPE YOUR MOTHER IS VERY PROUD.
STAY BACK! I'LL FIRE!
I'M WARNING YOU, I WAS A MEDICAL STUDENT, SO, I... I KNOW WHERE TO SHOOT.
A RATHER UNORTHODOX INTERPRETATION OF THE HIPPOCRATIC OATH.
AND BEFORE YOU FIRE, BEFORE YOU SQUEEZE THAT TRIGGER AND TAKE A LIFE, THERE'S A LITTLE THING CALLED A SAFETY-CATCH...
I'M THE DOCTOR, SO THAT MEANS I OUTRANK YOU.
ONE LITTLE SWITCH ON THE SIDE...
...THAT'S ALL THAT STANDS BETWEEN YOU AND ANOTHER DEPRESSING STATISTIC.

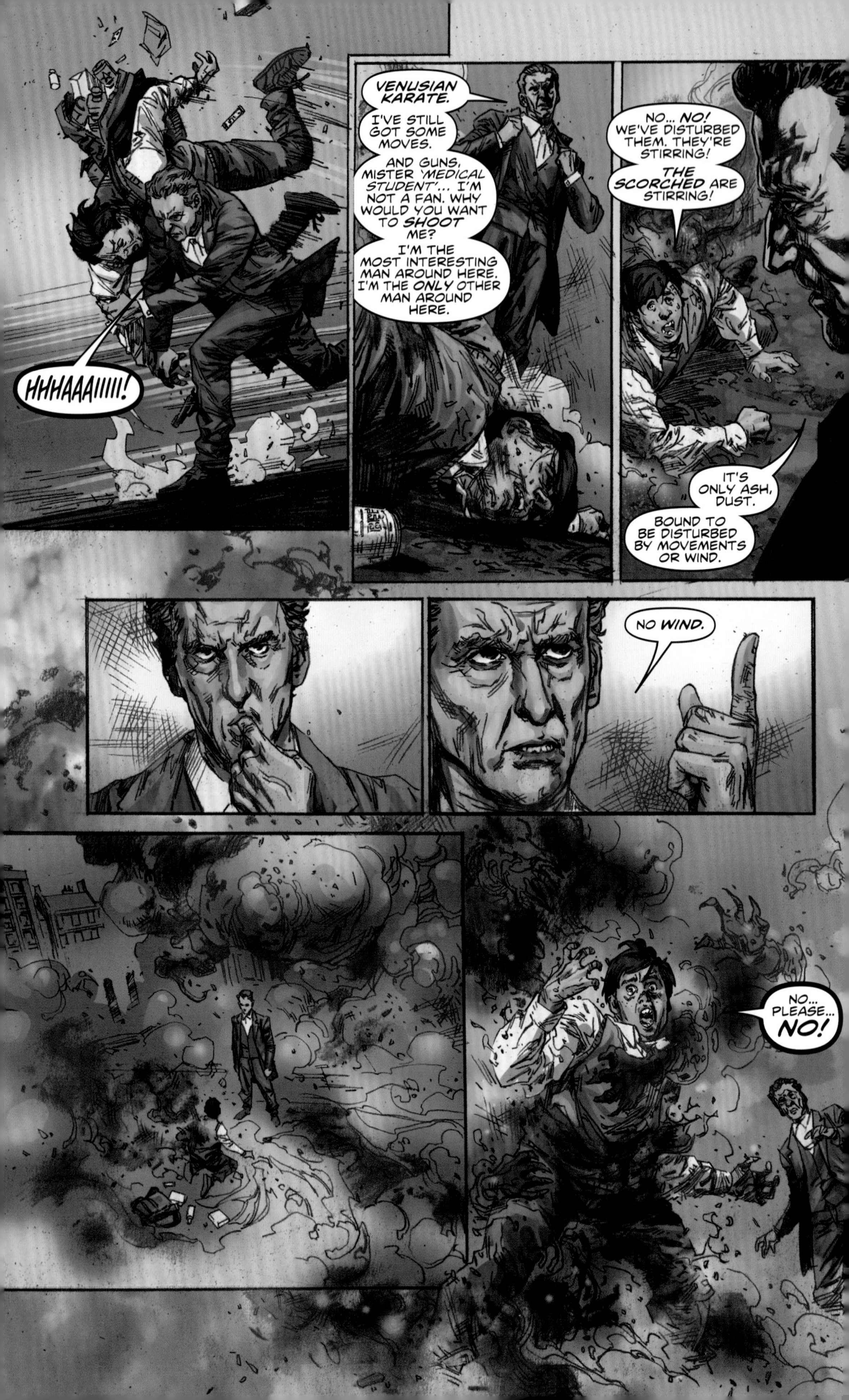
HHHAAAIIIIII!
VENUSIAN KARATE.
I'VE STILL GOT SOME MOVES.
AND GUNS, MISTER 'MEDICAL STUDENT'... I'M NOT A FAN. WHY WOULD YOU WANT TO SHOOT ME?
I'M THE MOST INTERESTING MAN AROUND HERE. I'M THE ONLY OTHER MAN AROUND HERE.
NO... NO! WE'VE DISTURBED THEM. THEY'RE STIRRING!
THE SCORCHED ARE STIRRING!
IT'S ONLY ASH, DUST.
BOUND TO BE DISTURBED BY MOVEMENTS OR WIND.
NO WIND.
NO... PLEASE... NO!

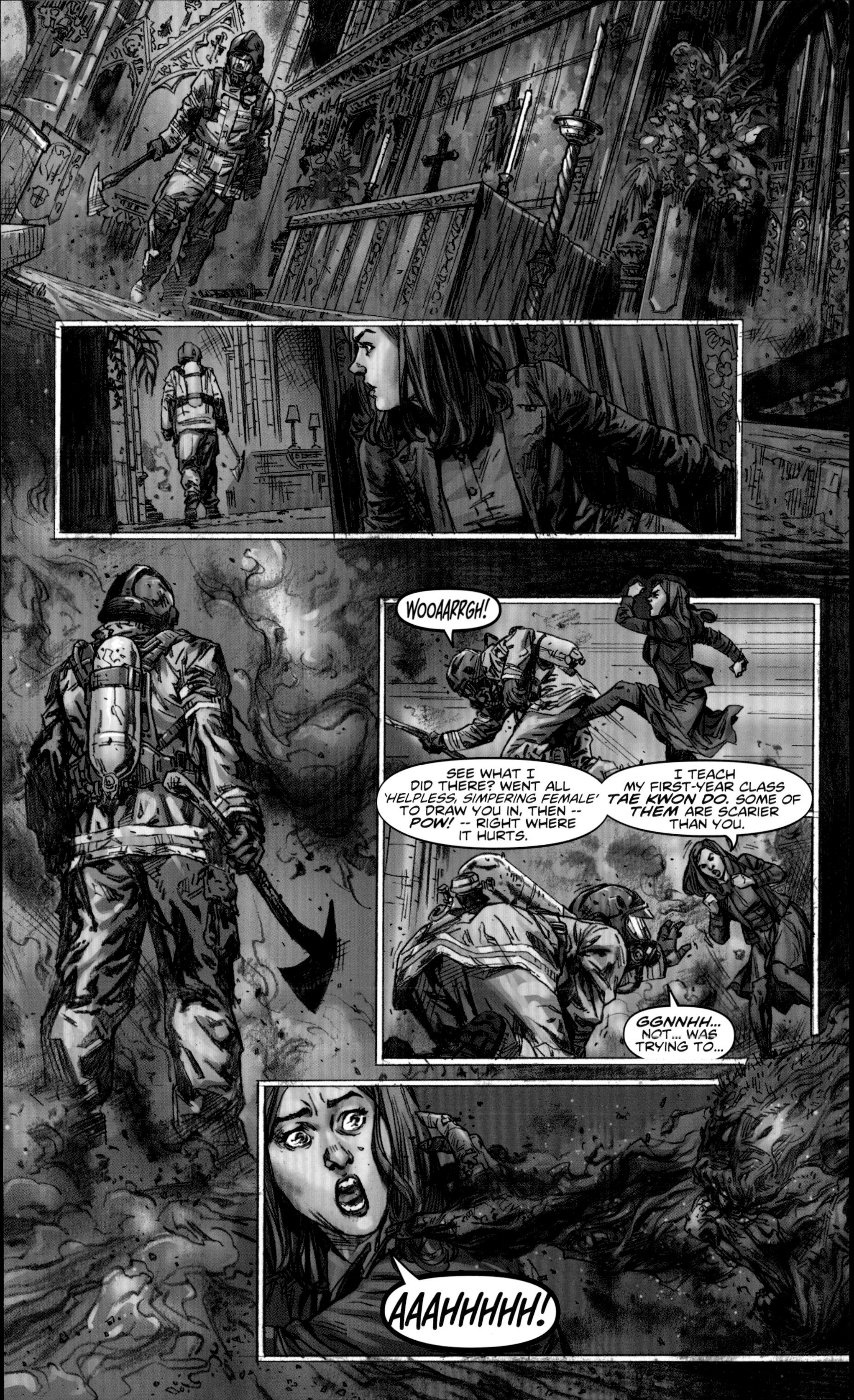
WOOAARRGH!
SEE WHAT I DID THERE? WENT ALL 'HELPLESS, SIMPERING FEMALE' TO DRAW YOU IN, THEN -- POW! -- RIGHT WHERE IT HURTS.
I TEACH MY FIRST-YEAR CLASS TAE KWON DO. SOME OF THEM ARE SCARIER THAN YOU.
GGNNHH... NOT... WAS TRYING TO...
AAAHHHHH!

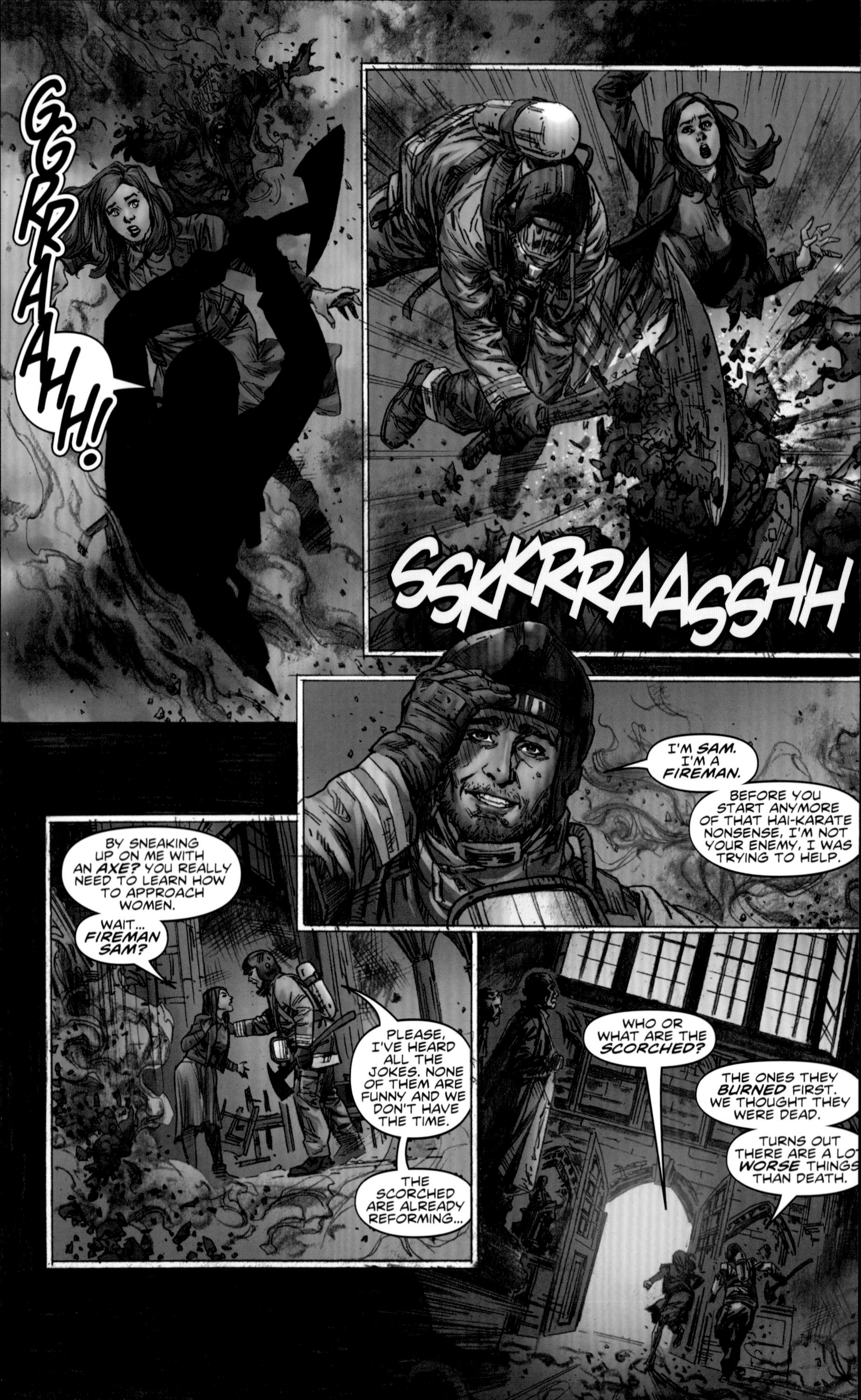
GGRRAAHH!
SSKKRRAASSHH
I'M SAM. I'M A FIREMAN.
BEFORE YOU START ANYMORE OF THAT HAI-KARATE NONSENSE, I'M NOT YOUR ENEMY, I WAS TRYING TO HELP.
BY SNEAKING UP ON ME WITH AN AXE? YOU REALLY NEED TO LEARN HOW TO APPROACH WOMEN.
WAIT... FIREMAN SAM?
PLEASE, I'VE HEARD ALL THE JOKES. NONE OF THEM ARE FUNNY AND WE DON'T HAVE THE TIME.
THE SCORCHED ARE ALREADY REFORMING...
WHO OR WHAT ARE THE SCORCHED?
THE ONES THEY BURNED FIRST. WE THOUGHT THEY WERE DEAD.
TURNS OUT THERE ARE A LOT WORSE THINGS THAN DEATH.

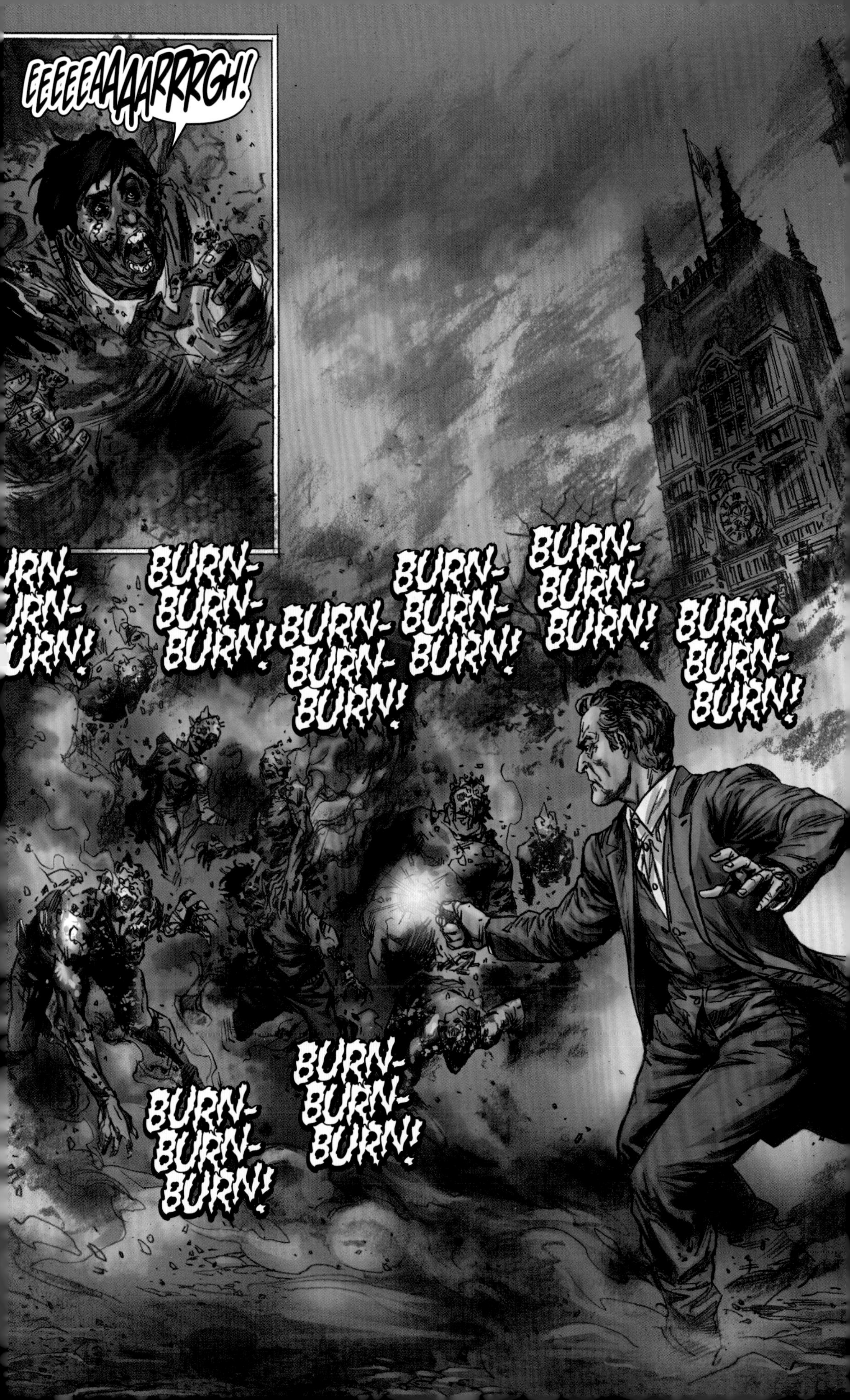
EEEEEAAAARRRGH!
BURN-
BURN-
BURN!
BURN-
BURN-
BURN!
BURN-
BURN-
BURN!
BURN-
BURN-
BURN!
BURN-
BURN-
BURN!
BURN-
BURN-
BURN!
BURN-
BURN-
BURN!

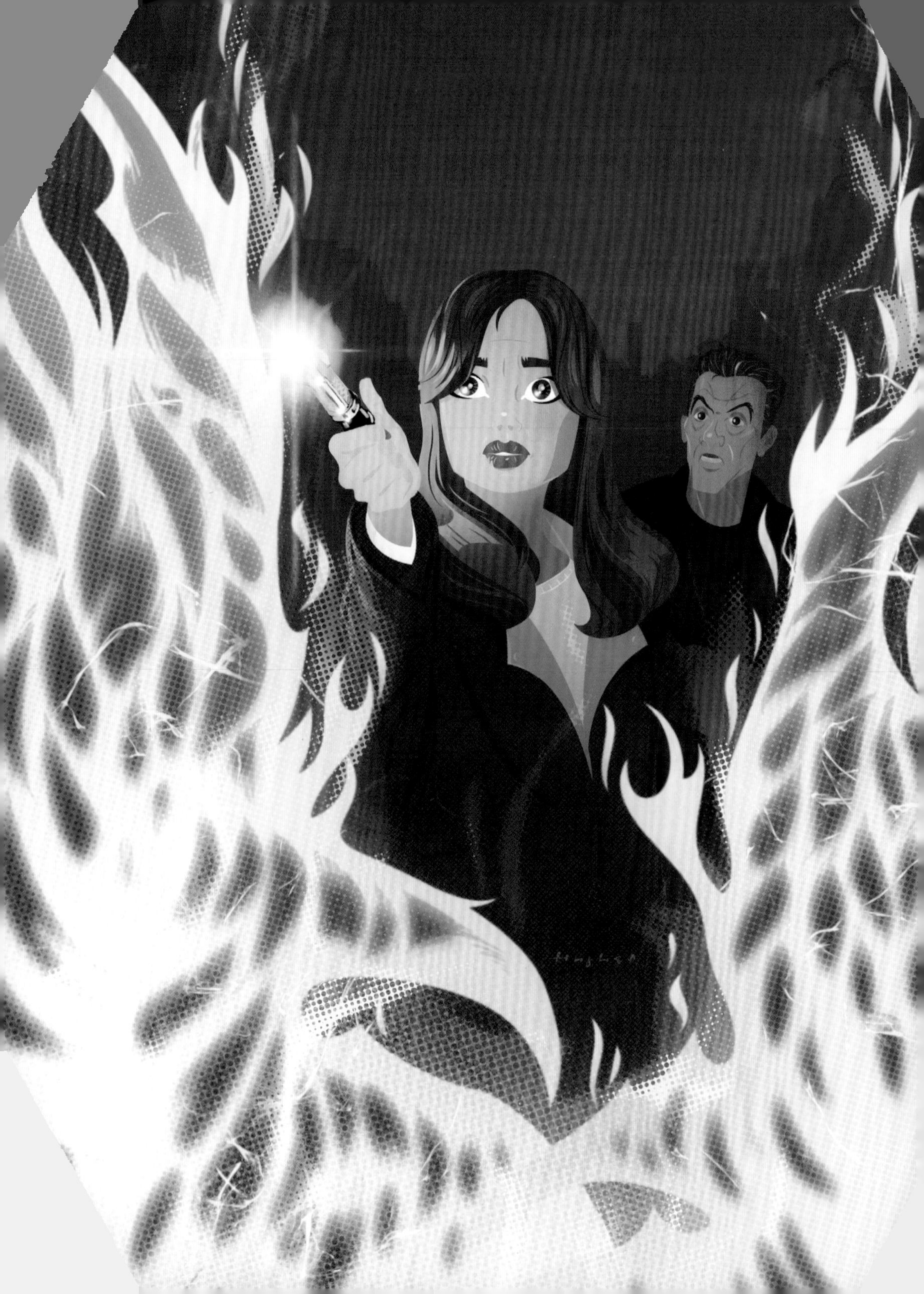

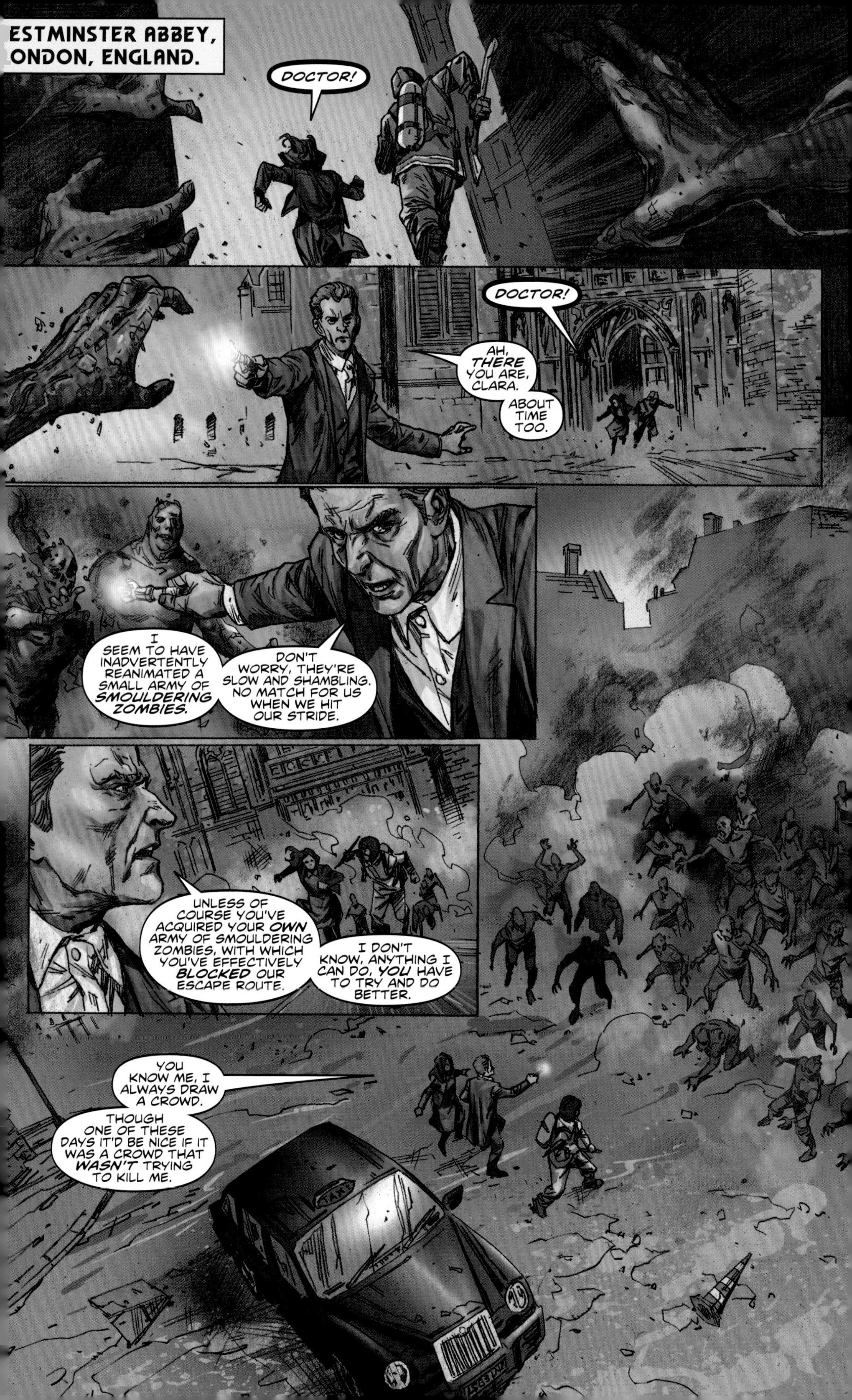

ESTMINSTER ABBEY, ONDON, ENGLAND.
DOCTOR!
DOCTOR!
AH, THERE YOU ARE, CLARA.
ABOUT TIME TOO.
I SEEM TO HAVE INADVERTENTLY REANIMATED A SMALL ARMY OF SMOULDERING ZOMBIES.
DON'T WORRY, THEY'RE SLOW AND SHAMBLING. NO MATCH FOR US WHEN WE HIT OUR STRIDE.
UNLESS OF COURSE YOU'VE ACQUIRED YOUR OWN ARMY OF SMOULDERING ZOMBIES, WITH WHICH YOU'VE EFFECTIVELY BLOCKED OUR ESCAPE ROUTE.
I DON'T KNOW, ANYTHING I CAN DO, YOU HAVE TO TRY AND DO BETTER.
YOU KNOW ME, I ALWAYS DRAW A CROWD.
THOUGH ONE OF THESE DAYS IT'D BE NICE IF IT WAS A CROWD THAT WASN'T TRYING TO KILL ME.
TAXI

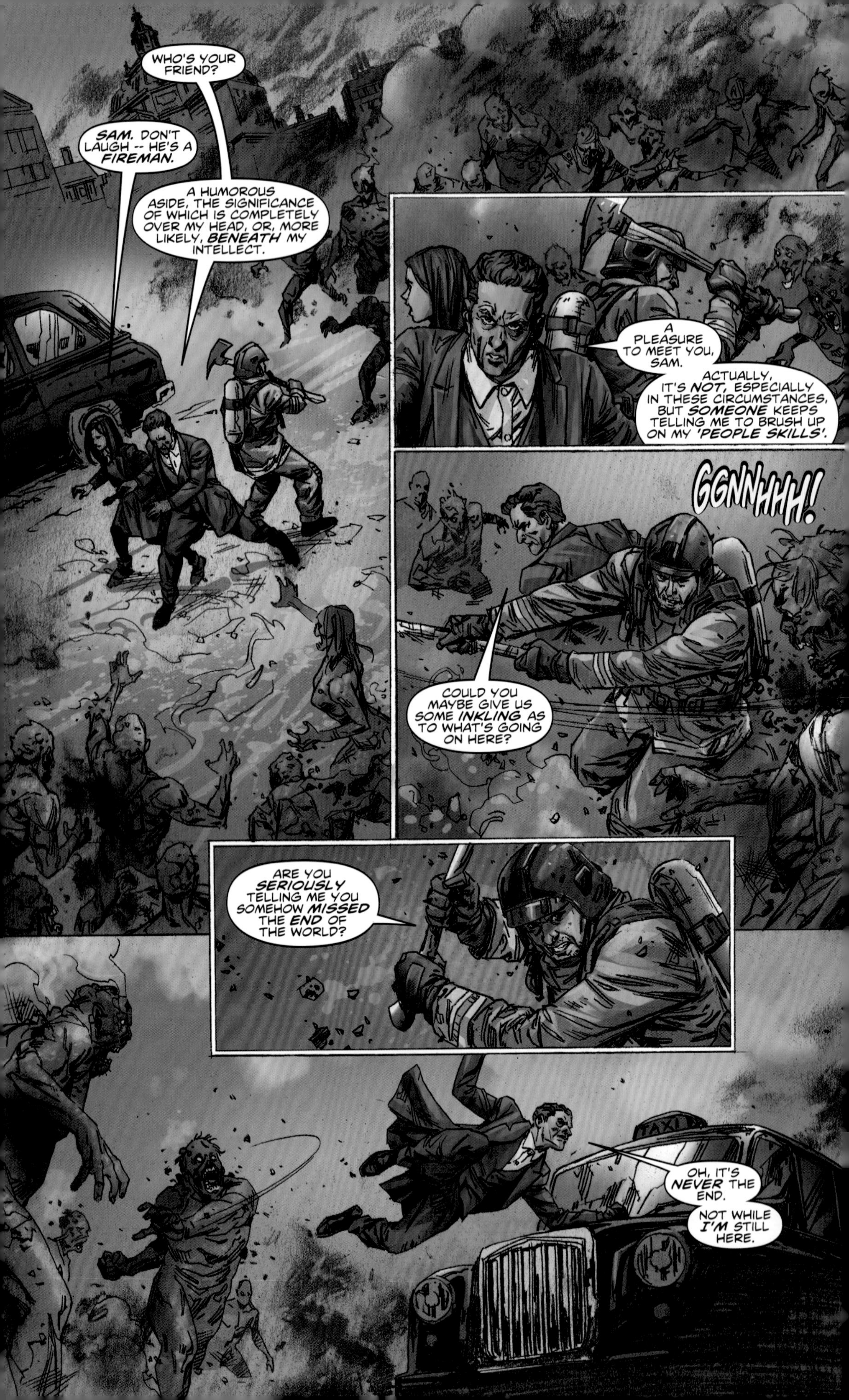
WHO'S YOUR FRIEND?
SAM. DON'T LAUGH -- HE'S A FIREMAN.
A HUMOROUS ASIDE, THE SIGNIFICANCE OF WHICH IS COMPLETELY OVER MY HEAD, OR, MORE LIKELY, BENEATH MY INTELLECT.
A PLEASURE TO MEET YOU, SAM.
ACTUALLY, IT'S NOT, ESPECIALLY IN THESE CIRCUMSTANCES, BUT SOMEONE KEEPS TELLING ME TO BRUSH UP ON MY 'PEOPLE SKILLS'.
GGNNHHH!
COULD YOU MAYBE GIVE US SOME INKLING AS TO WHAT'S GOING ON HERE?
ARE YOU SERIOUSLY TELLING ME YOU SOMEHOW MISSED THE END OF THE WORLD?
TAXI
OH, IT'S NEVER THE END.
NOT WHILE I'M STILL HERE.

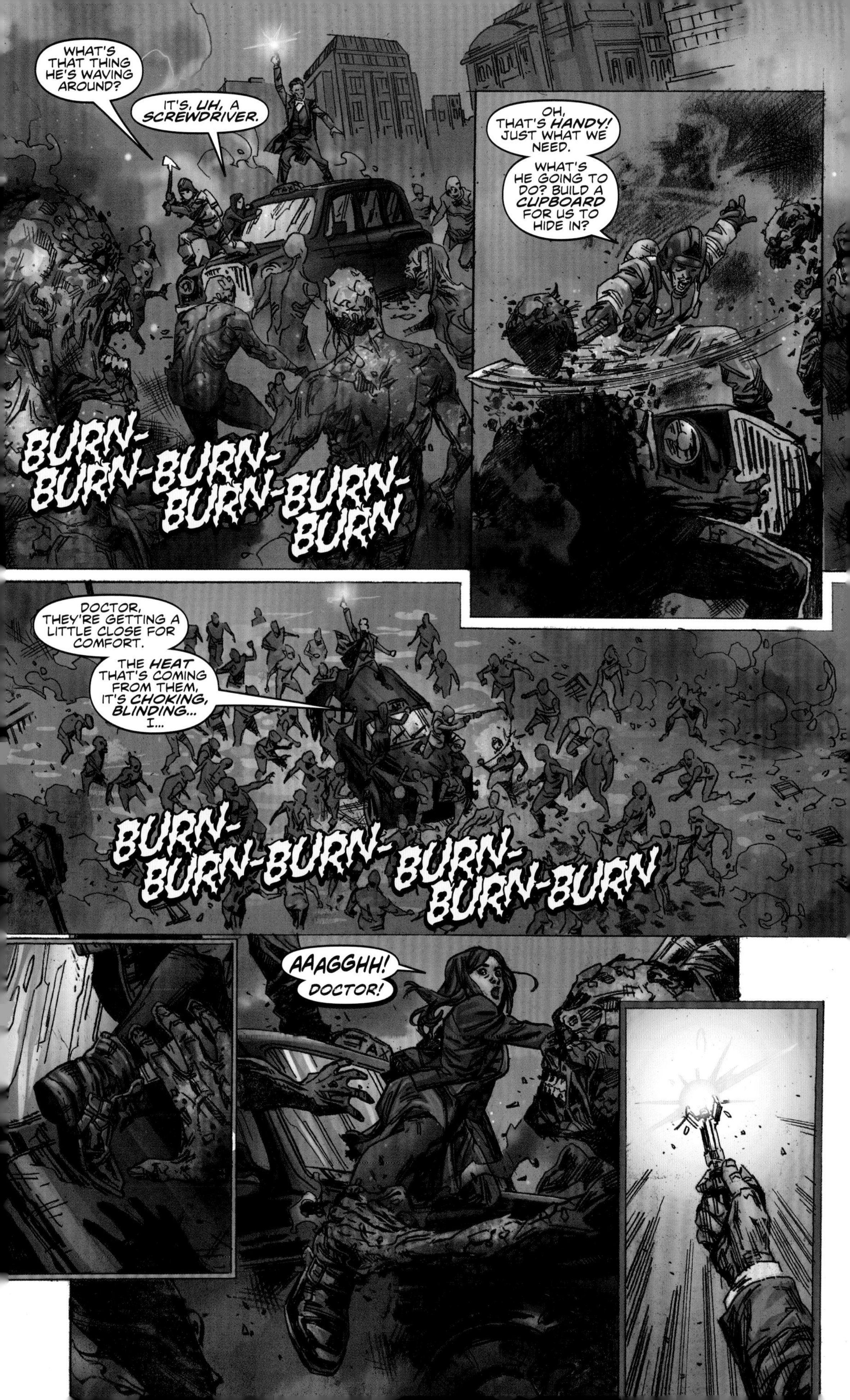
WHAT'S THAT THING HE'S WAVING AROUND?
IT'S, UH, A SCREWDRIVER.
BURN-BURN-BURN-BURN-BURN-BURN
OH, THAT'S HANDY! JUST WHAT WE NEED.
WHAT'S HE GOING TO DO? BUILD A CUPBOARD FOR US TO HIDE IN?
DOCTOR, THEY'RE GETTING A LITTLE CLOSE FOR COMFORT.
THE HEAT THAT'S COMING FROM THEM, IT'S CHOKING, BLINDING... I...
BURN-BURN-BURN-BURN-BURN-BURN
AAAGGHH! DOCTOR!

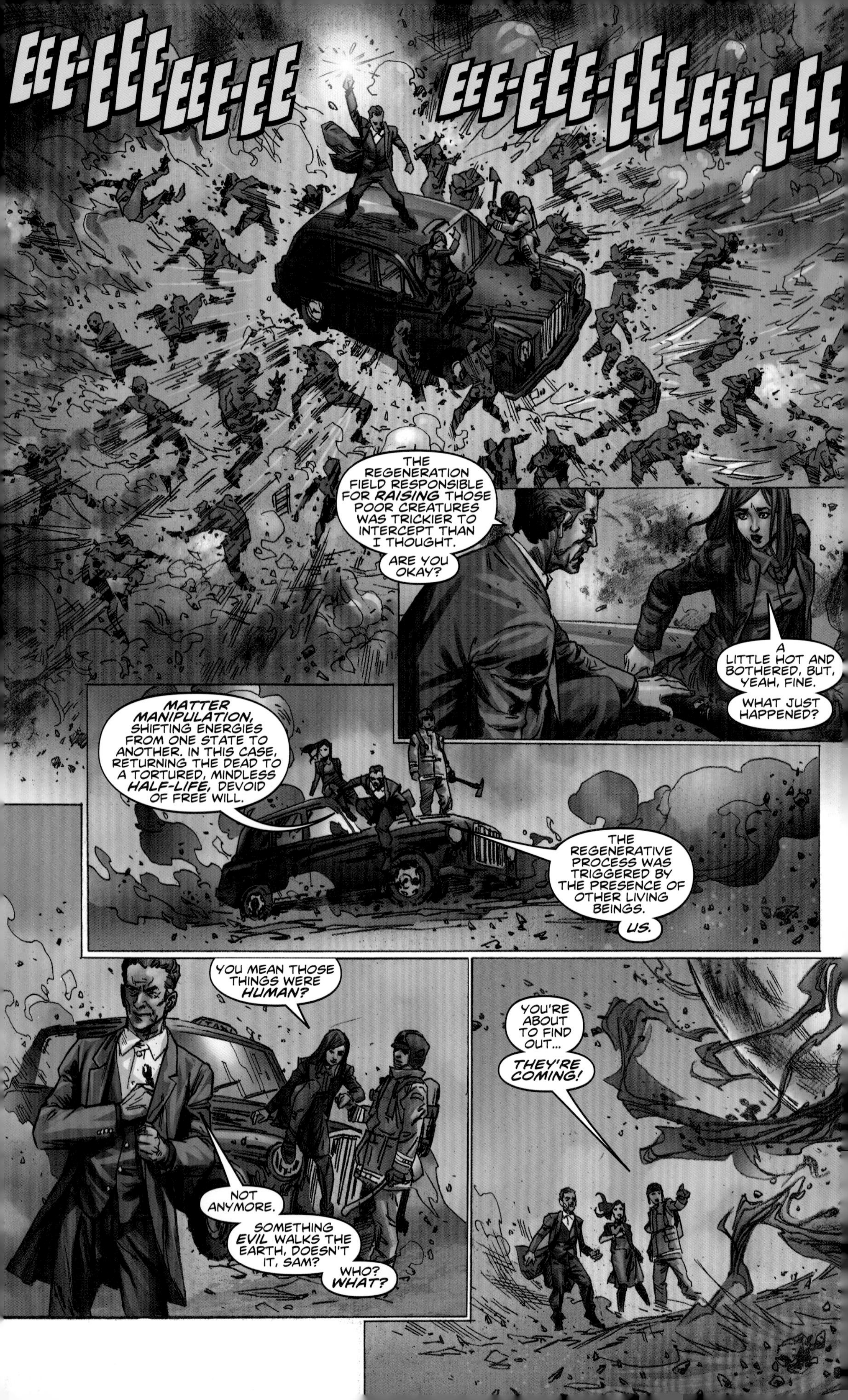
EEE-EEEEEE-EE
EEE-EEE-EEEEEE-EEE
THE REGENERATION FIELD RESPONSIBLE FOR RAISING THOSE POOR CREATURES WAS TRICKIER TO INTERCEPT THAN I THOUGHT.
ARE YOU OKAY?
A LITTLE HOT AND BOTHERED, BUT, YEAH, FINE.
WHAT JUST HAPPENED?
MATTER MANIPULATION, SHIFTING ENERGIES FROM ONE STATE TO ANOTHER. IN THIS CASE, RETURNING THE DEAD TO A TORTURED, MINDLESS HALF-LIFE, DEVOID OF FREE WILL.
THE REGENERATIVE PROCESS WAS TRIGGERED BY THE PRESENCE OF OTHER LIVING BEINGS.
US.
YOU MEAN THOSE THINGS WERE HUMAN?
NOT ANYMORE.
SOMETHING EVIL WALKS THE EARTH, DOESN'T IT, SAM?
WHO? WHAT?
YOU'RE ABOUT TO FIND OUT...
THEY'RE COMING!

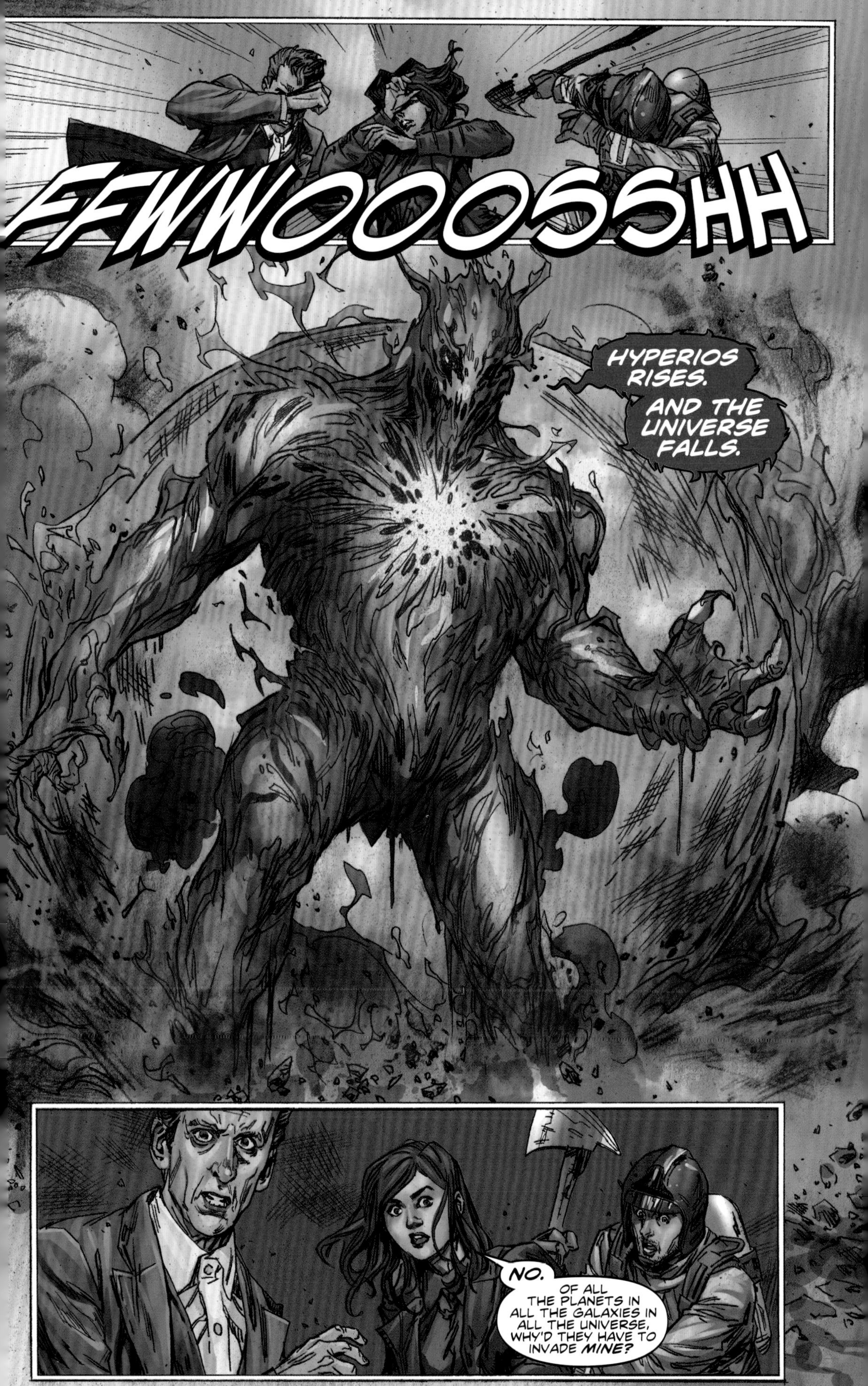
FFWOOOSSHH
HYPERIOS RISES.
AND THE UNIVERSE FALLS.
NO.
OF ALL THE PLANETS IN ALL THE GALAXIES IN ALL THE UNIVERSE, WHY'D THEY HAVE TO INVADE MINE?

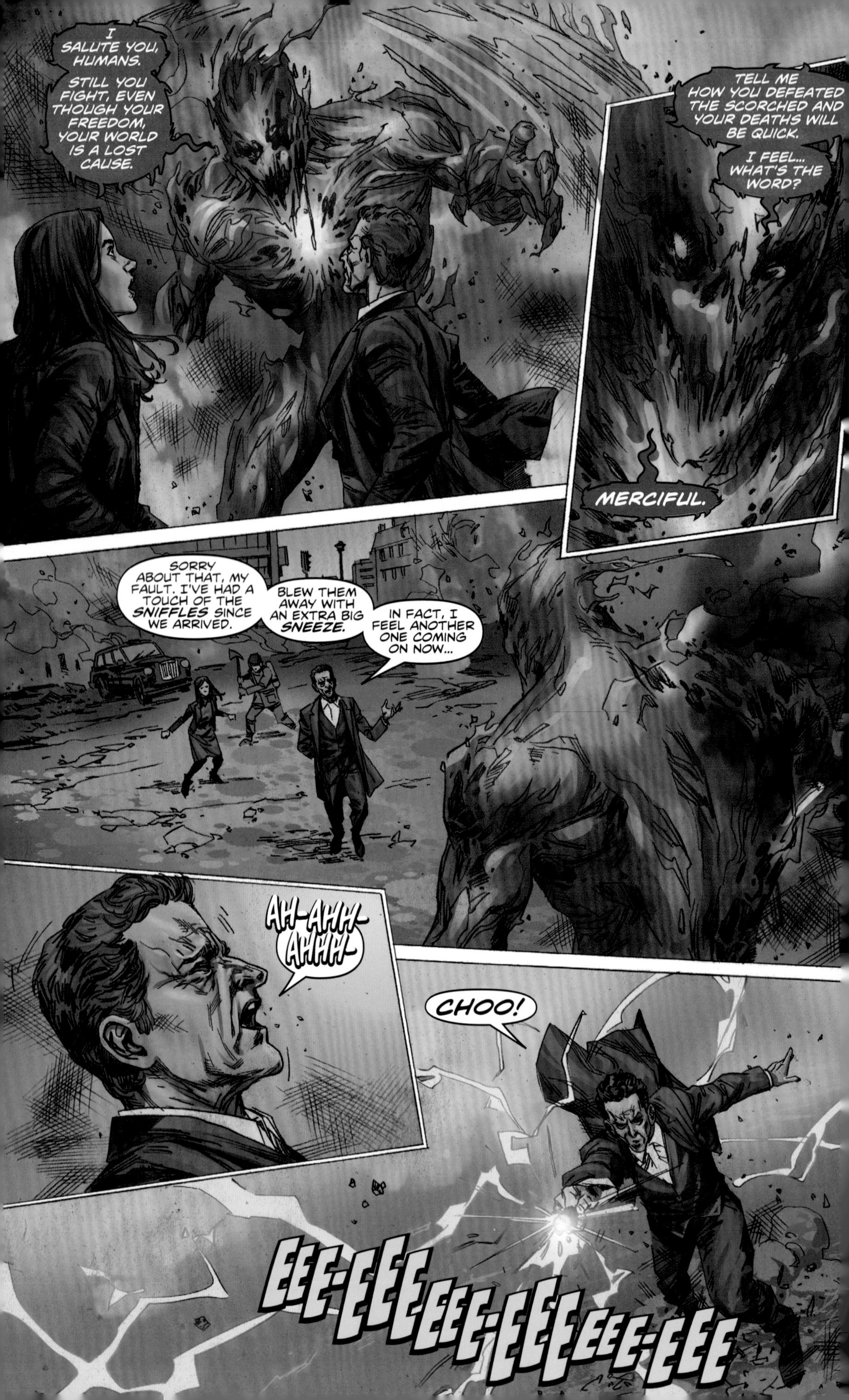
I SALUTE YOU, HUMANS.
STILL YOU FIGHT, EVEN THOUGH YOUR FREEDOM, YOUR WORLD IS A LOST CAUSE.
TELL ME HOW YOU DEFEATED THE SCORCHED AND YOUR DEATHS WILL BE QUICK.
I FEEL... WHAT'S THE WORD?
MERCIFUL.
SORRY ABOUT THAT, MY FAULT. I'VE HAD A TOUCH OF THE SNIFFLES SINCE WE ARRIVED.
BLEW THEM AWAY WITH AN EXTRA BIG SNEEZE.
IN FACT, I FEEL ANOTHER ONE COMING ON NOW...
AH-AHH-AHHH-
CHOO!
EEE-EEEEEE-EEEEEEE-EEE

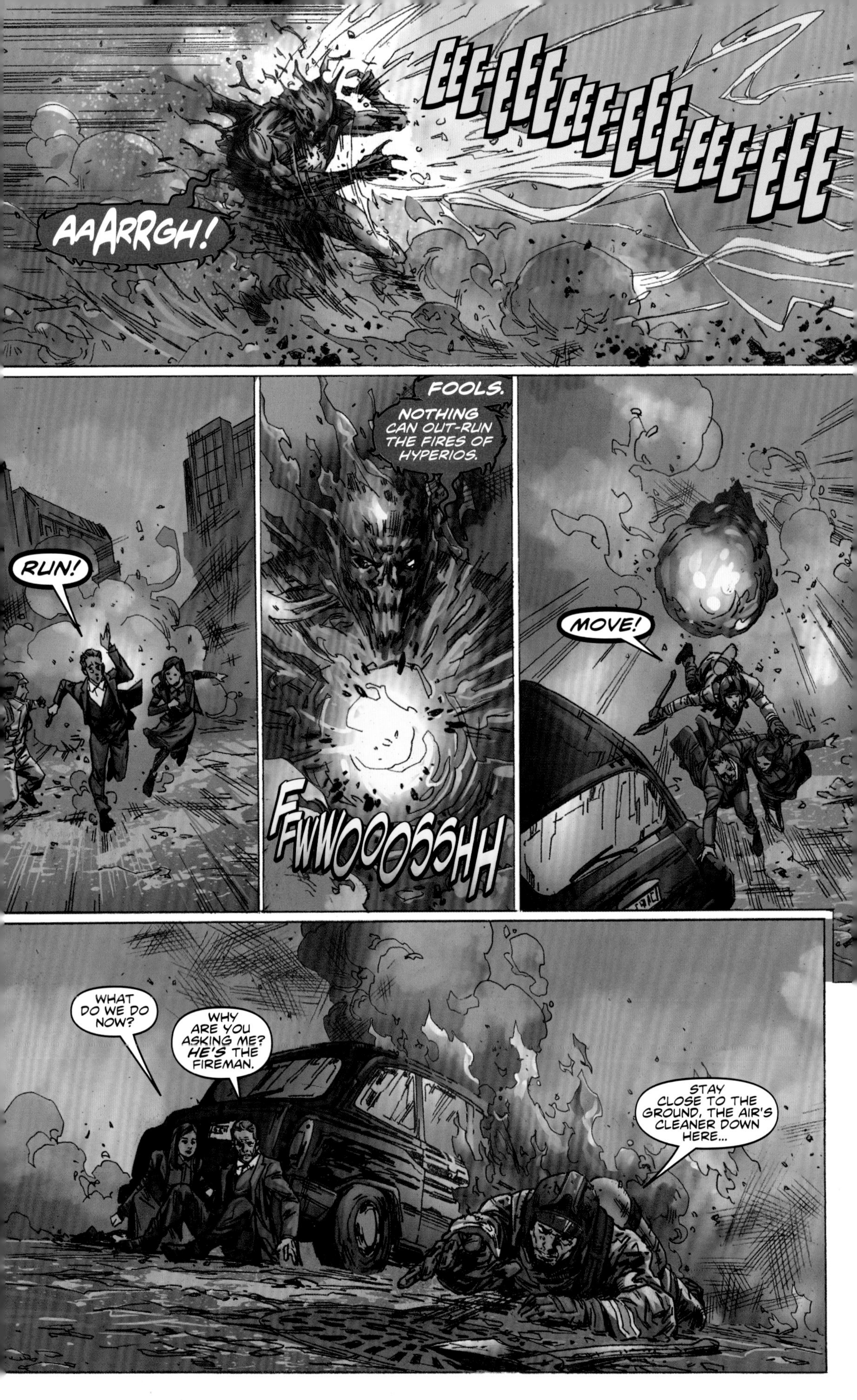
EEE-EEEEEE-EEEEEE-EEE
AAARRGH!
RUN!
FOOLS.
NOTHING CAN OUT-RUN THE FIRES OF HYPERIOS.
FFWWOOOSSHH
MOVE!
WHAT DO WE DO NOW?
WHY ARE YOU ASKING ME? HE'S THE FIREMAN.
STAY CLOSE TO THE GROUND, THE AIR'S CLEANER DOWN HERE...

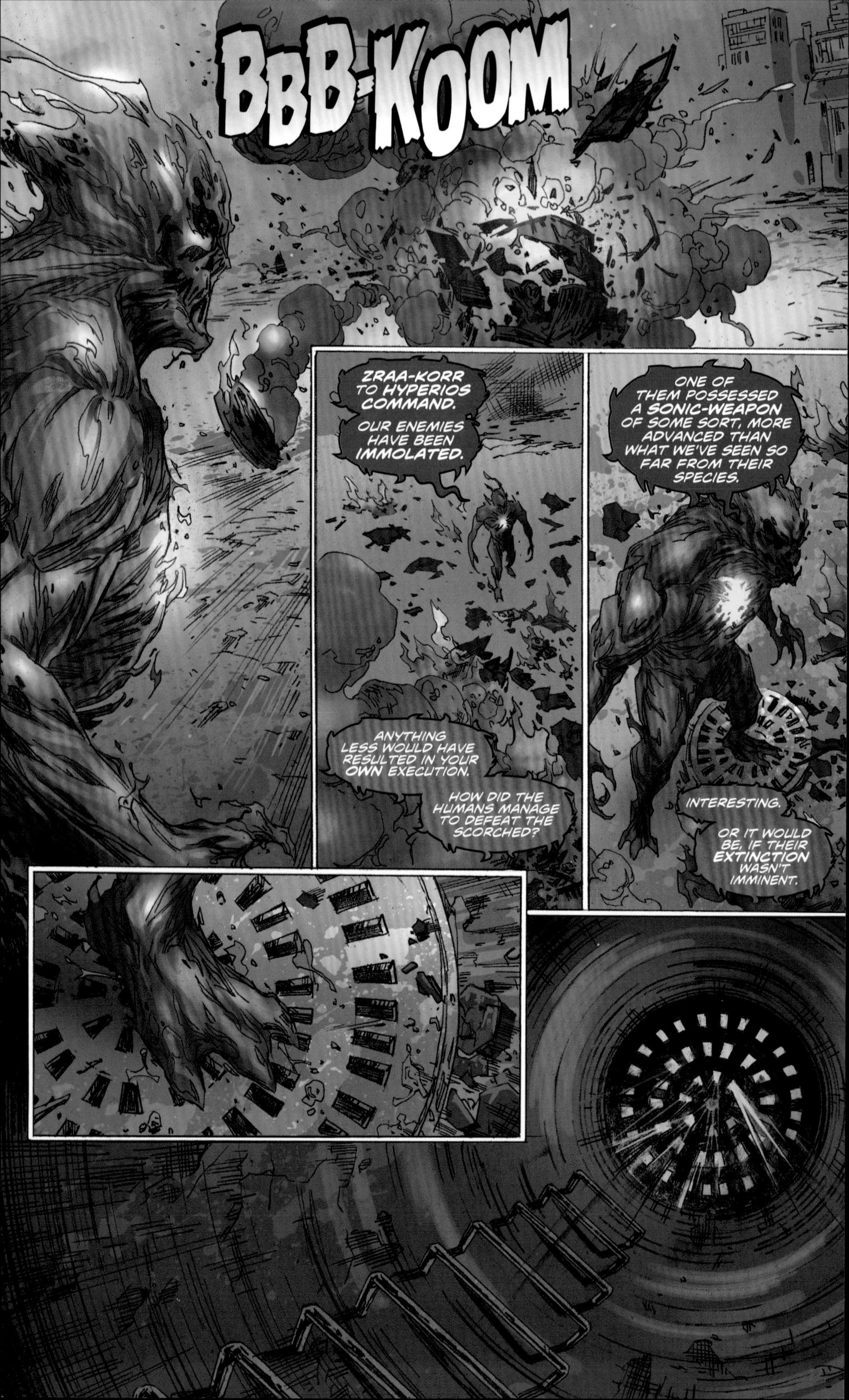
BBB-KOOM
ZRAA-KORR TO HYPERIOS COMMAND.
OUR ENEMIES HAVE BEEN IMMOLATED.
ANYTHING LESS WOULD HAVE RESULTED IN YOUR OWN EXECUTION.
HOW DID THE HUMANS MANAGE TO DEFEAT THE SCORCHED?
ONE OF THEM POSSESSED A SONIC-WEAPON OF SOME SORT, MORE ADVANCED THAN WHAT WE'VE SEEN SO FAR FROM THEIR SPECIES.
INTERESTING.
OR IT WOULD BE, IF THEIR EXTINCTION WASN'T IMMINENT.

WHAT WAS THAT YOU WERE SAYING ABOUT THE AIR BEING *CLEANER* DOWN HERE?

SHH!

HE'S GONE.

'COURSE HE HAS, WE'RE *MARINATING* IN *SEWAGE!*

WHY WOULD HE WANT TO BARBEQUE US *NOW?*

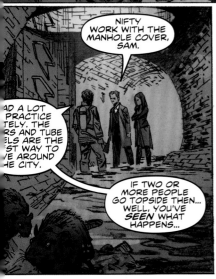

NIFTY WORK WITH THE MANHOLE COVER, SAM.

...AD A LOT ...PRACTICE ...TELY. THE ...RS AND TUBE ...ELS ARE THE ...ST WAY TO ...VE AROUND ...E CITY.

IF TWO OR MORE PEOPLE GO TOPSIDE THEN... WELL, YOU'VE *SEEN* WHAT HAPPENS...

SOMETHING I DON'T UNDERSTAND...

YOU DIDN'T SEEM TO KNOW WHAT HAD HAPPENED HERE, BUT YOU *RECOGNIZED* THOSE CREATURES. *HOW?*

OH, WE MAY LOOK LIKE A *GRUMPY OLD MAN* AND HIS *CARER,* BUT WE'VE BEEN ABOUT A BIT.

I'M *CLARA.* HE'S *THE DOCTOR.*

WHEN DID THE HYPERIONS ARRIVE?

HARD TO SAY, A FEW WEEKS AT MOST.

YOU KIND OF LOSE TRACK OF TIME. TOO BUSY TRYING TO SURVIVE. EVERYTHING ELSE JUST FADES AWAY.

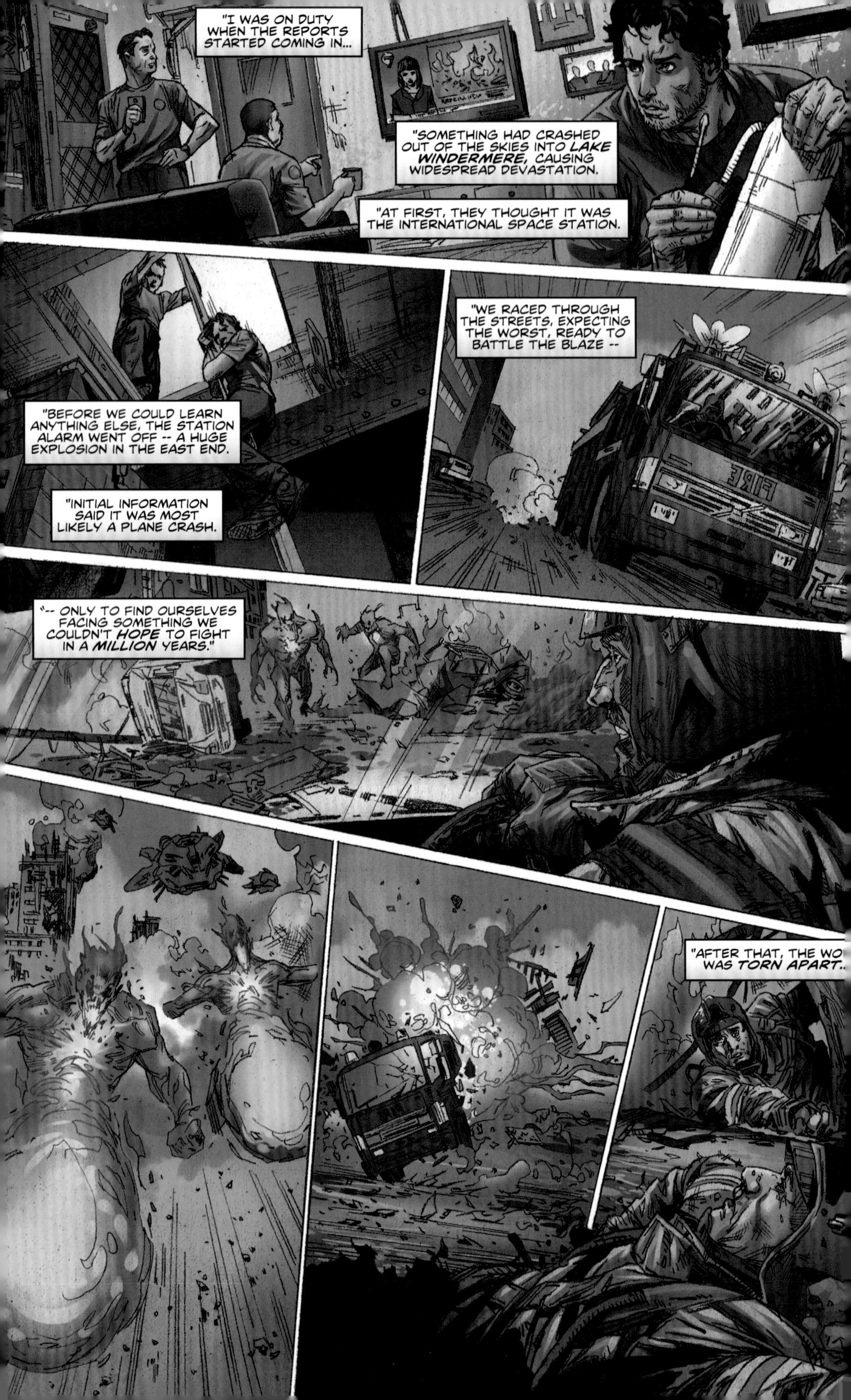
"I WAS ON DUTY WHEN THE REPORTS STARTED COMING IN...
"SOMETHING HAD CRASHED OUT OF THE SKIES INTO LAKE WINDERMERE, CAUSING WIDESPREAD DEVASTATION.
"AT FIRST, THEY THOUGHT IT WAS THE INTERNATIONAL SPACE STATION.
"BEFORE WE COULD LEARN ANYTHING ELSE, THE STATION ALARM WENT OFF -- A HUGE EXPLOSION IN THE EAST END.
"INITIAL INFORMATION SAID IT WAS MOST LIKELY A PLANE CRASH.
"WE RACED THROUGH THE STREETS, EXPECTING THE WORST, READY TO BATTLE THE BLAZE --
FIRE
"-- ONLY TO FIND OURSELVES FACING SOMETHING WE COULDN'T HOPE TO FIGHT IN A MILLION YEARS."
"AFTER THAT, THE WO
WAS TORN APART...

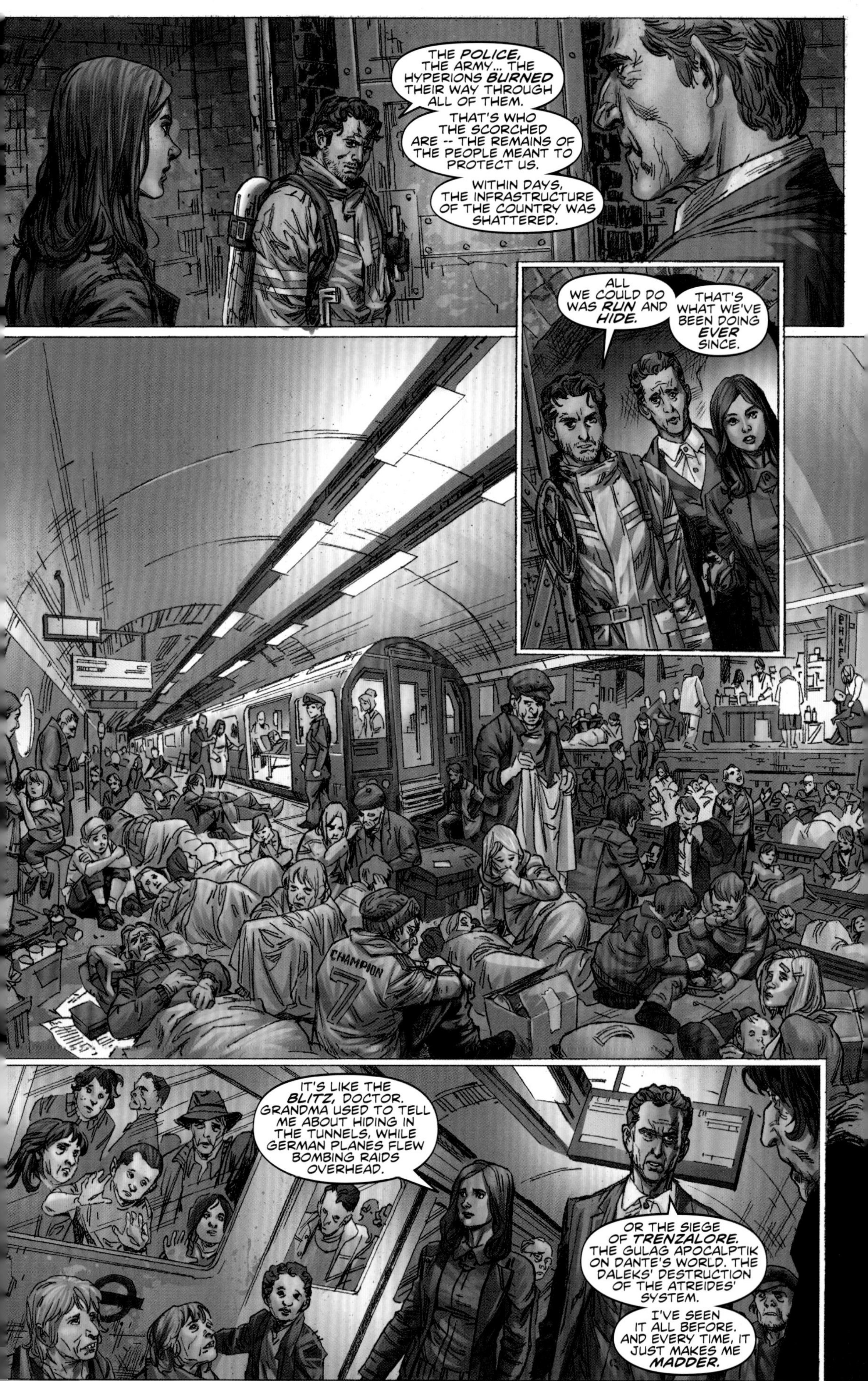
THE POLICE, THE ARMY... THE HYPERIONS BURNED THEIR WAY THROUGH ALL OF THEM.
THAT'S WHO THE SCORCHED ARE -- THE REMAINS OF THE PEOPLE MEANT TO PROTECT US.
WITHIN DAYS, THE INFRASTRUCTURE OF THE COUNTRY WAS SHATTERED.
ALL WE COULD DO WAS RUN AND HIDE.
THAT'S WHAT WE'VE BEEN DOING EVER SINCE.
CHAMPION
7
IT'S LIKE THE BLITZ, DOCTOR. GRANDMA USED TO TELL ME ABOUT HIDING IN THE TUNNELS, WHILE GERMAN PLANES FLEW BOMBING RAIDS OVERHEAD.
OR THE SIEGE OF TRENZALORE. THE GULAG APOCALPTIK ON DANTE'S WORLD. THE DALEKS' DESTRUCTION OF THE ATREIDES' SYSTEM.
I'VE SEEN IT ALL BEFORE. AND EVERY TIME, IT JUST MAKES ME MADDER.

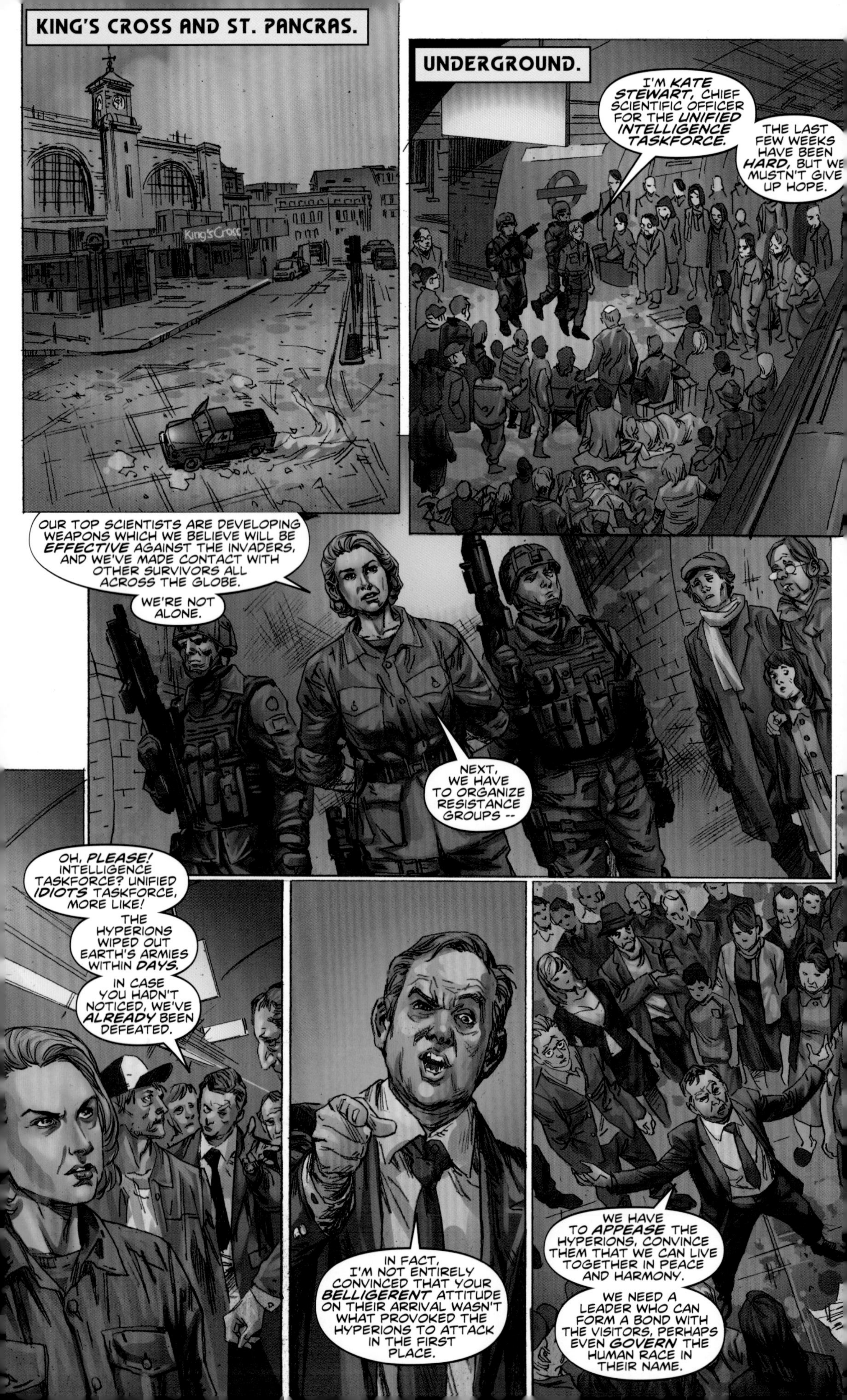
KING'S CROSS AND ST. PANCRAS.
King's Cross
UNDERGROUND.
I'M KATE STEWART, CHIEF SCIENTIFIC OFFICER FOR THE UNIFIED INTELLIGENCE TASKFORCE.
THE LAST FEW WEEKS HAVE BEEN HARD, BUT WE MUSTN'T GIVE UP HOPE.
OUR TOP SCIENTISTS ARE DEVELOPING WEAPONS WHICH WE BELIEVE WILL BE EFFECTIVE AGAINST THE INVADERS, AND WE'VE MADE CONTACT WITH OTHER SURVIVORS ALL ACROSS THE GLOBE.
WE'RE NOT ALONE.
NEXT, WE HAVE TO ORGANIZE RESISTANCE GROUPS --
OH, PLEASE! INTELLIGENCE TASKFORCE? UNIFIED IDIOTS TASKFORCE, MORE LIKE!
THE HYPERIONS WIPED OUT EARTH'S ARMIES WITHIN DAYS.
IN CASE YOU HADN'T NOTICED, WE'VE ALREADY BEEN DEFEATED.
IN FACT, I'M NOT ENTIRELY CONVINCED THAT YOUR BELLIGERENT ATTITUDE ON THEIR ARRIVAL WASN'T WHAT PROVOKED THE HYPERIONS TO ATTACK IN THE FIRST PLACE.
WE HAVE TO APPEASE THE HYPERIONS, CONVINCE THEM THAT WE CAN LIVE TOGETHER IN PEACE AND HARMONY.
WE NEED A LEADER WHO CAN FORM A BOND WITH THE VISITORS, PERHAPS EVEN GOVERN THE HUMAN RACE IN THEIR NAME.

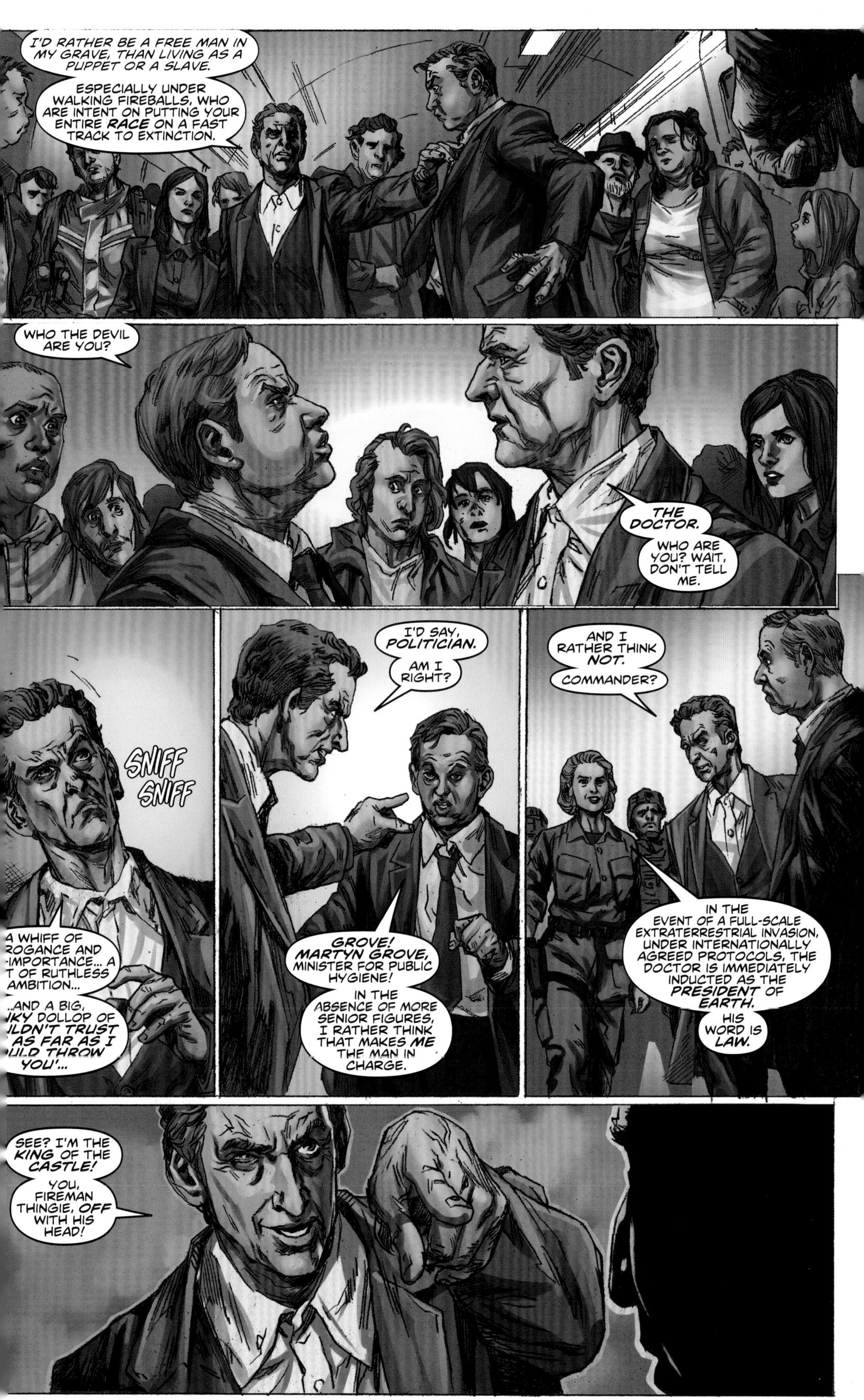
I'D RATHER BE A FREE MAN IN MY GRAVE, THAN LIVING AS A PUPPET OR A SLAVE.
ESPECIALLY UNDER WALKING FIREBALLS, WHO ARE INTENT ON PUTTING YOUR ENTIRE RACE ON A FAST TRACK TO EXTINCTION.
WHO THE DEVIL ARE YOU?
THE DOCTOR.
WHO ARE YOU? WAIT, DON'T TELL ME.
SNIFF SNIFF
A WHIFF OF ROGANCE AND -IMPORTANCE... A T OF RUTHLESS AMBITION...
...AND A BIG, NKY DOLLOP OF ULDN'T TRUST AS FAR AS I ULD THROW YOU'...
I'D SAY, POLITICIAN.
AM I RIGHT?
GROVE! MARTYN GROVE, MINISTER FOR PUBLIC HYGIENE!
IN THE ABSENCE OF MORE SENIOR FIGURES, I RATHER THINK THAT MAKES ME THE MAN IN CHARGE.
AND I RATHER THINK NOT.
COMMANDER?
IN THE EVENT OF A FULL-SCALE EXTRATERRESTRIAL INVASION, UNDER INTERNATIONALLY AGREED PROTOCOLS, THE DOCTOR IS IMMEDIATELY INDUCTED AS THE PRESIDENT OF EARTH.
HIS WORD IS LAW.
SEE? I'M THE KING OF THE CASTLE!
YOU, FIREMAN THINGIE, OFF WITH HIS HEAD!

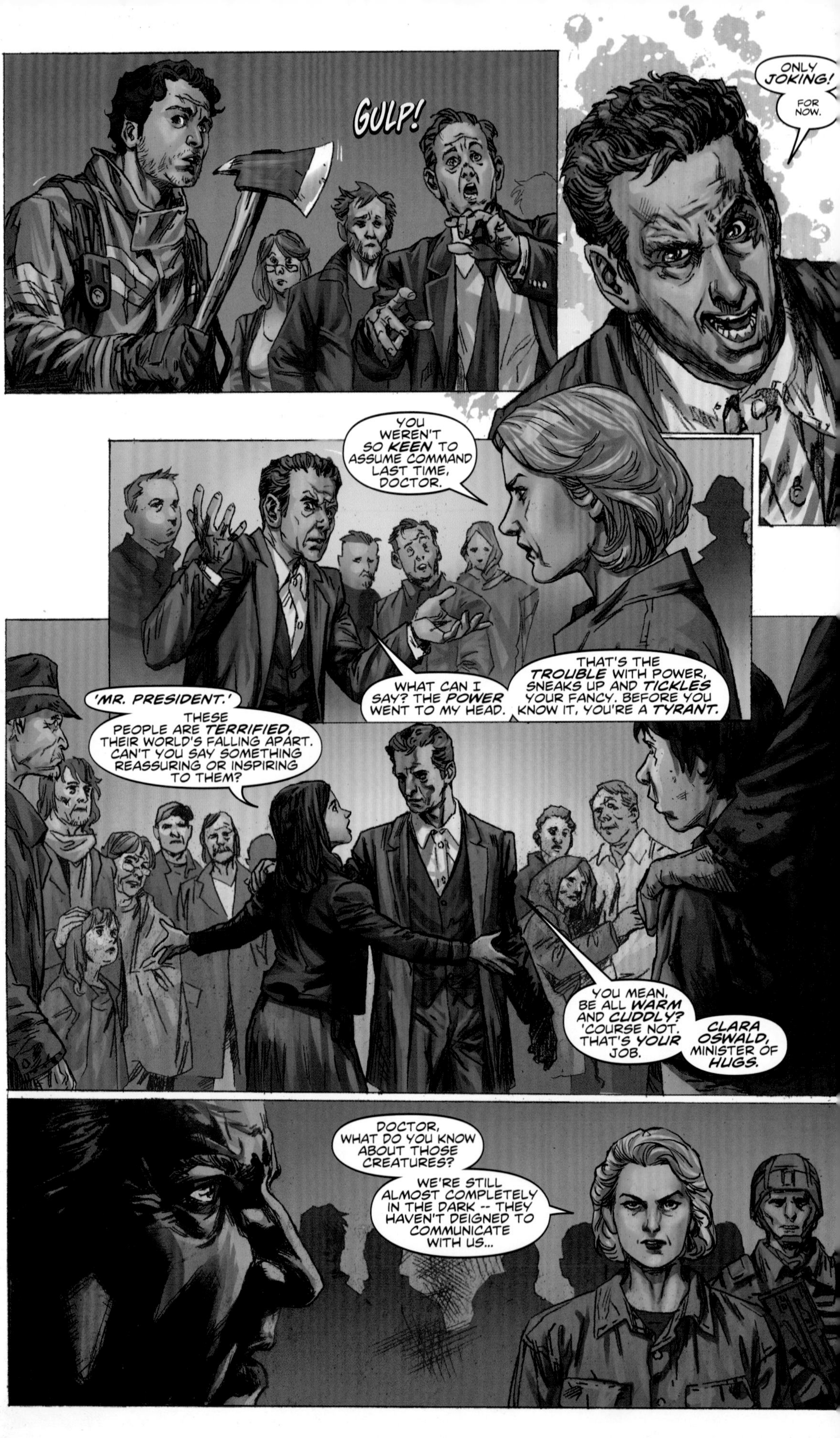
GULP!
ONLY JOKING!
FOR NOW.
YOU WEREN'T SO KEEN TO ASSUME COMMAND LAST TIME, DOCTOR.
WHAT CAN I SAY? THE POWER WENT TO MY HEAD.
THAT'S THE TROUBLE WITH POWER, SNEAKS UP AND TICKLES YOUR FANCY. BEFORE YOU KNOW IT, YOU'RE A TYRANT.
'MR. PRESIDENT.'
THESE PEOPLE ARE TERRIFIED, THEIR WORLD'S FALLING APART. CAN'T YOU SAY SOMETHING REASSURING OR INSPIRING TO THEM?
YOU MEAN, BE ALL WARM AND CUDDLY? 'COURSE NOT. THAT'S YOUR JOB.
CLARA OSWALD, MINISTER OF HUGS.
DOCTOR, WHAT DO YOU KNOW ABOUT THOSE CREATURES?
WE'RE STILL ALMOST COMPLETELY IN THE DARK -- THEY HAVEN'T DEIGNED TO COMMUNICATE WITH US...

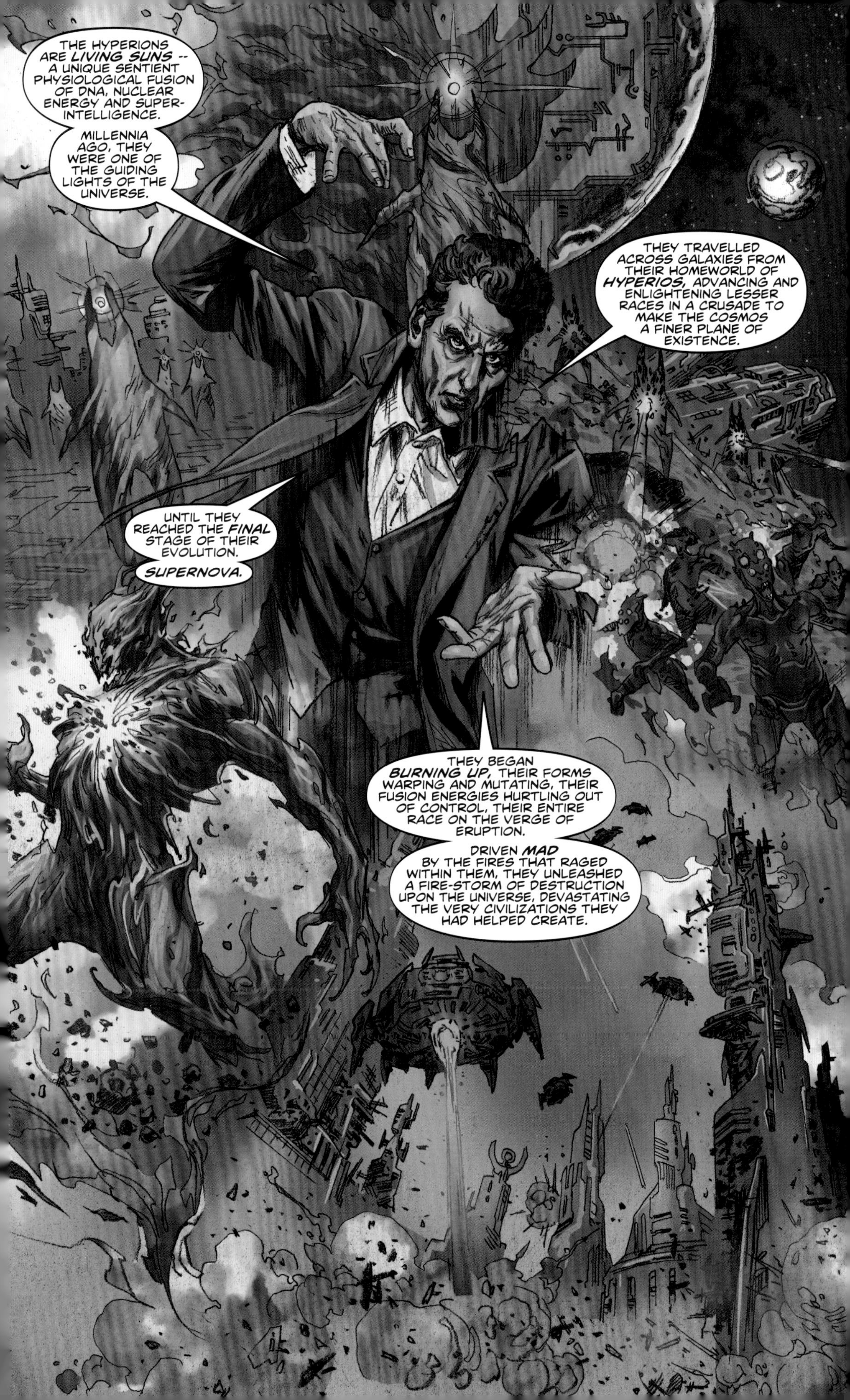
THE HYPERIONS ARE LIVING SUNS -- A UNIQUE SENTIENT PHYSIOLOGICAL FUSION OF DNA, NUCLEAR ENERGY AND SUPER-INTELLIGENCE.
MILLENNIA AGO, THEY WERE ONE OF THE GUIDING LIGHTS OF THE UNIVERSE.
THEY TRAVELLED ACROSS GALAXIES FROM THEIR HOMEWORLD OF HYPERIOS, ADVANCING AND ENLIGHTENING LESSER RACES IN A CRUSADE TO MAKE THE COSMOS A FINER PLANE OF EXISTENCE.
UNTIL THEY REACHED THE FINAL STAGE OF THEIR EVOLUTION.
SUPERNOVA.
THEY BEGAN BURNING UP, THEIR FORMS WARPING AND MUTATING, THEIR FUSION ENERGIES HURTLING OUT OF CONTROL, THEIR ENTIRE RACE ON THE VERGE OF ERUPTION.
DRIVEN MAD BY THE FIRES THAT RAGED WITHIN THEM, THEY UNLEASHED A FIRE-STORM OF DESTRUCTION UPON THE UNIVERSE, DEVASTATING THE VERY CIVILIZATIONS THEY HAD HELPED CREATE.

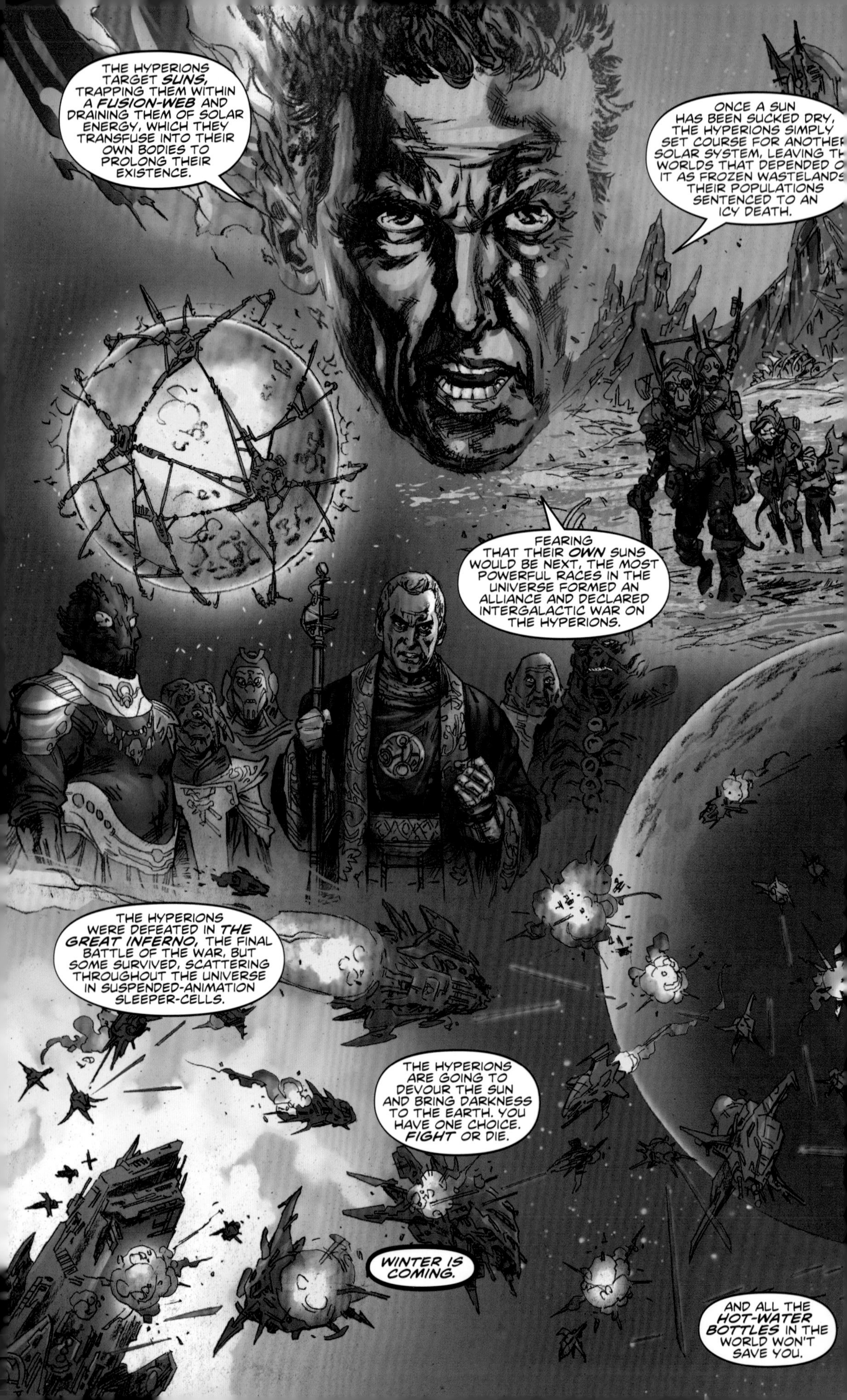
THE HYPERIONS TARGET SUNS, TRAPPING THEM WITHIN A FUSION-WEB AND DRAINING THEM OF SOLAR ENERGY, WHICH THEY TRANSFUSE INTO THEIR OWN BODIES TO PROLONG THEIR EXISTENCE.
ONCE A SUN HAS BEEN SUCKED DRY, THE HYPERIONS SIMPLY SET COURSE FOR ANOTHER SOLAR SYSTEM, LEAVING TH WORLDS THAT DEPENDED O IT AS FROZEN WASTELANDS THEIR POPULATIONS SENTENCED TO AN ICY DEATH.
FEARING THAT THEIR OWN SUNS WOULD BE NEXT, THE MOST POWERFUL RACES IN THE UNIVERSE FORMED AN ALLIANCE AND DECLARED INTERGALACTIC WAR ON THE HYPERIONS.
THE HYPERIONS WERE DEFEATED IN THE GREAT INFERNO, THE FINAL BATTLE OF THE WAR, BUT SOME SURVIVED, SCATTERING THROUGHOUT THE UNIVERSE IN SUSPENDED-ANIMATION SLEEPER-CELLS.
THE HYPERIONS ARE GOING TO DEVOUR THE SUN AND BRING DARKNESS TO THE EARTH. YOU HAVE ONE CHOICE. FIGHT OR DIE.
WINTER IS COMING.
AND ALL THE HOT-WATER BOTTLES IN THE WORLD WON'T SAVE YOU.

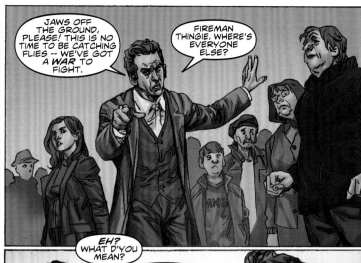

VERY REASSURING, DOCTOR.

YOU'VE *'INSPIRED'* THEM HALF TO DEATH.

JAWS OFF THE GROUND, PLEASE! THIS IS NO TIME TO BE CATCHING FLIES -- WE'VE GOT A *WAR* TO FIGHT.

FIREMAN THINGIE, WHERE'S EVERYONE ELSE?

I TOLD THEM THE *TRUTH.* SOONER OR LATER, EVERYONE HAS TO FACE THE TRUTH.

EH? WHAT D'YOU MEAN?

ARE YOU TRYING TO TELL ME THE *ENTIRE* POPULATION OF LONDON IS DOWN HERE?

IT'S BUSY, BUT HARDLY RUSH HOUR. I DON'T HAVE MY NOSE JAMMED IN SOME *HYGIENE-DEFICIENT* PUDDING-HEAD'S ARMPIT FOR A START.

ONLY SOME OF US MADE IT DOWN HERE, THE MAJORITY WERE TAKEN CAPTIVE.

THE HYPERIONS HAVE ERECTED *FIREWALLS* THROUGHOUT THE COUNTRY, ISOLATING ENTIRE CITIES AND REGIONS.

THE HEAT THEY GENERATE IS INCREDIBLE. GET TOO CLOSE AND YOU'RE *INCINERATED* IMMEDIATELY.

THE NEAREST ONE'S IN *SUSSEX.* BEHIND THE FLAMES YOU CAN HEAR *SCREAMS,* THE *ROAR* OF STRANGE MACHINERY.

IT... IT SOUNDS LIKE *HELL.*

THEN *THAT'S* WHERE WE HAVE TO GO. *INTO THE FIRE.*

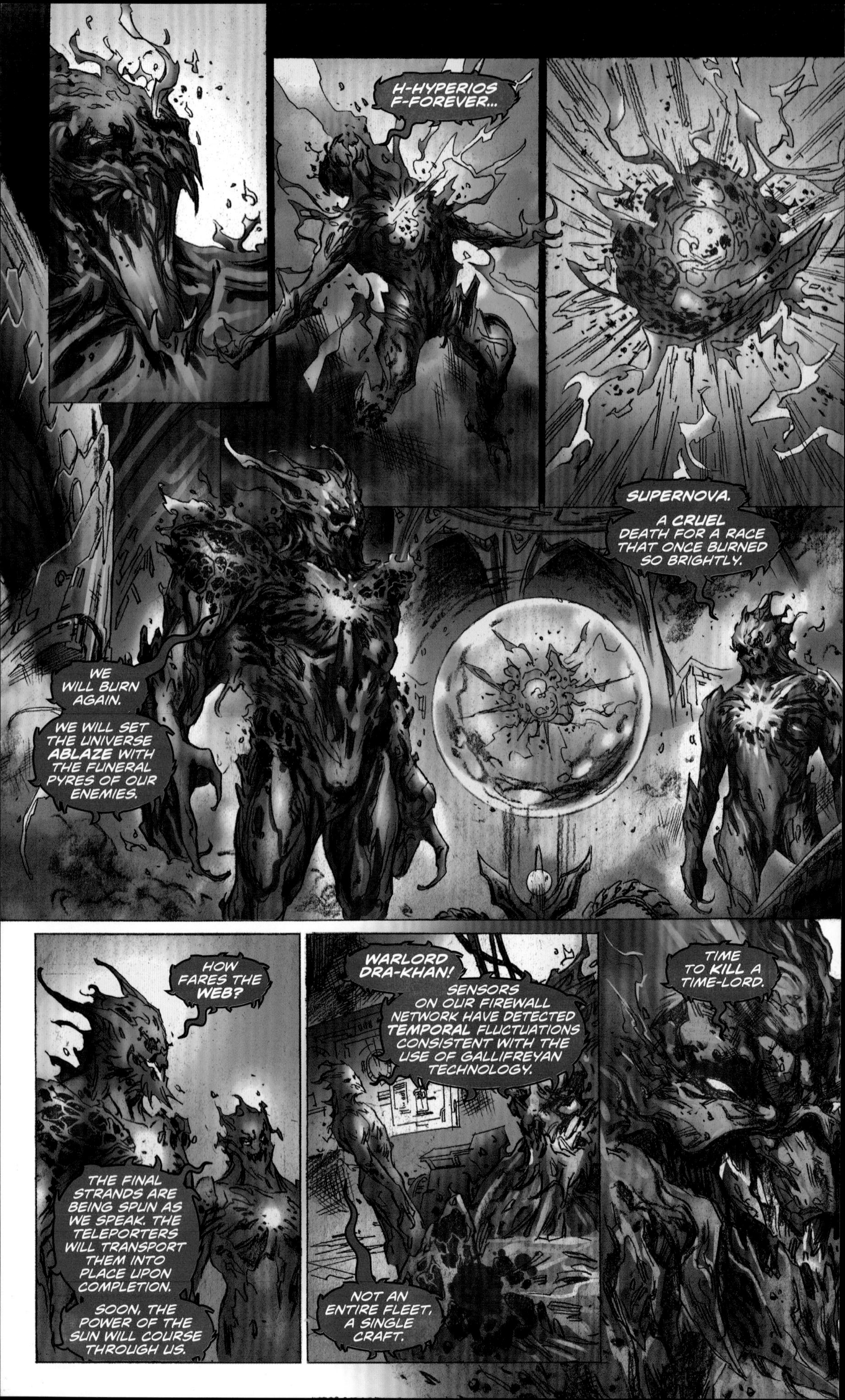
H-HYPERIOS F-FOREVER...
SUPERNOVA.
A CRUEL DEATH FOR A RACE THAT ONCE BURNED SO BRIGHTLY.
WE WILL BURN AGAIN.
WE WILL SET THE UNIVERSE ABLAZE WITH THE FUNERAL PYRES OF OUR ENEMIES.
HOW FARES THE WEB?
THE FINAL STRANDS ARE BEING SPUN AS WE SPEAK. THE TELEPORTERS WILL TRANSPORT THEM INTO PLACE UPON COMPLETION.
SOON, THE POWER OF THE SUN WILL COURSE THROUGH US.
WARLORD DRA-KHAN!
SENSORS ON OUR FIREWALL NETWORK HAVE DETECTED TEMPORAL FLUCTUATIONS CONSISTENT WITH THE USE OF GALLIFREYAN TECHNOLOGY.
NOT AN ENTIRE FLEET, A SINGLE CRAFT.
TIME TO KILL A TIME-LORD.

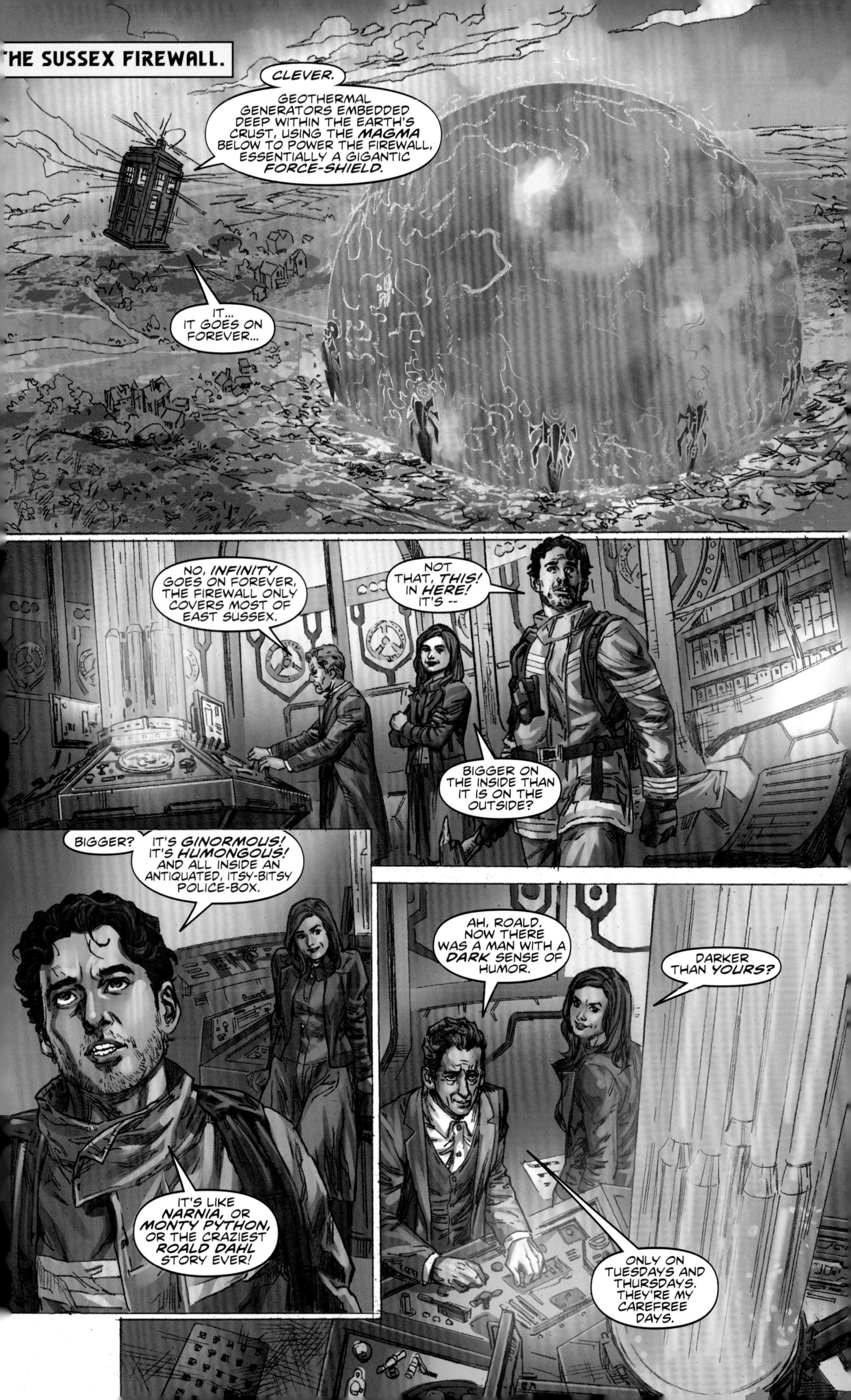
THE SUSSEX FIREWALL.
CLEVER.
GEOTHERMAL GENERATORS EMBEDDED DEEP WITHIN THE EARTH'S CRUST, USING THE MAGMA BELOW TO POWER THE FIREWALL, ESSENTIALLY A GIGANTIC FORCE-SHIELD.
IT... IT GOES ON FOREVER...
NO, INFINITY GOES ON FOREVER, THE FIREWALL ONLY COVERS MOST OF EAST SUSSEX.
NOT THAT, THIS! IN HERE! IT'S --
BIGGER ON THE INSIDE THAN IT IS ON THE OUTSIDE?
BIGGER?
IT'S GINORMOUS! IT'S HUMONGOUS! AND ALL INSIDE AN ANTIQUATED, ITSY-BITSY POLICE-BOX.
IT'S LIKE NARNIA, OR MONTY PYTHON, OR THE CRAZIEST ROALD DAHL STORY EVER!
AH, ROALD. NOW THERE WAS A MAN WITH A DARK SENSE OF HUMOR.
DARKER THAN YOURS?
ONLY ON TUESDAYS AND THURSDAYS. THEY'RE MY CAREFREE DAYS.

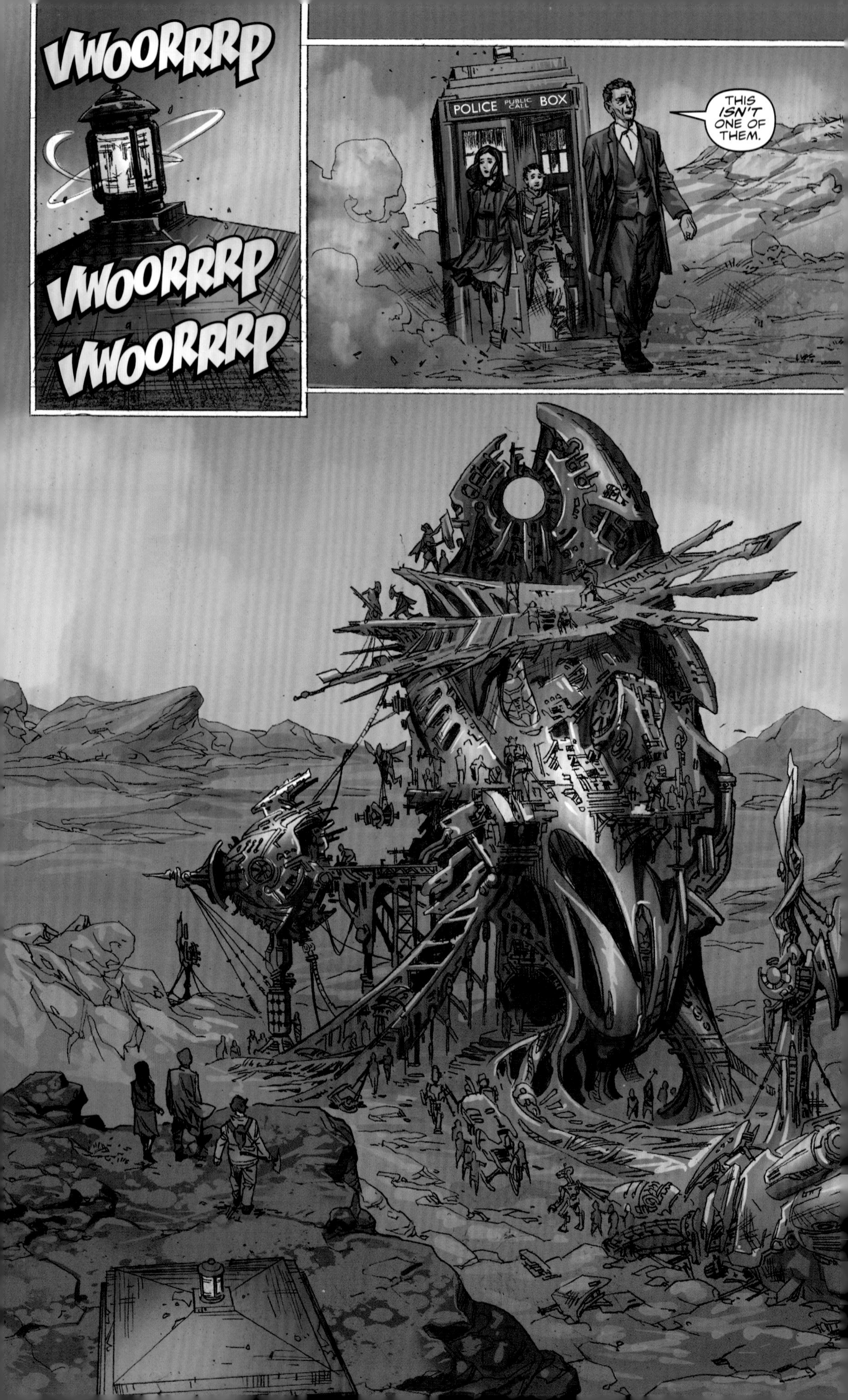
VWOORRRP
VWOORRRP
VWOORRRP
POLICE PUBLIC CALL BOX
THIS ISN'T ONE OF THEM.

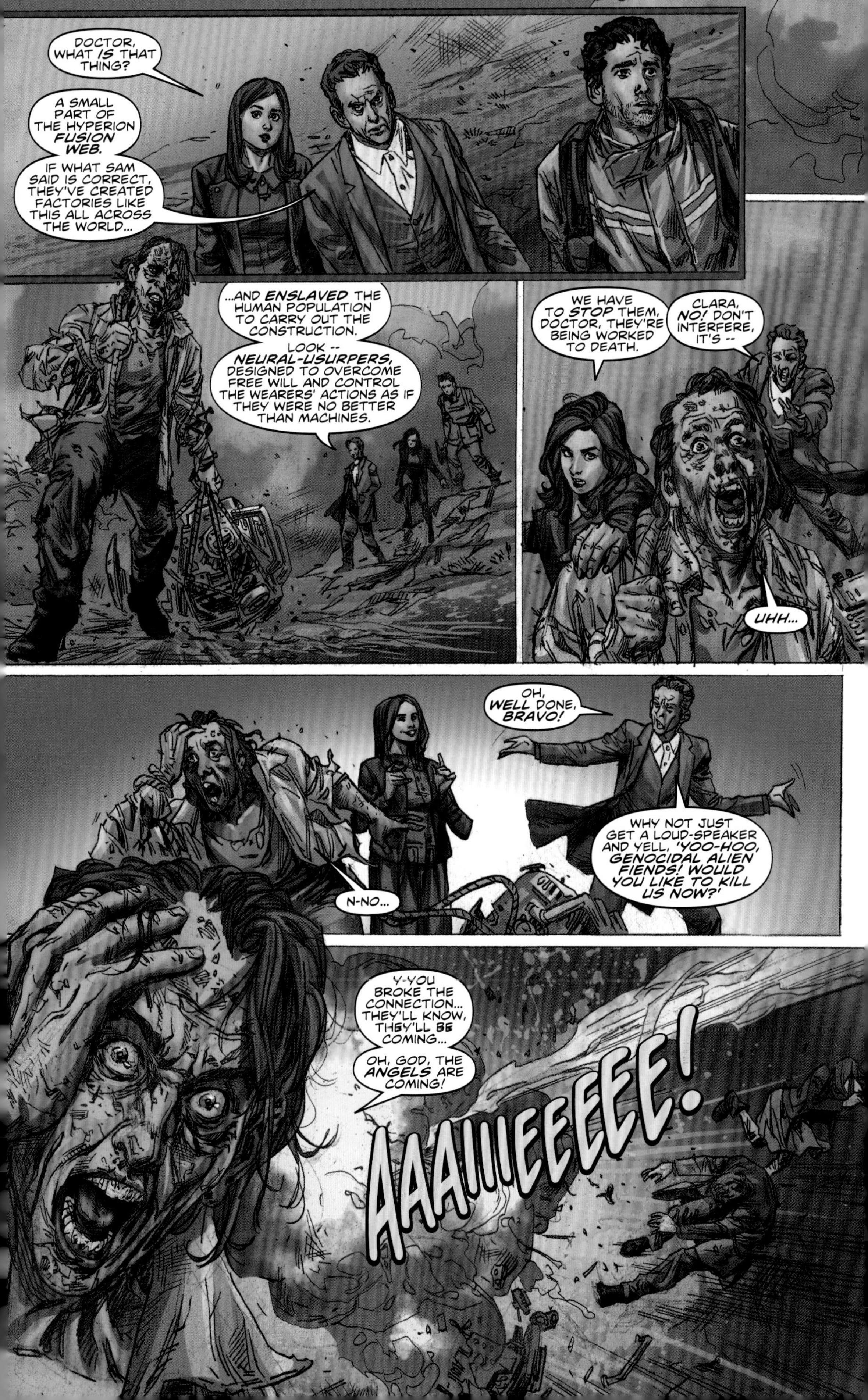
DOCTOR, WHAT IS THAT THING?
A SMALL PART OF THE HYPERION FUSION WEB.
IF WHAT SAM SAID IS CORRECT, THEY'VE CREATED FACTORIES LIKE THIS ALL ACROSS THE WORLD...
...AND ENSLAVED THE HUMAN POPULATION TO CARRY OUT THE CONSTRUCTION.
LOOK -- NEURAL-USURPERS, DESIGNED TO OVERCOME FREE WILL AND CONTROL THE WEARERS' ACTIONS AS IF THEY WERE NO BETTER THAN MACHINES.
WE HAVE TO STOP THEM, DOCTOR, THEY'RE BEING WORKED TO DEATH.
CLARA, NO! DON'T INTERFERE, IT'S --
UHH...
OH, WELL DONE, BRAVO!
WHY NOT JUST GET A LOUD-SPEAKER AND YELL, 'YOO-HOO, GENOCIDAL ALIEN FIENDS! WOULD YOU LIKE TO KILL US NOW?'
N-NO...
Y-YOU BROKE THE CONNECTION... THEY'LL KNOW, THEY'LL BE COMING...
OH, GOD, THE ANGELS ARE COMING!
AAAIIIEEEEE!

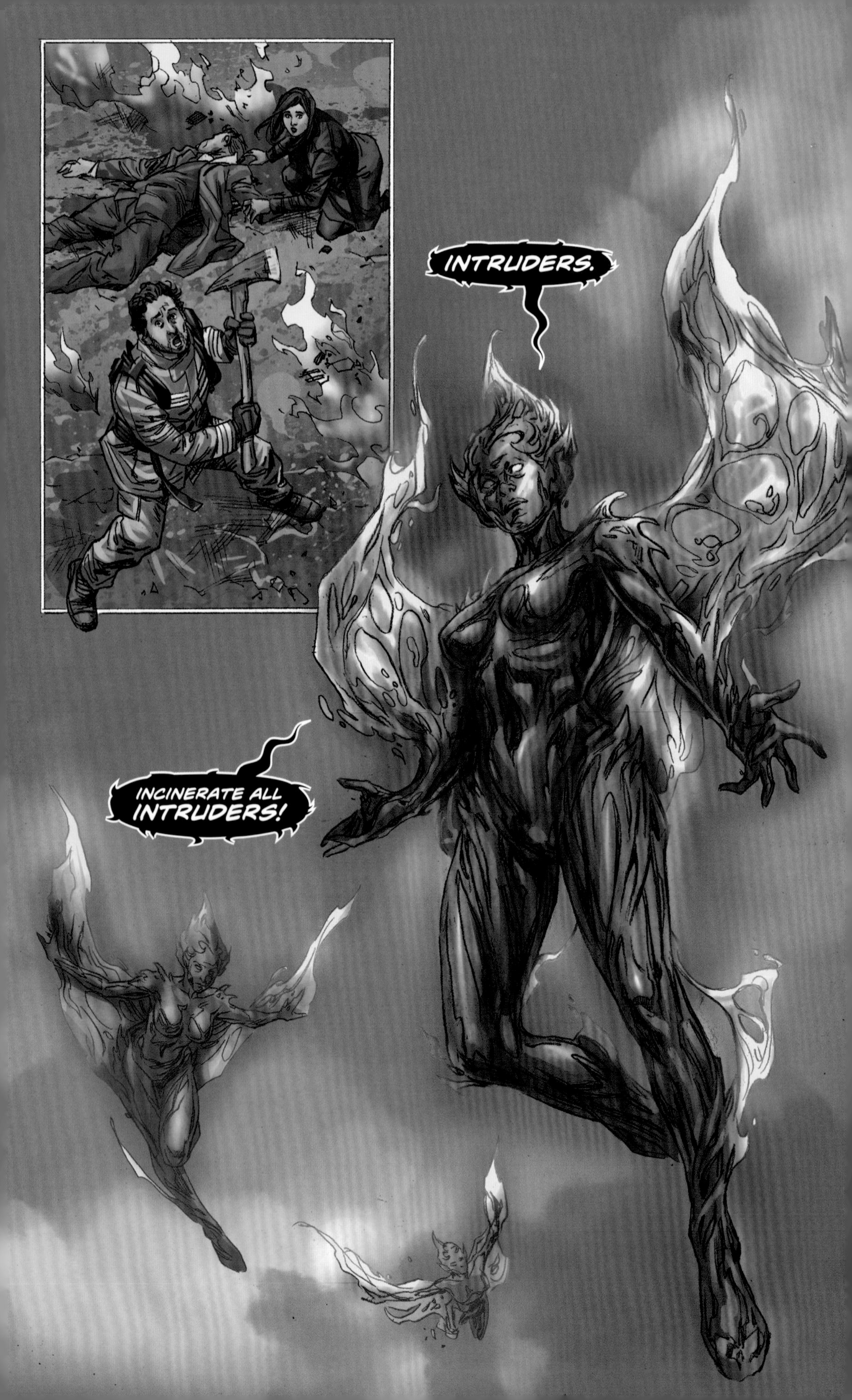
INTRUDERS.
INCINERATE ALL INTRUDERS!

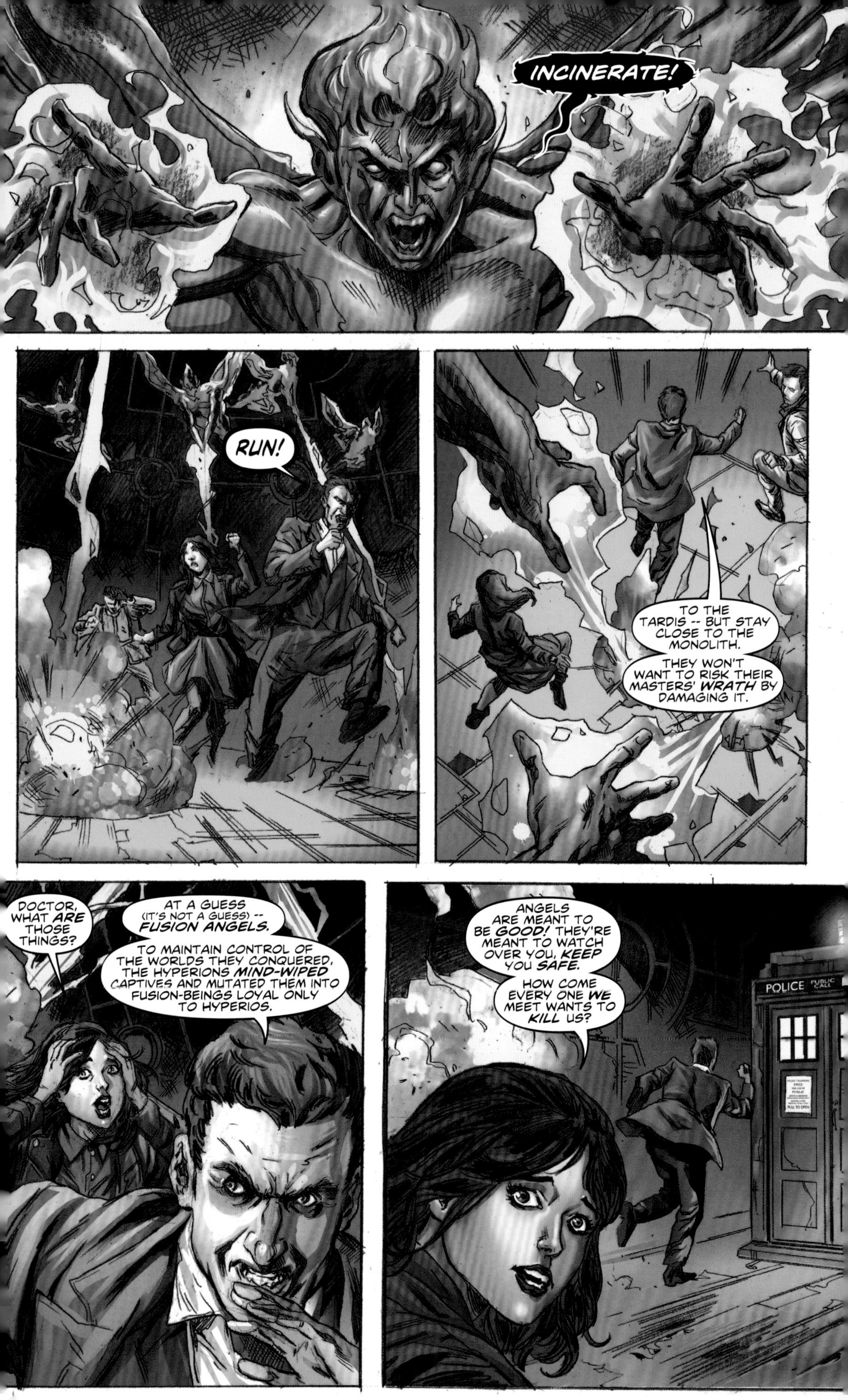
INCINERATE!
RUN!
TO THE TARDIS -- BUT STAY CLOSE TO THE MONOLITH.
THEY WON'T WANT TO RISK THEIR MASTERS' WRATH BY DAMAGING IT.
DOCTOR, WHAT ARE THOSE THINGS?
AT A GUESS (IT'S NOT A GUESS) -- FUSION ANGELS.
TO MAINTAIN CONTROL OF THE WORLDS THEY CONQUERED, THE HYPERIONS MIND-WIPED CAPTIVES AND MUTATED THEM INTO FUSION-BEINGS LOYAL ONLY TO HYPERIOS.
ANGELS ARE MEANT TO BE GOOD! THEY'RE MEANT TO WATCH OVER YOU, KEEP YOU SAFE.
HOW COME EVERY ONE WE MEET WANTS TO KILL US?
POLICE PUBLIC CALL

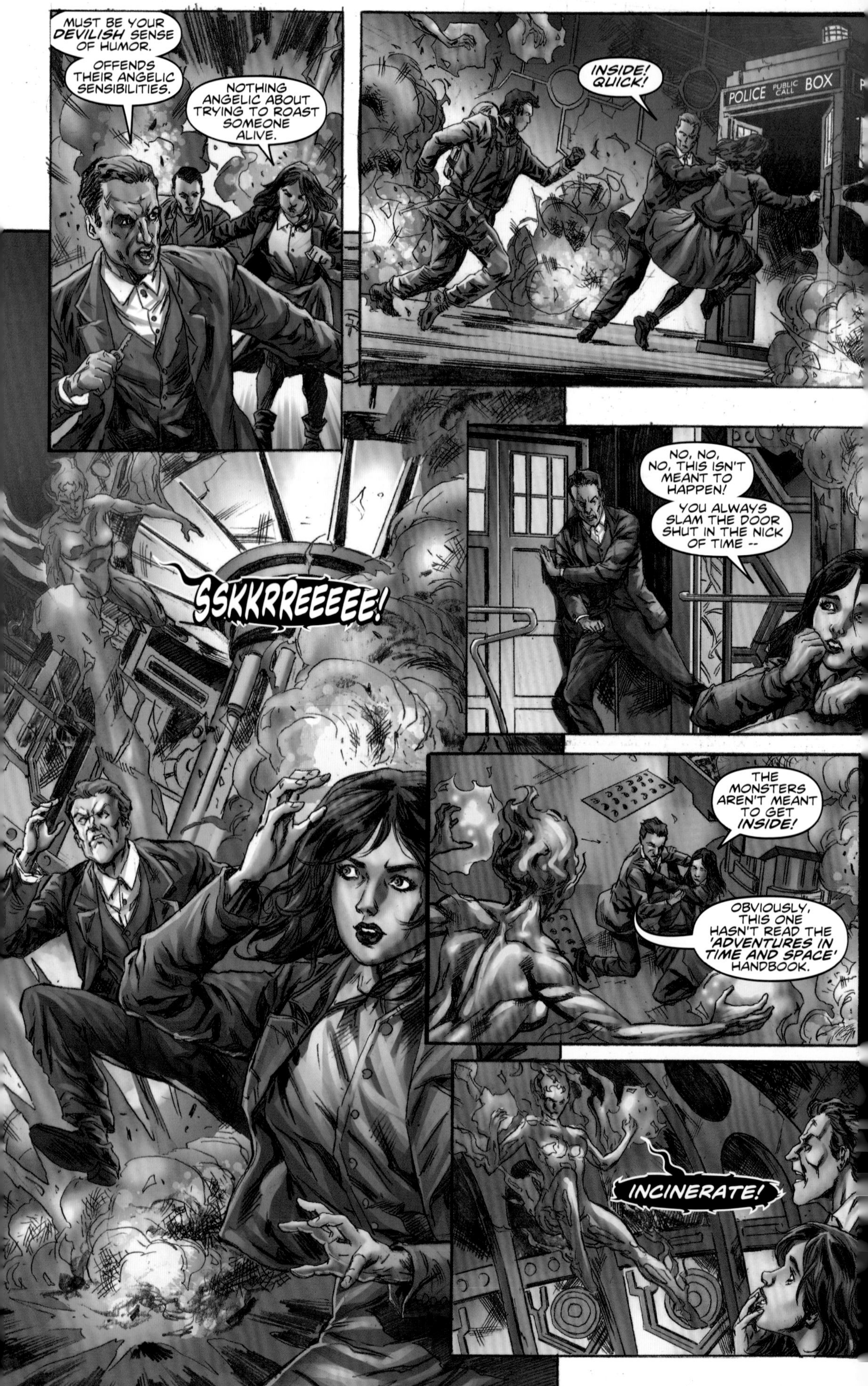
MUST BE YOUR DEVILISH SENSE OF HUMOR.
OFFENDS THEIR ANGELIC SENSIBILITIES.
NOTHING ANGELIC ABOUT TRYING TO ROAST SOMEONE ALIVE.
INSIDE! QUICK!
POLICE PUBLIC CALL BOX
SSKKRREEEEEE!
NO, NO, NO, THIS ISN'T MEANT TO HAPPEN!
YOU ALWAYS SLAM THE DOOR SHUT IN THE NICK OF TIME --
THE MONSTERS AREN'T MEANT TO GET INSIDE!
OBVIOUSLY, THIS ONE HASN'T READ THE 'ADVENTURES IN TIME AND SPACE' HANDBOOK.
INCINERATE!

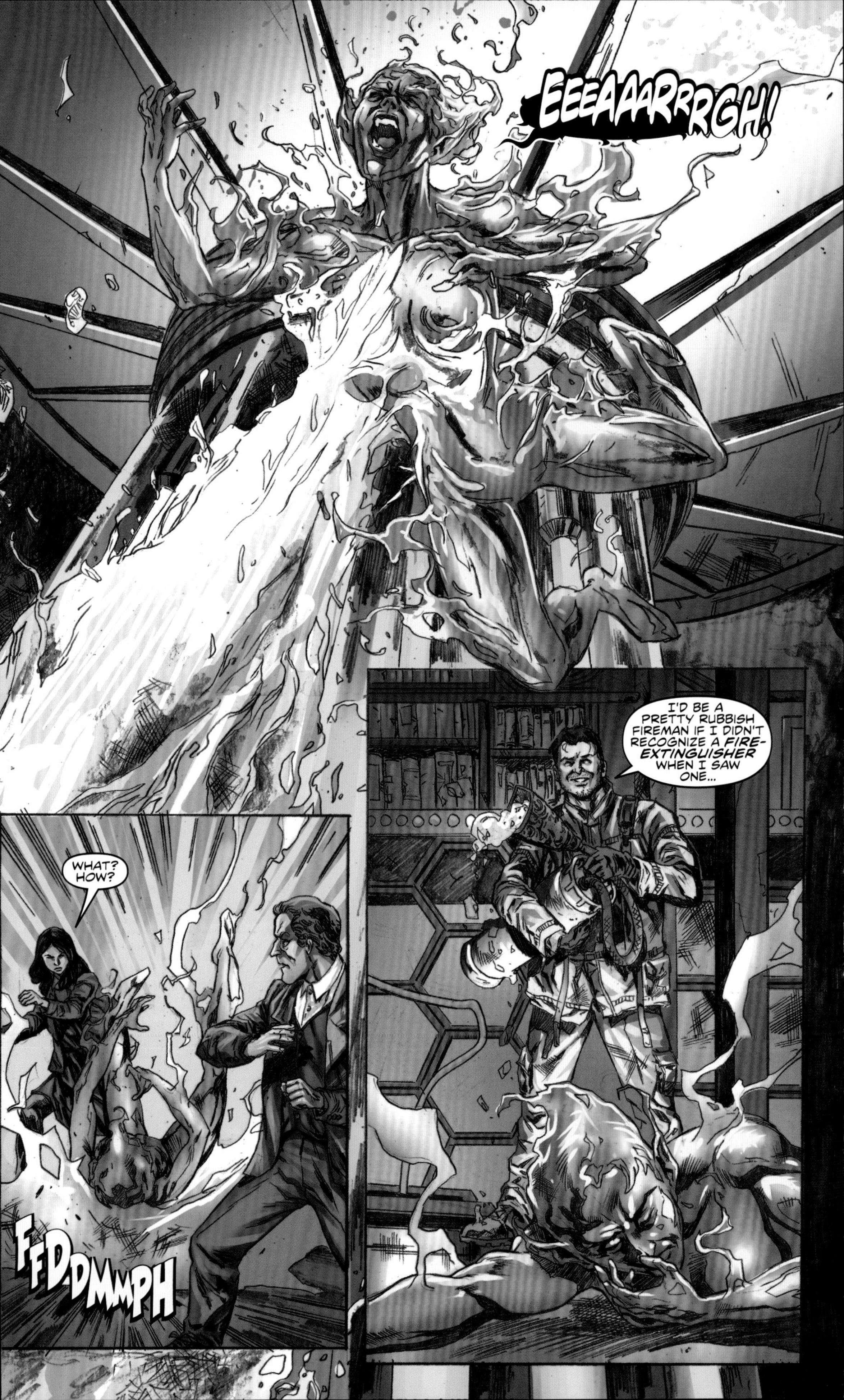
EEEAAARRRRGH!
I'D BE A PRETTY RUBBISH FIREMAN IF I DIDN'T RECOGNIZE A *FIRE-EXTINGUISHER* WHEN I SAW ONE...
WHAT? HOW?
FFDDMMMPH

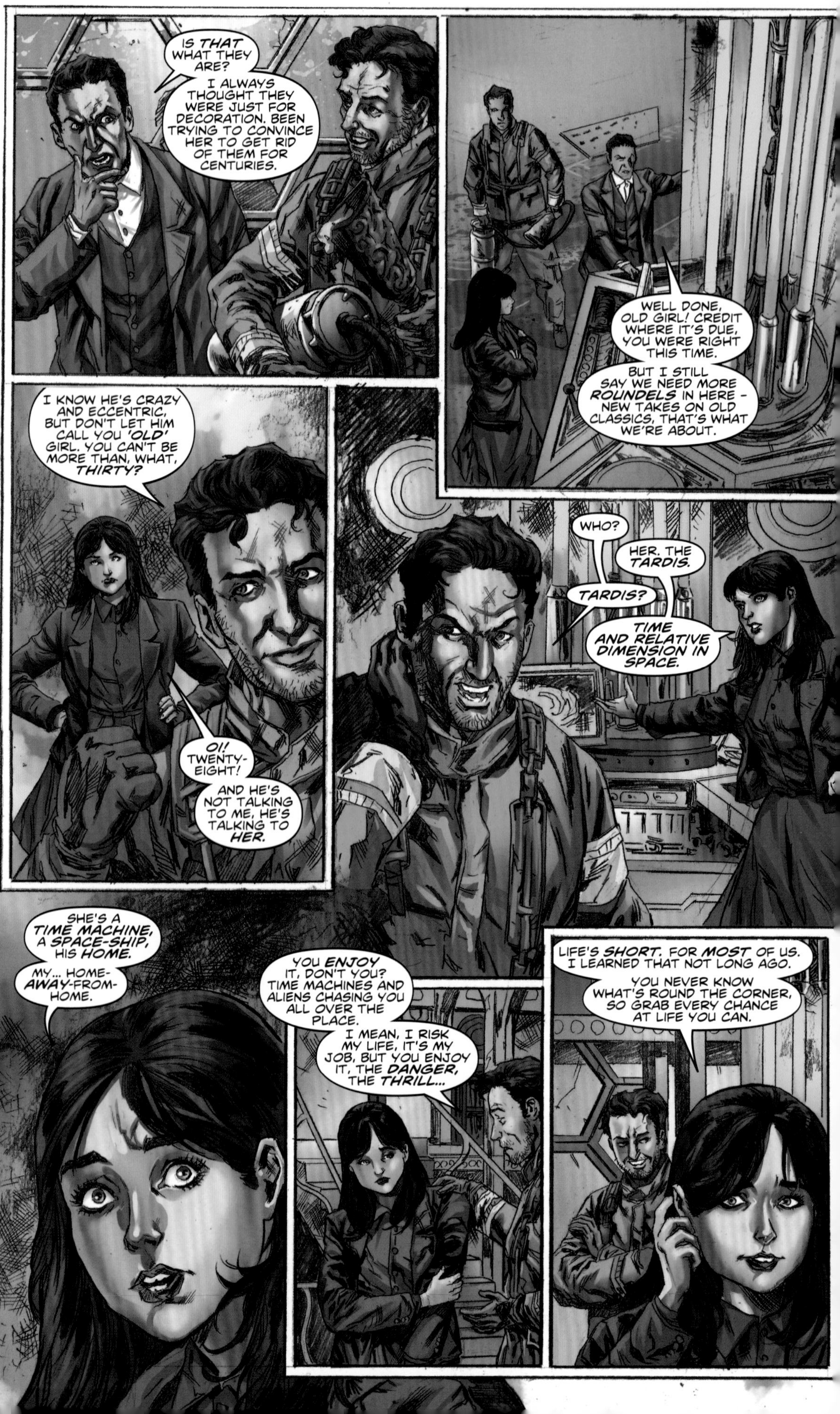
IS THAT WHAT THEY ARE?
I ALWAYS THOUGHT THEY WERE JUST FOR DECORATION. BEEN TRYING TO CONVINCE HER TO GET RID OF THEM FOR CENTURIES.
WELL DONE, OLD GIRL! CREDIT WHERE IT'S DUE, YOU WERE RIGHT THIS TIME.
BUT I STILL SAY WE NEED MORE ROUNDELS IN HERE - NEW TAKES ON OLD CLASSICS, THAT'S WHAT WE'RE ABOUT.
I KNOW HE'S CRAZY AND ECCENTRIC, BUT DON'T LET HIM CALL YOU 'OLD' GIRL. YOU CAN'T BE MORE THAN, WHAT, THIRTY?
OI! TWENTY-EIGHT!
AND HE'S NOT TALKING TO ME, HE'S TALKING TO HER.
WHO?
HER. THE TARDIS.
TARDIS?
TIME AND RELATIVE DIMENSION IN SPACE.
SHE'S A TIME MACHINE, A SPACE-SHIP, HIS HOME.
MY... HOME-AWAY-FROM-HOME.
YOU ENJOY IT, DON'T YOU? TIME MACHINES AND ALIENS CHASING YOU ALL OVER THE PLACE.
I MEAN, I RISK MY LIFE, IT'S MY JOB, BUT YOU ENJOY IT, THE DANGER, THE THRILL...
LIFE'S SHORT. FOR MOST OF US. I LEARNED THAT NOT LONG AGO.
YOU NEVER KNOW WHAT'S ROUND THE CORNER, SO GRAB EVERY CHANCE AT LIFE YOU CAN.

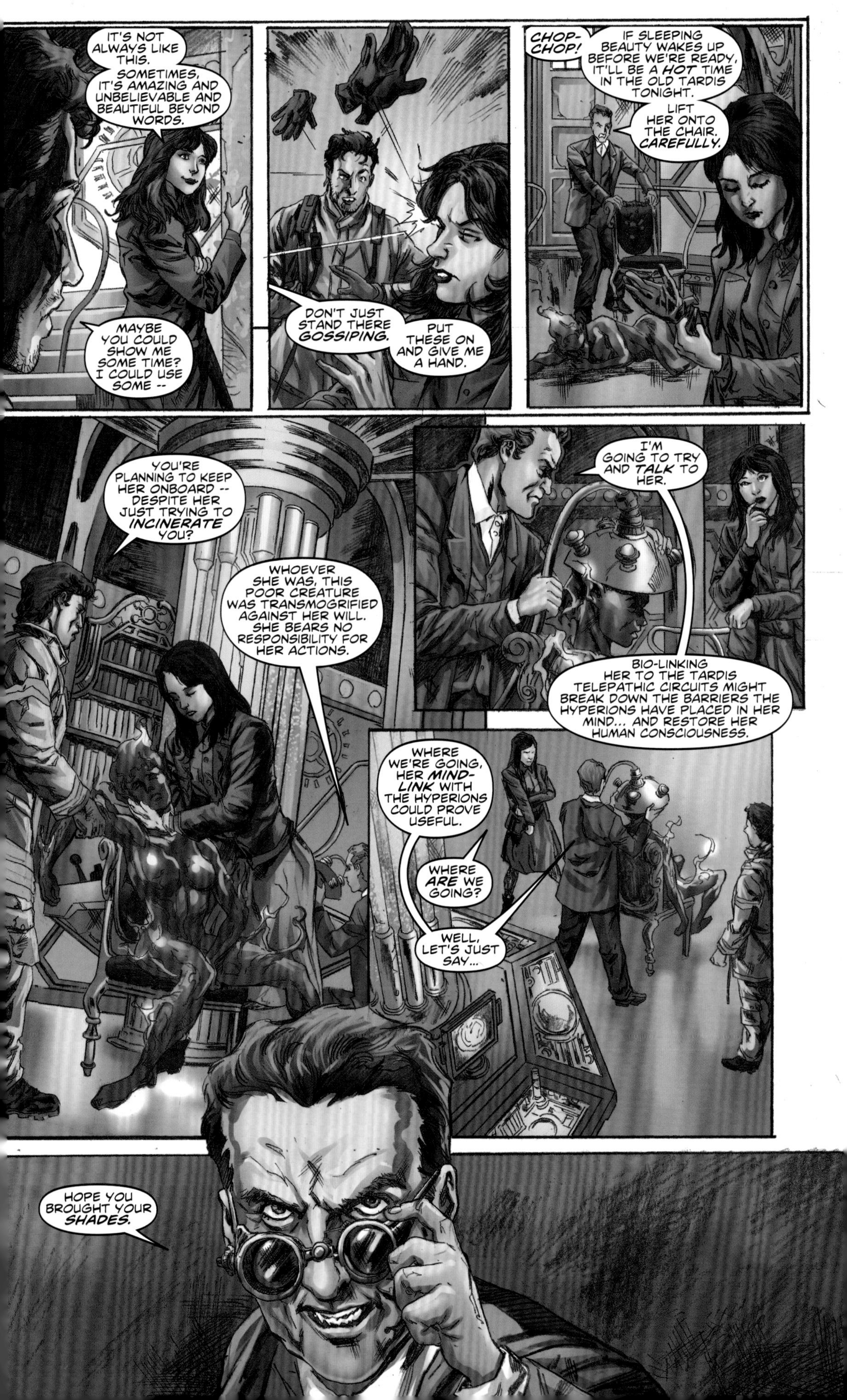

IT'S NOT ALWAYS LIKE THIS. SOMETIMES, IT'S AMAZING AND UNBELIEVABLE AND BEAUTIFUL BEYOND WORDS.
MAYBE YOU COULD SHOW ME SOME TIME? I COULD USE SOME --
DON'T JUST STAND THERE GOSSIPING.
PUT THESE ON AND GIVE ME A HAND.
CHOP-CHOP!
IF SLEEPING BEAUTY WAKES UP BEFORE WE'RE READY, IT'LL BE A HOT TIME IN THE OLD TARDIS TONIGHT.
LIFT HER ONTO THE CHAIR. CAREFULLY.
YOU'RE PLANNING TO KEEP HER ONBOARD -- DESPITE HER JUST TRYING TO INCINERATE YOU?
WHOEVER SHE WAS, THIS POOR CREATURE WAS TRANSMOGRIFIED AGAINST HER WILL. SHE BEARS NO RESPONSIBILITY FOR HER ACTIONS.
I'M GOING TO TRY AND TALK TO HER.
BIO-LINKING HER TO THE TARDIS TELEPATHIC CIRCUITS MIGHT BREAK DOWN THE BARRIERS THE HYPERIONS HAVE PLACED IN HER MIND... AND RESTORE HER HUMAN CONSCIOUSNESS.
WHERE WE'RE GOING, HER MIND-LINK WITH THE HYPERIONS COULD PROVE USEFUL.
WHERE ARE WE GOING?
WELL, LET'S JUST SAY...
HOPE YOU BROUGHT YOUR SHADES.

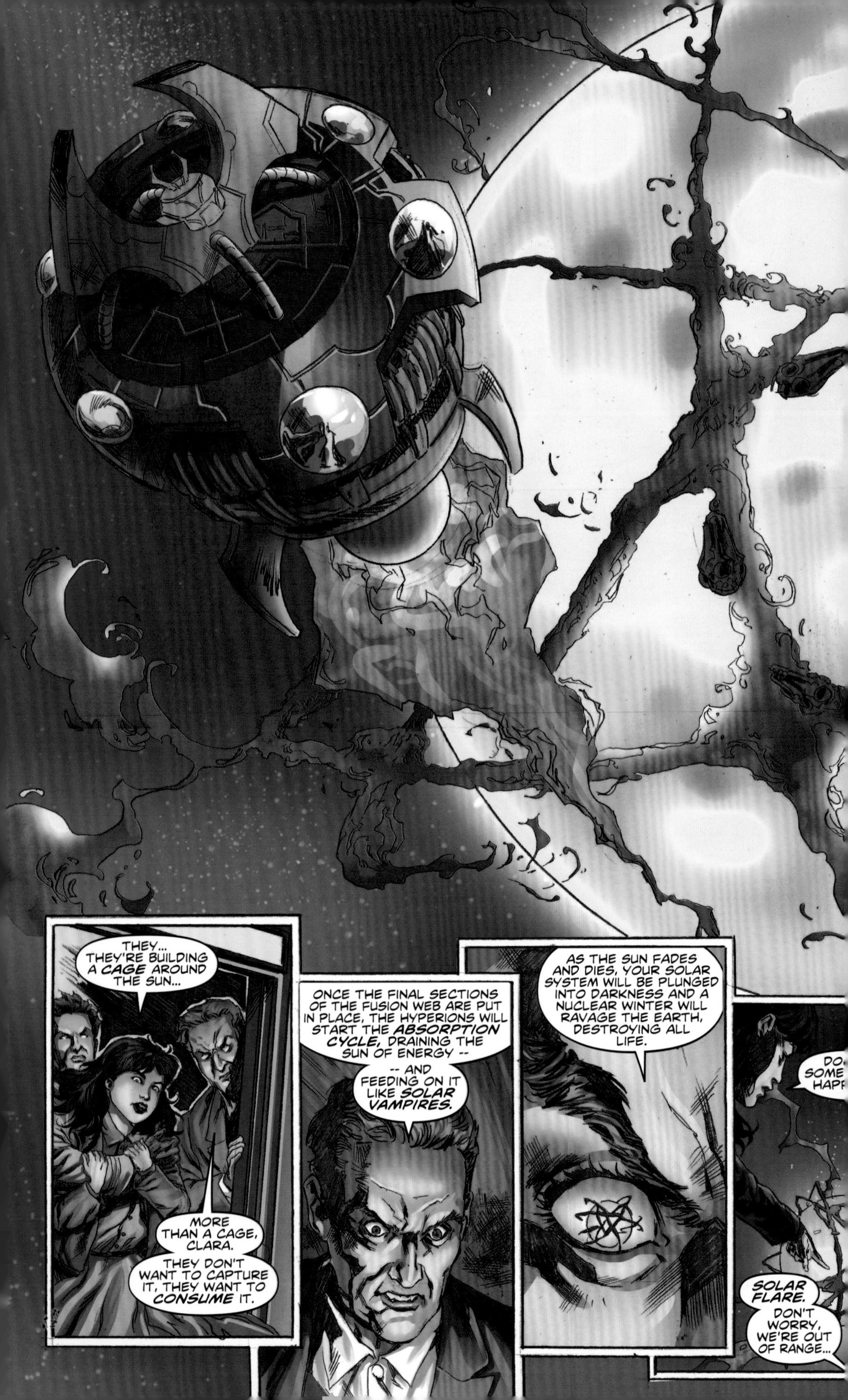

THEY... THEY'RE BUILDING A CAGE AROUND THE SUN...
MORE THAN A CAGE, CLARA.
THEY DON'T WANT TO CAPTURE IT, THEY WANT TO CONSUME IT.
ONCE THE FINAL SECTIONS OF THE FUSION WEB ARE PUT IN PLACE, THE HYPERIONS WILL START THE ABSORPTION CYCLE, DRAINING THE SUN OF ENERGY --
-- AND FEEDING ON IT LIKE SOLAR VAMPIRES.
AS THE SUN FADES AND DIES, YOUR SOLAR SYSTEM WILL BE PLUNGED INTO DARKNESS AND A NUCLEAR WINTER WILL RAVAGE THE EARTH, DESTROYING ALL LIFE.
SOLAR FLARE.
DON'T WORRY, WE'RE OUT OF RANGE...

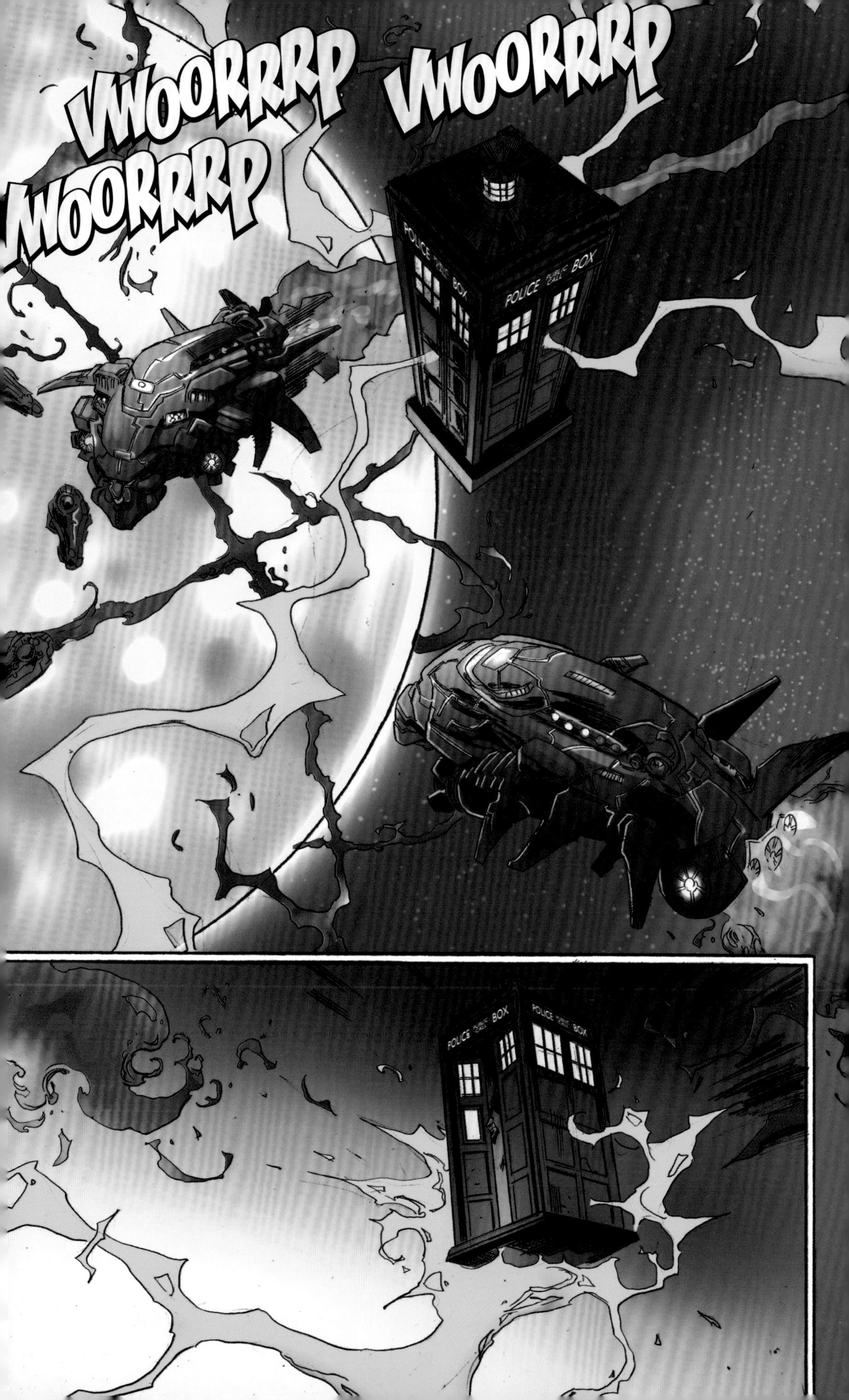
VWOORRRP
VWOORRRP
WOORRRP
POLICE PUBLIC CALL BOX

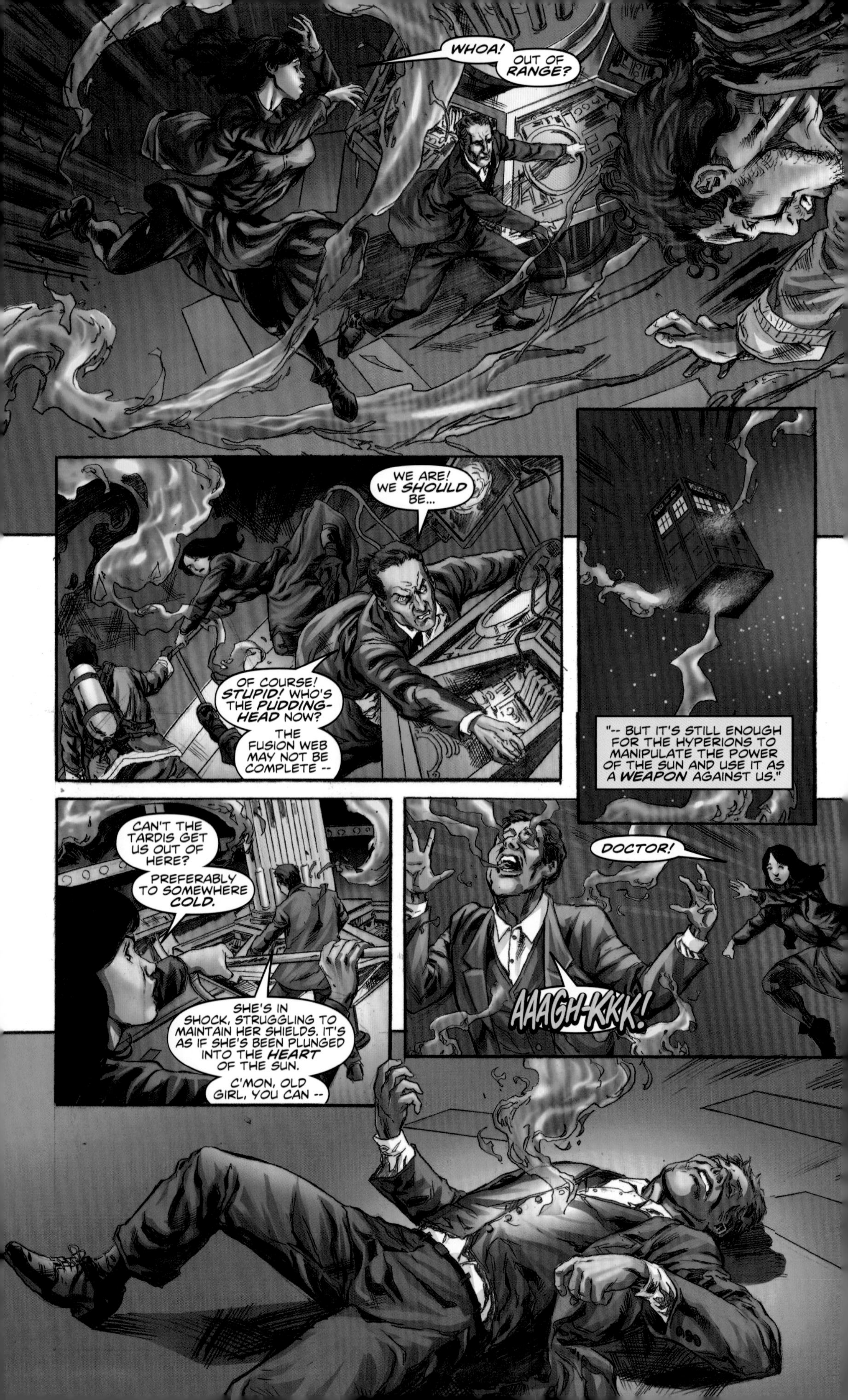
WHOA! OUT OF RANGE?
WE ARE! WE SHOULD BE...
OF COURSE! STUPID! WHO'S THE PUDDING-HEAD NOW?
THE FUSION WEB MAY NOT BE COMPLETE --
"-- BUT IT'S STILL ENOUGH FOR THE HYPERIONS TO MANIPULATE THE POWER OF THE SUN AND USE IT AS A WEAPON AGAINST US."
CAN'T THE TARDIS GET US OUT OF HERE?
PREFERABLY TO SOMEWHERE COLD.
SHE'S IN SHOCK, STRUGGLING TO MAINTAIN HER SHIELDS. IT'S AS IF SHE'S BEEN PLUNGED INTO THE HEART OF THE SUN.
C'MON, OLD GIRL, YOU CAN --
DOCTOR!
AAAGH-KKK!

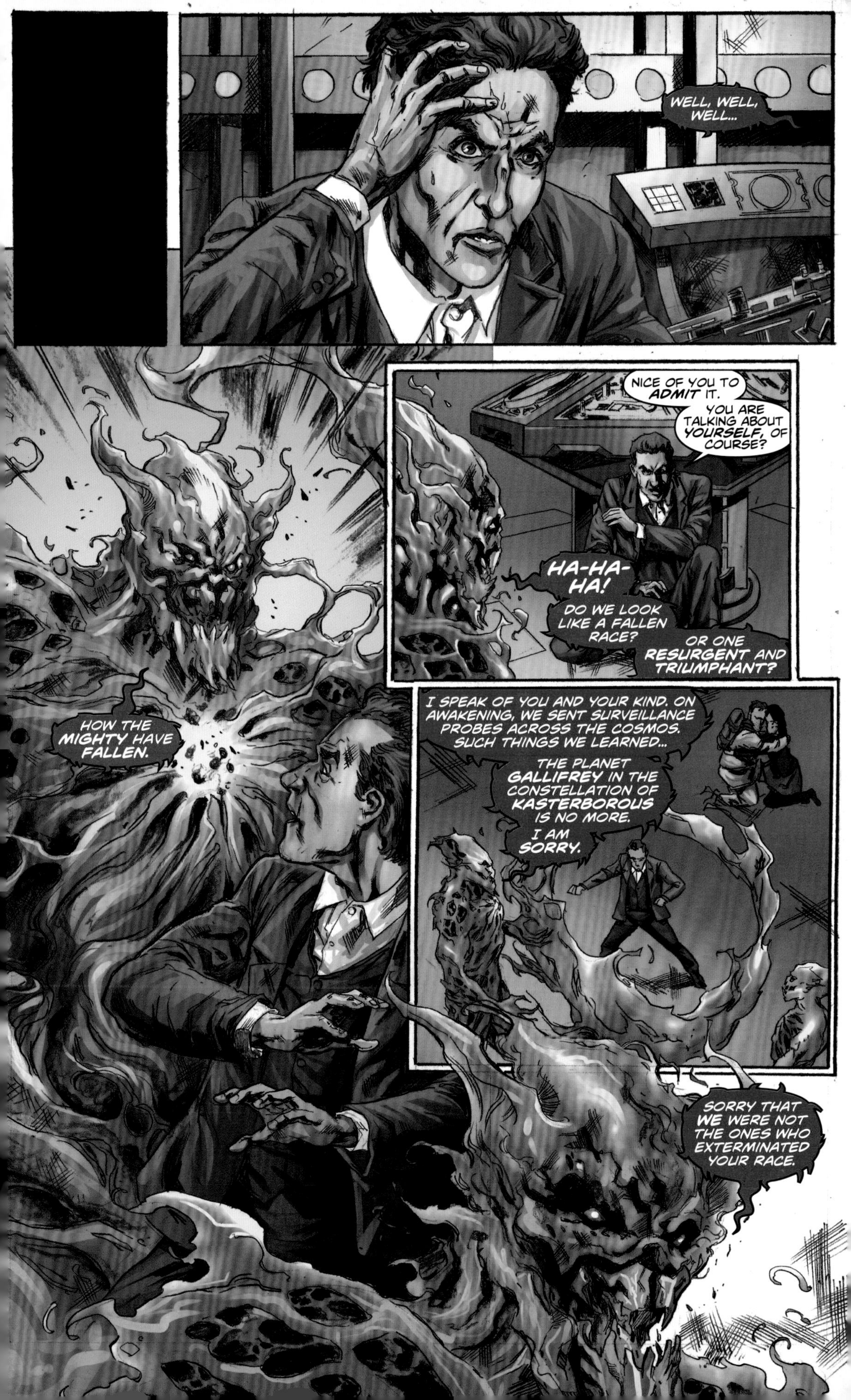
WELL, WELL, WELL...
HOW THE MIGHTY HAVE FALLEN.
NICE OF YOU TO ADMIT IT.
YOU ARE TALKING ABOUT YOURSELF, OF COURSE?
HA-HA-HA!
DO WE LOOK LIKE A FALLEN RACE?
OR ONE RESURGENT AND TRIUMPHANT?
I SPEAK OF YOU AND YOUR KIND. ON AWAKENING, WE SENT SURVEILLANCE PROBES ACROSS THE COSMOS. SUCH THINGS WE LEARNED...
THE PLANET GALLIFREY IN THE CONSTELLATION OF KASTERBOROUS IS NO MORE.
I AM SORRY.
SORRY THAT WE WERE NOT THE ONES WHO EXTERMINATED YOUR RACE.

THE *LAST* OF THE *TIME LORDS.*

STILL MORE THAN ENOUGH TO *HUFF* AND *PUFF* AND BLOW YOU LOT OUT LIKE *CANDLES* ON A BIRTHDAY CAKE.

I AM *WARLORD DRA-KHAN* OF THE *HYPERION EMPIRE.* WHAT DO THEY CALL YOU?

THE *DOCTOR.*

A *HEALER.* NOT EVEN A *WARRIOR.* A *POOR* TESTAMENT TO YOUR RACE

HOW *DID* YOU ESCAPE THE GREAT INFERNO? HYPERIOS WAS DESTROYED.

EVERYTHING WE DID WAS FOR SURVIVAL.

DO YOU SERIOUSLY THINK WE'D THROW ALL THAT AWAY IN ONE FINAL BLAZE OF GLORY?

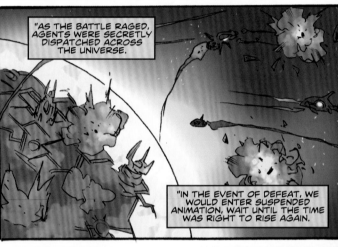

"AS THE BATTLE RAGED, AGENTS WERE SECRETLY DISPATCHED ACROSS THE UNIVERSE.

"IN THE EVENT OF DEFEAT, WE WOULD ENTER SUSPENDED ANIMATION, WAIT UNTIL THE TIME WAS RIGHT TO RISE AGAIN.

"WE CONCEALED OURSELVES ON THE ICE PLANET THE HUMANS CALL *NEPTUNE,* THE LAST PLACE ANYONE WOULD SEARCH FOR US.

"FEW WILL EVEN NOTICE WHEN THIS BACKWATER SOLAR SYSTEM BLINKS OUT OF EXISTENCE."

HOW CAN YOU CONDEMN AN INNOCENT SPECIES TO DEATH?

HAVE YOU NEVER STEPPED ON AN *INSECT* WITHOUT A SECOND THOUGHT?

SENTIENT OR NOT, AND YOU ARE *BARELY* THAT... YOU ARE *BENEATH* SIGNIFICANCE.

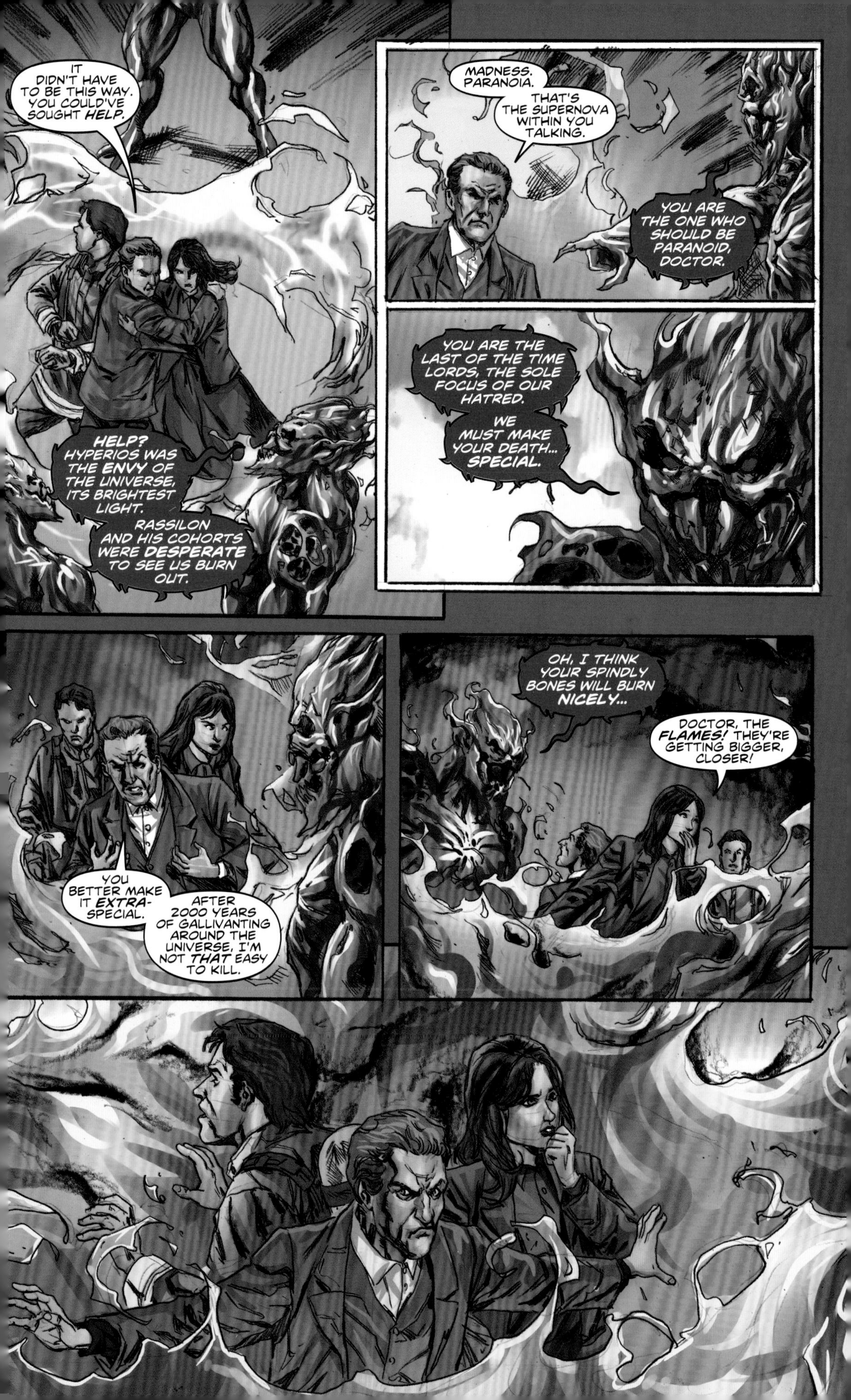
IT DIDN'T HAVE TO BE THIS WAY. YOU COULD'VE SOUGHT HELP.
HELP? HYPERIOS WAS THE ENVY OF THE UNIVERSE, ITS BRIGHTEST LIGHT.
RASSILON AND HIS COHORTS WERE DESPERATE TO SEE US BURN OUT.
MADNESS. PARANOIA.
THAT'S THE SUPERNOVA WITHIN YOU TALKING.
YOU ARE THE ONE WHO SHOULD BE PARANOID, DOCTOR.
YOU ARE THE LAST OF THE TIME LORDS, THE SOLE FOCUS OF OUR HATRED.
WE MUST MAKE YOUR DEATH... SPECIAL.
YOU BETTER MAKE IT EXTRA-SPECIAL.
AFTER 2000 YEARS OF GALLIVANTING AROUND THE UNIVERSE, I'M NOT THAT EASY TO KILL.
OH, I THINK YOUR SPINDLY BONES WILL BURN NICELY...
DOCTOR, THE FLAMES! THEY'RE GETTING BIGGER, CLOSER!

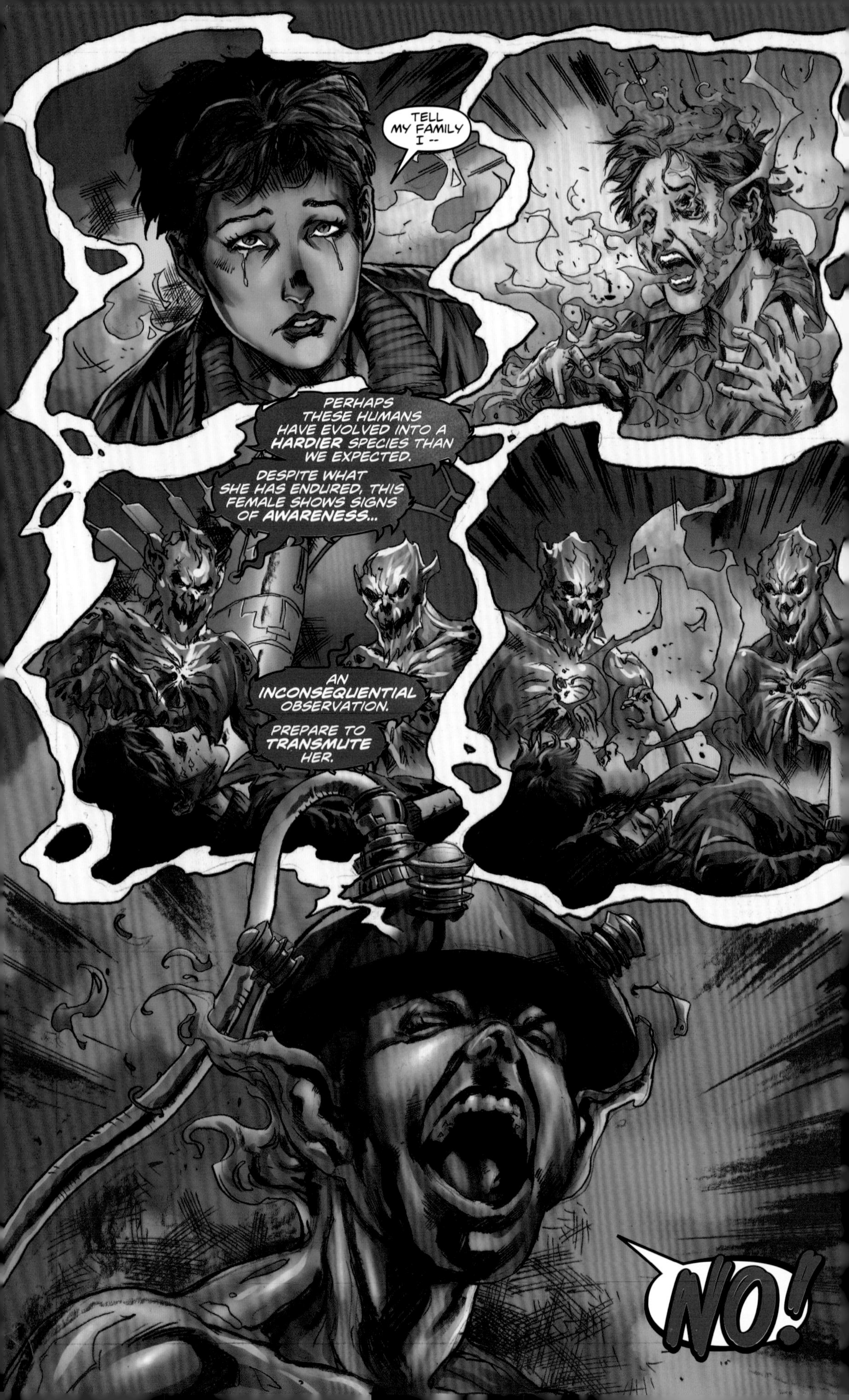
TELL MY FAMILY I --
PERHAPS THESE HUMANS HAVE EVOLVED INTO A HARDIER SPECIES THAN WE EXPECTED.
DESPITE WHAT SHE HAS ENDURED, THIS FEMALE SHOWS SIGNS OF AWARENESS...
AN INCONSEQUENTIAL OBSERVATION.
PREPARE TO TRANSMUTE HER.
NO!

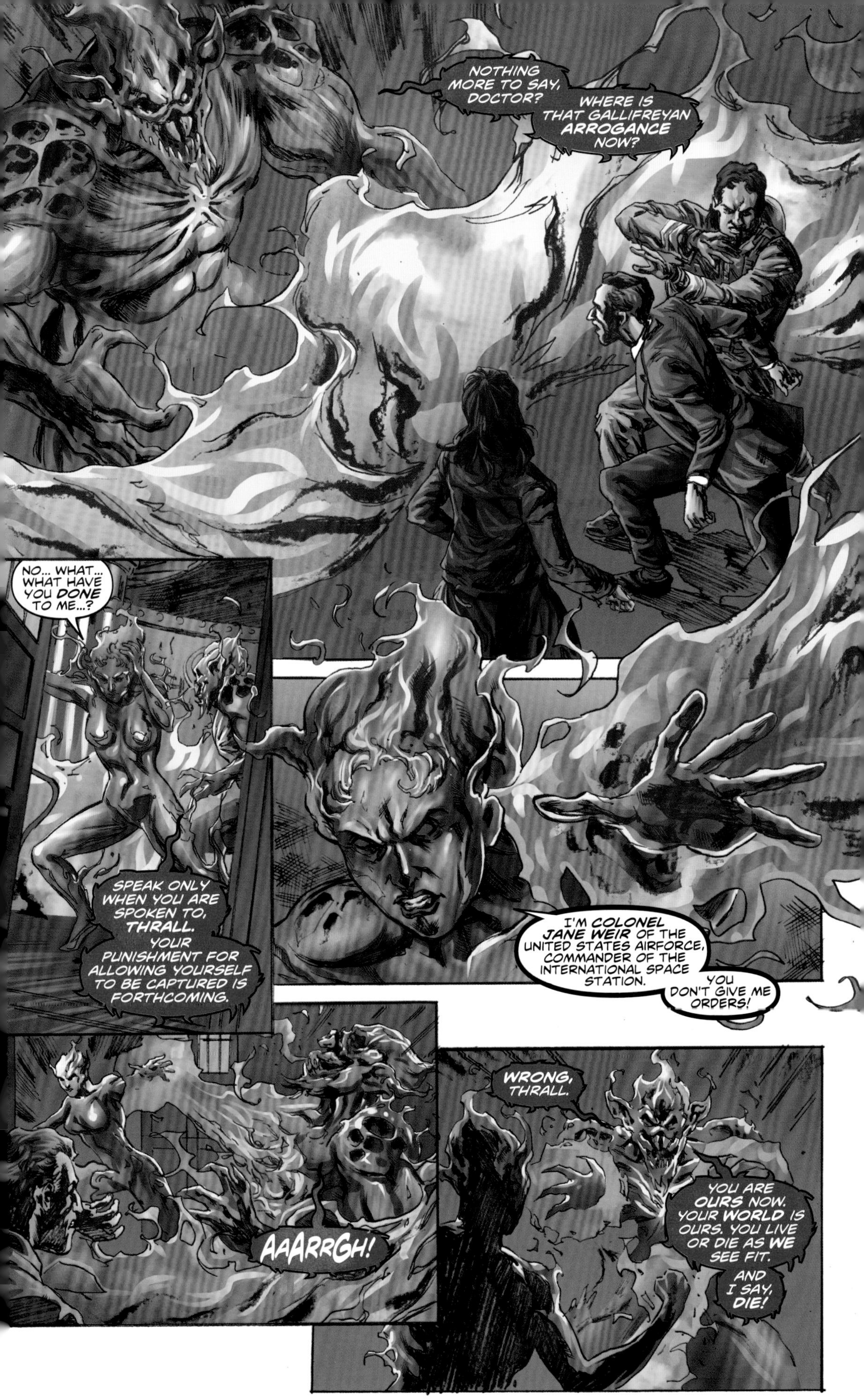
NOTHING MORE TO SAY, DOCTOR?
WHERE IS THAT GALLIFREYAN ARROGANCE NOW?
NO... WHAT... WHAT HAVE YOU DONE TO ME...?
SPEAK ONLY WHEN YOU ARE SPOKEN TO, THRALL. YOUR PUNISHMENT FOR ALLOWING YOURSELF TO BE CAPTURED IS FORTHCOMING.
I'M COLONEL JANE WEIR OF THE UNITED STATES AIRFORCE, COMMANDER OF THE INTERNATIONAL SPACE STATION.
YOU DON'T GIVE ME ORDERS!
AAARRGH!
WRONG, THRALL.
YOU ARE OURS NOW. YOUR WORLD IS OURS. YOU LIVE OR DIE AS WE SEE FIT.
AND I SAY, DIE!

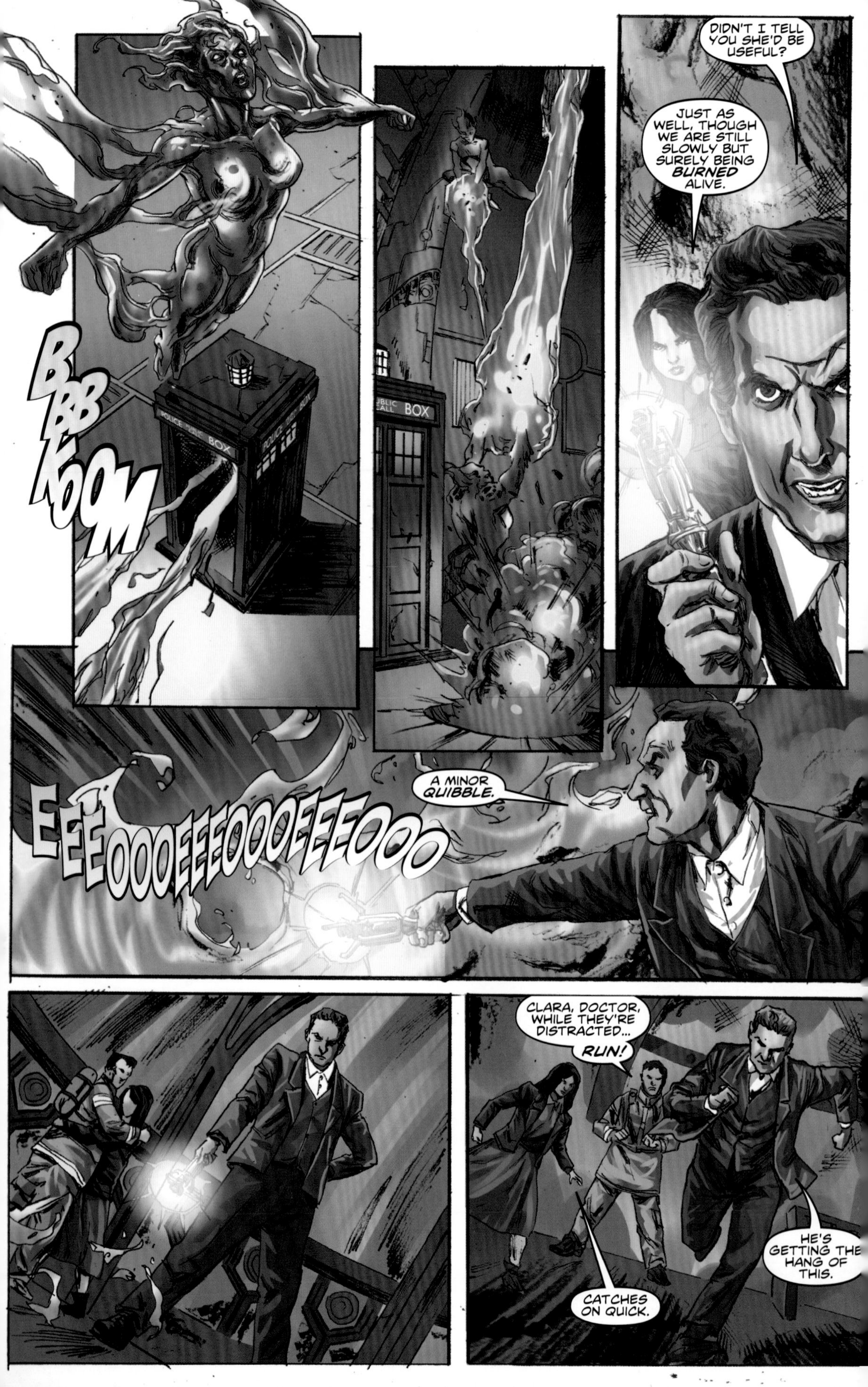

BBB
KOOM
DIDN'T I TELL YOU SHE'D BE USEFUL?
JUST AS WELL, THOUGH WE ARE STILL SLOWLY BUT SURELY BEING BURNED ALIVE.
A MINOR QUIBBLE.
EEEOOOEEEOOOEEEOOO
CLARA, DOCTOR, WHILE THEY'RE DISTRACTED... RUN!
HE'S GETTING THE HANG OF THIS.
CATCHES ON QUICK.

IF YOU WANT TO FIGHT THE HYPERIONS, COME WITH US!

COLONEL WEIR! THIS ISN'T THE WAY! YOU DON'T HAVE A CHANCE ON YOUR OWN!

VVOORRRD VVOORRRP

VVOORRRP

DOCTOR!

TRAFALGAR SQUARE, LONDON.

IF WE WANT TO BE *LEADERS* IN THE NEW WORLD ORDER, WE MUST BE *BOLD*, SHAPE EVENTS TO OUR ADVANTAGE.

THERE *ISN'T* NEW WORLD ORD SIR, JUST THE C ONE. AND THAT WELL, A BIT OF *MESS* AT --

AS MINISTER OF PUBLIC HYGIENE, IT'S MY JOB TO CLEAN UP MESSES, TO LEAD HUMANITY IN A PHOENIX-LIKE RISE FROM THE --

S-SIR, I REALLY DON'T THINK THIS IS ADVISABLE...

WHO DARES WINS, *TRISTRAM*, AS OUR LADS IN THE S.A.S. SAY.

AAAIIIEEEEE!

ULP! DON'T BE *HASTY!* I -- I KNOW YOU'RE OUT THERE, THAT YOU'RE LISTENING...

PLEASE, I CAN *HELP.*

DO YOU *HEAR* ME?

THE DOCTOR!

-- ASHES...

I HAVE INFORMATION ABOUT THE MAN THEY CALL THE DOCTOR.

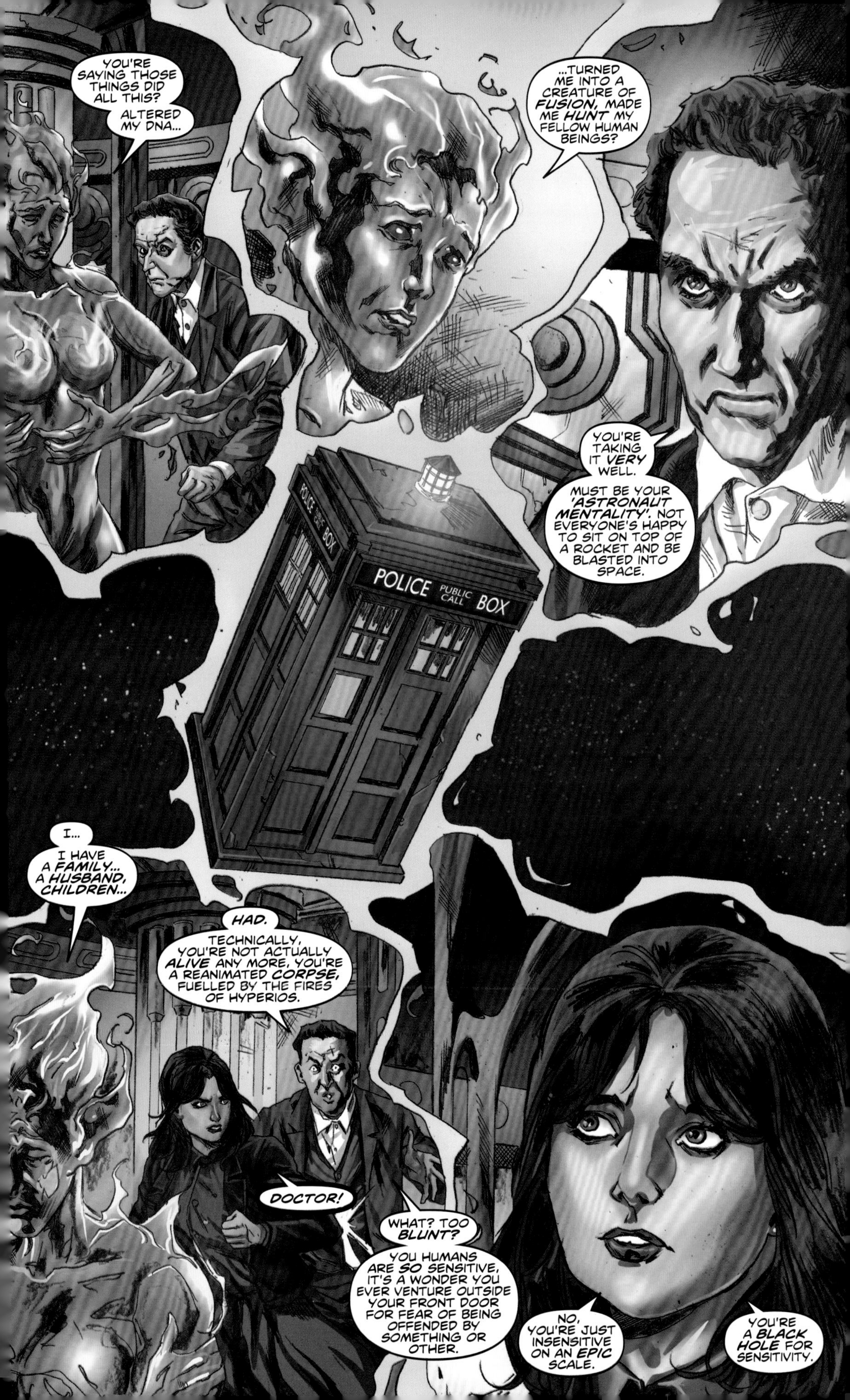
YOU'RE SAYING THOSE THINGS DID ALL THIS?
ALTERED MY DNA...
...TURNED ME INTO A CREATURE OF FUSION, MADE ME HUNT MY FELLOW HUMAN BEINGS?
YOU'RE TAKING IT VERY WELL.
MUST BE YOUR 'ASTRONAUT MENTALITY'. NOT EVERYONE'S HAPPY TO SIT ON TOP OF A ROCKET AND BE BLASTED INTO SPACE.
POLICE PUBLIC CALL BOX
I...
I HAVE A FAMILY... A HUSBAND, CHILDREN...
HAD.
TECHNICALLY, YOU'RE NOT ACTUALLY ALIVE ANY MORE, YOU'RE A REANIMATED CORPSE, FUELLED BY THE FIRES OF HYPERIOS.
DOCTOR!
WHAT? TOO BLUNT?
YOU HUMANS ARE SO SENSITIVE, IT'S A WONDER YOU EVER VENTURE OUTSIDE YOUR FRONT DOOR FOR FEAR OF BEING OFFENDED BY SOMETHING OR OTHER.
NO, YOU'RE JUST INSENSITIVE ON AN EPIC SCALE.
YOU'RE A BLACK HOLE FOR SENSITIVITY.

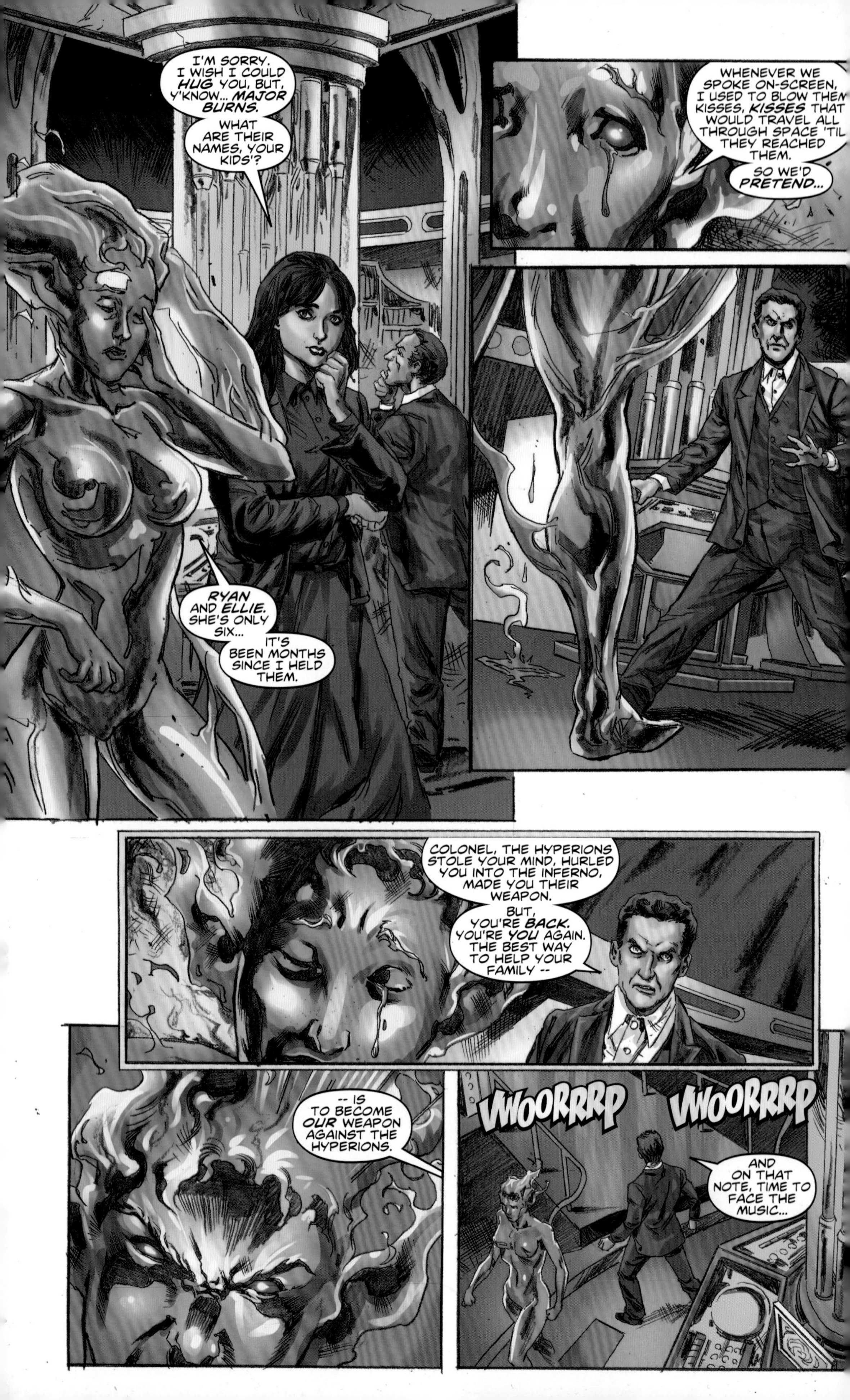
I'M SORRY. I WISH I COULD HUG YOU, BUT, Y'KNOW... MAJOR BURNS.
WHAT ARE THEIR NAMES, YOUR KIDS'?
RYAN AND ELLIE. SHE'S ONLY SIX...
IT'S BEEN MONTHS SINCE I HELD THEM.
WHENEVER WE SPOKE ON-SCREEN, I USED TO BLOW THEM KISSES, KISSES THAT WOULD TRAVEL ALL THROUGH SPACE 'TIL THEY REACHED THEM.
SO WE'D PRETEND...
COLONEL, THE HYPERIONS STOLE YOUR MIND, HURLED YOU INTO THE INFERNO, MADE YOU THEIR WEAPON.
BUT, YOU'RE BACK. YOU'RE YOU AGAIN. THE BEST WAY TO HELP YOUR FAMILY --
-- IS TO BECOME OUR WEAPON AGAINST THE HYPERIONS.
VWOORRRP
VWOORRRP
AND ON THAT NOTE, TIME TO FACE THE MUSIC...

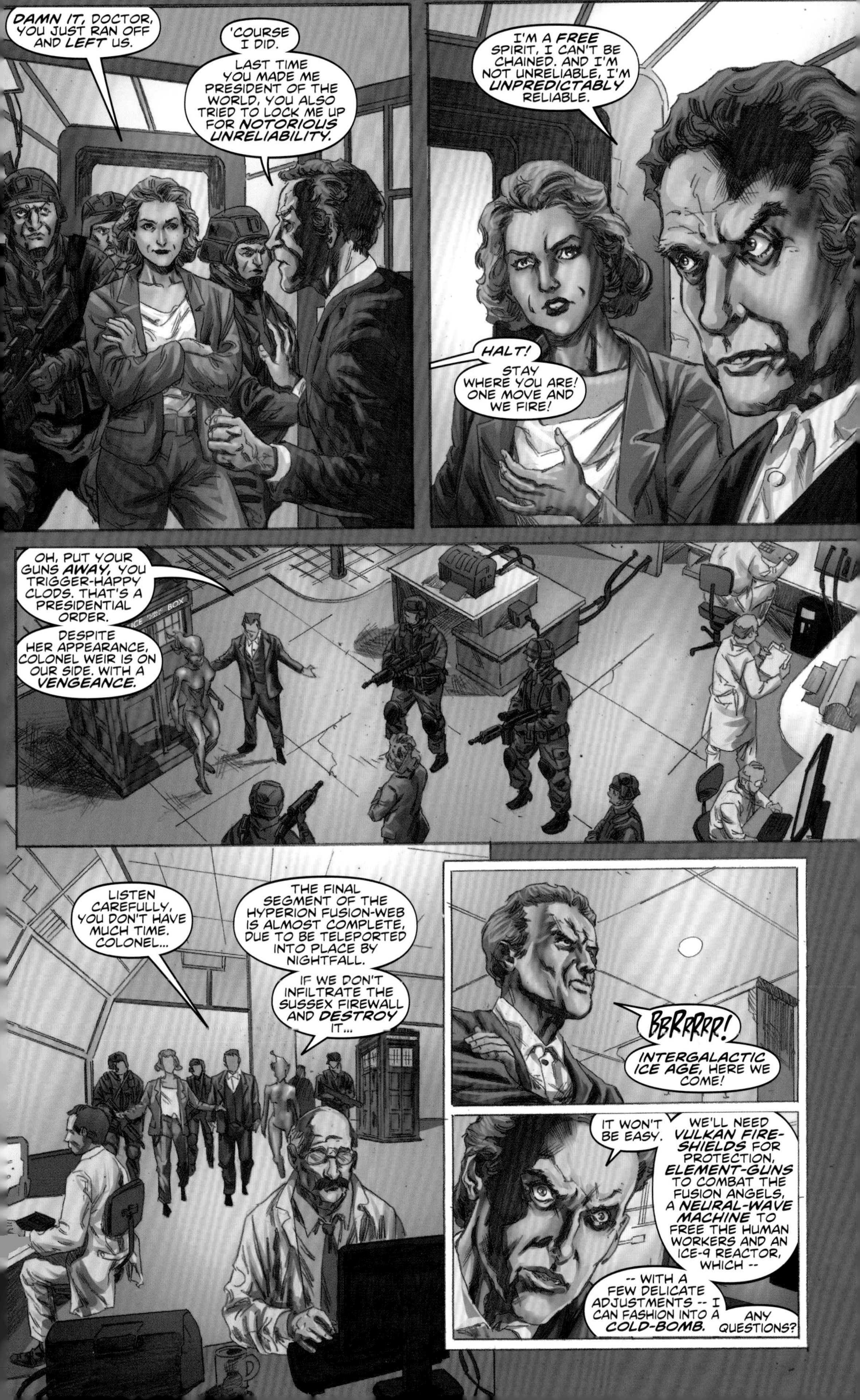
DAMN IT, DOCTOR, YOU JUST RAN OFF AND LEFT US.
'COURSE I DID.
LAST TIME YOU MADE ME PRESIDENT OF THE WORLD, YOU ALSO TRIED TO LOCK ME UP FOR NOTORIOUS UNRELIABILITY.
I'M A FREE SPIRIT, I CAN'T BE CHAINED. AND I'M NOT UNRELIABLE, I'M UNPREDICTABLY RELIABLE.
HALT!
STAY WHERE YOU ARE! ONE MOVE AND WE FIRE!
OH, PUT YOUR GUNS AWAY, YOU TRIGGER-HAPPY CLODS. THAT'S A PRESIDENTIAL ORDER.
DESPITE HER APPEARANCE, COLONEL WEIR IS ON OUR SIDE. WITH A VENGEANCE.
LISTEN CAREFULLY, YOU DON'T HAVE MUCH TIME. COLONEL...
THE FINAL SEGMENT OF THE HYPERION FUSION-WEB IS ALMOST COMPLETE, DUE TO BE TELEPORTED INTO PLACE BY NIGHTFALL.
IF WE DON'T INFILTRATE THE SUSSEX FIREWALL AND DESTROY IT...
BBRRRRR!
INTERGALACTIC ICE AGE, HERE WE COME!
IT WON'T BE EASY.
WE'LL NEED VULKAN FIRE-SHIELDS FOR PROTECTION, ELEMENT-GUNS TO COMBAT THE FUSION ANGELS, A NEURAL-WAVE MACHINE TO FREE THE HUMAN WORKERS AND AN ICE-9 REACTOR, WHICH --
-- WITH A FEW DELICATE ADJUSTMENTS -- I CAN FASHION INTO A COLD-BOMB.
ANY QUESTIONS?

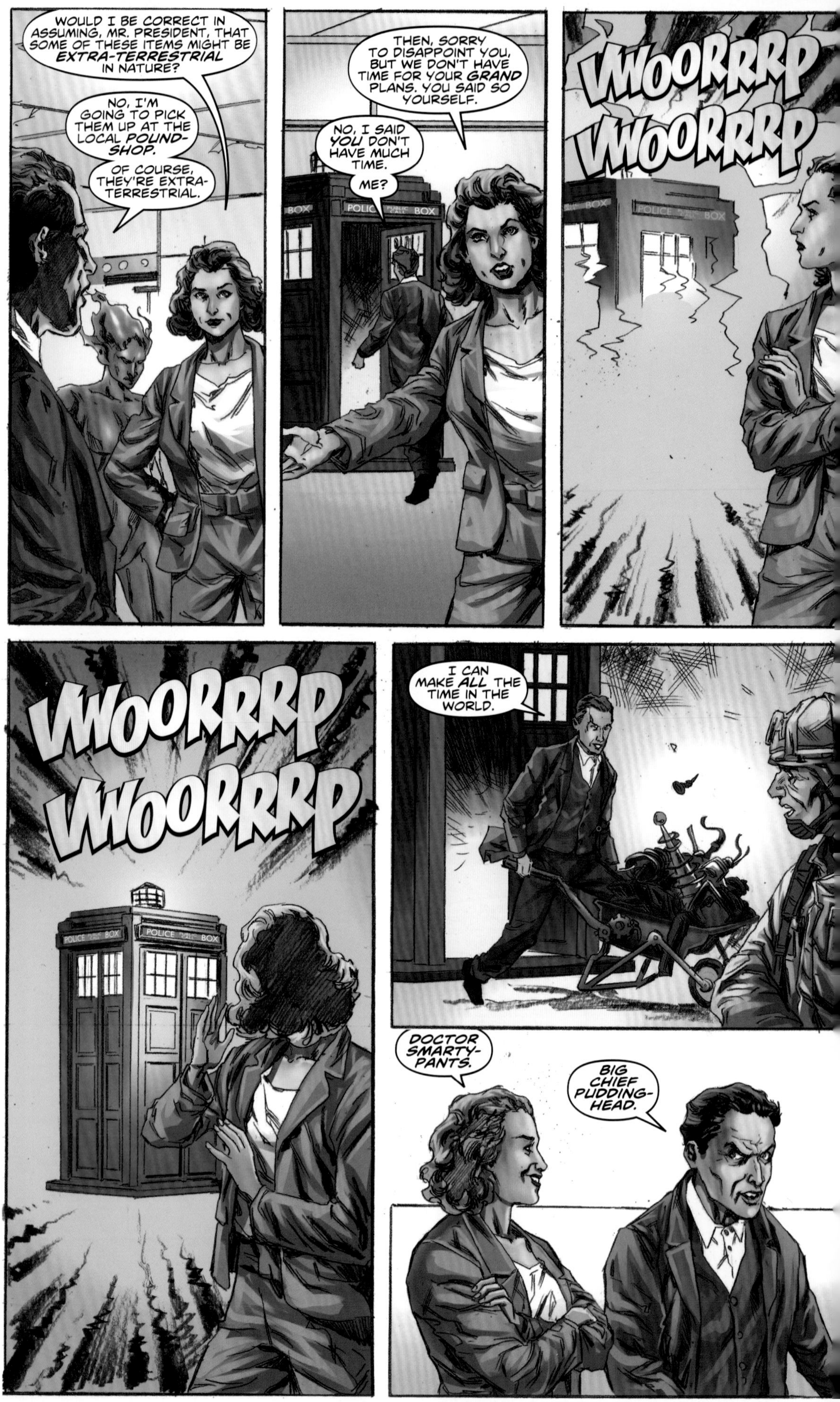
WOULD I BE CORRECT IN ASSUMING, MR. PRESIDENT, THAT SOME OF THESE ITEMS MIGHT BE EXTRA-TERRESTRIAL IN NATURE?
NO, I'M GOING TO PICK THEM UP AT THE LOCAL POUND-SHOP.
OF COURSE, THEY'RE EXTRA-TERRESTRIAL.
THEN, SORRY TO DISAPPOINT YOU, BUT WE DON'T HAVE TIME FOR YOUR GRAND PLANS. YOU SAID SO YOURSELF.
NO, I SAID YOU DON'T HAVE MUCH TIME.
ME?
POLICE PUBLIC CALL BOX
VWOORRRP
VWOORRRP
POLICE PUBLIC CALL BOX
VWOORRRP
VWOORRRP
POLICE PUBLIC CALL BOX
I CAN MAKE ALL THE TIME IN THE WORLD.
DOCTOR SMARTY-PANTS.
BIG CHIEF PUDDING-HEAD.

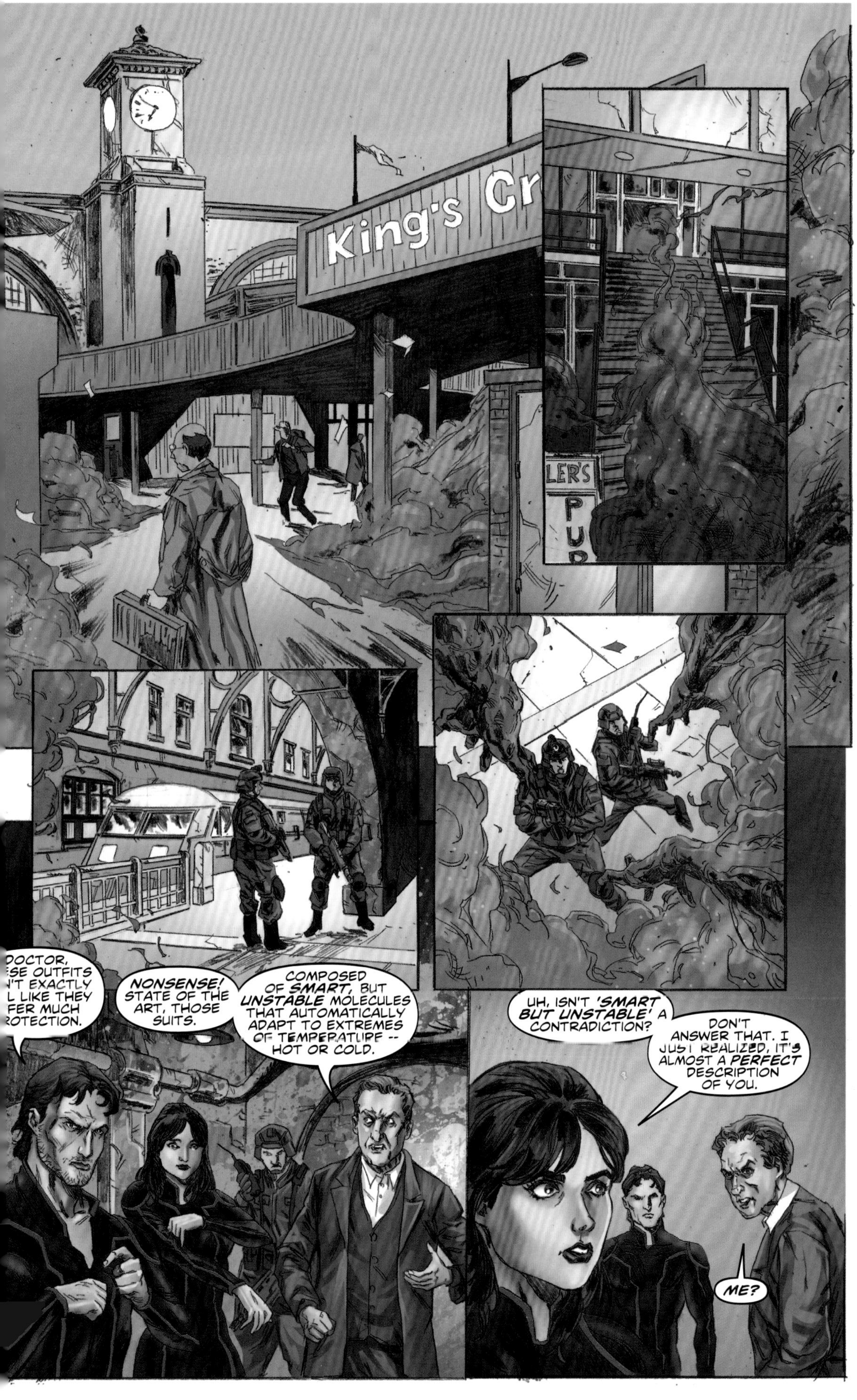
King's Cr
LER'S
PU
DOCTOR, ESE OUTFITS N'T EXACTLY L LIKE THEY FER MUCH ROTECTION.
NONSENSE! STATE OF THE ART, THOSE SUITS.
COMPOSED OF SMART, BUT UNSTABLE MOLECULES THAT AUTOMATICALLY ADAPT TO EXTREMES OF TEMPERATURE -- HOT OR COLD.
UH, ISN'T 'SMART BUT UNSTABLE' A CONTRADICTION?
DON'T ANSWER THAT. I JUST REALIZED, IT'S ALMOST A PERFECT DESCRIPTION OF YOU.
ME?

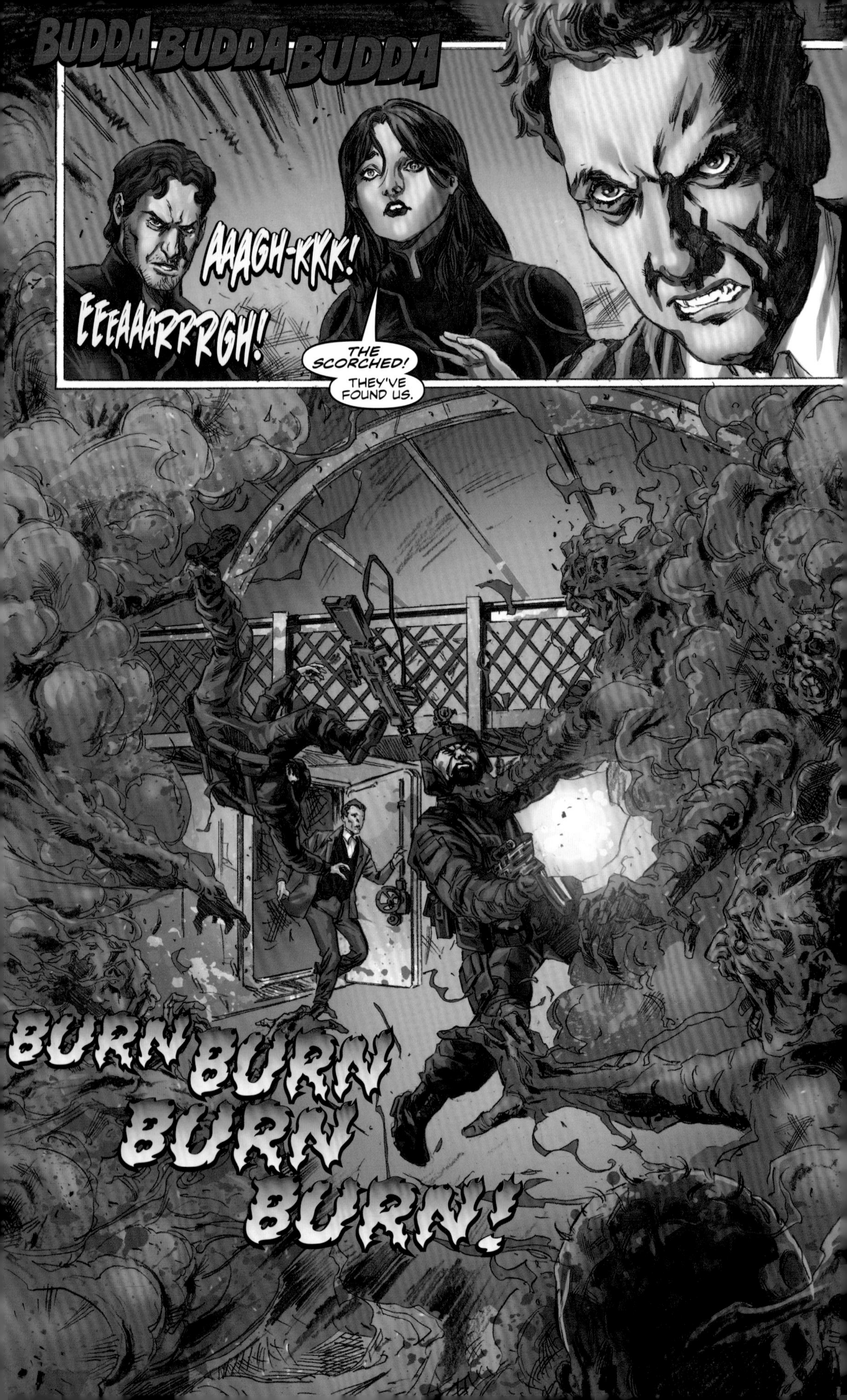
BUDDA BUDDA BUDDA
AAAGH-KKK!
EEEAAARRRGH!
THE SCORCHED!
THEY'VE FOUND US.
BURN BURN BURN BURN!

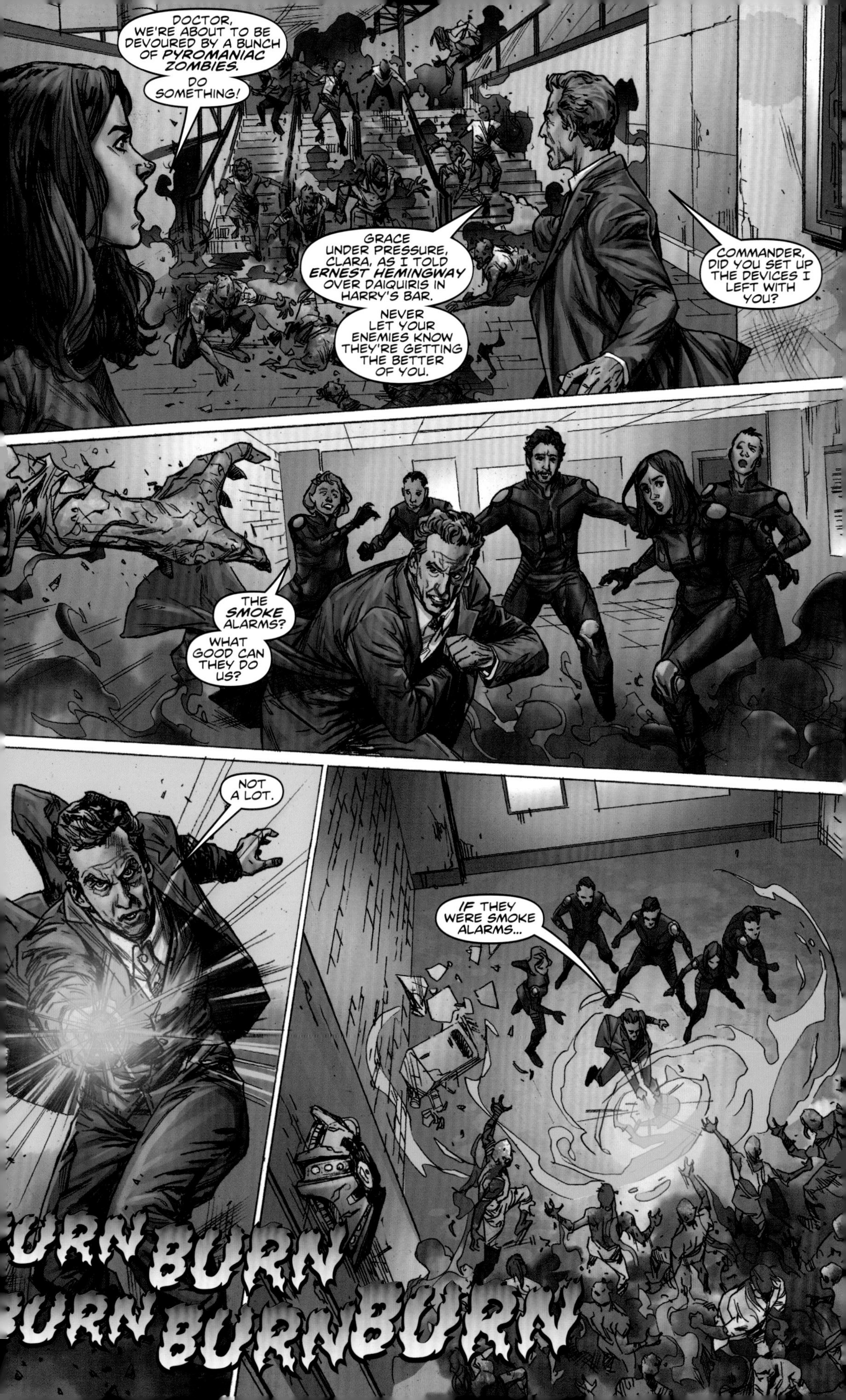
DOCTOR, WE'RE ABOUT TO BE DEVOURED BY A BUNCH OF *PYROMANIAC ZOMBIES.*
DO SOMETHING!
GRACE UNDER PRESSURE, CLARA, AS I TOLD *ERNEST HEMINGWAY* OVER DAIQUIRIS IN HARRY'S BAR.
NEVER LET YOUR ENEMIES KNOW THEY'RE GETTING THE BETTER OF YOU.
COMMANDER, DID YOU SET UP THE DEVICES I LEFT WITH YOU?
THE *SMOKE* ALARMS?
WHAT GOOD CAN THEY DO US?
NOT A LOT.
IF THEY WERE SMOKE ALARMS...
URN BURN
URN BURNBURN

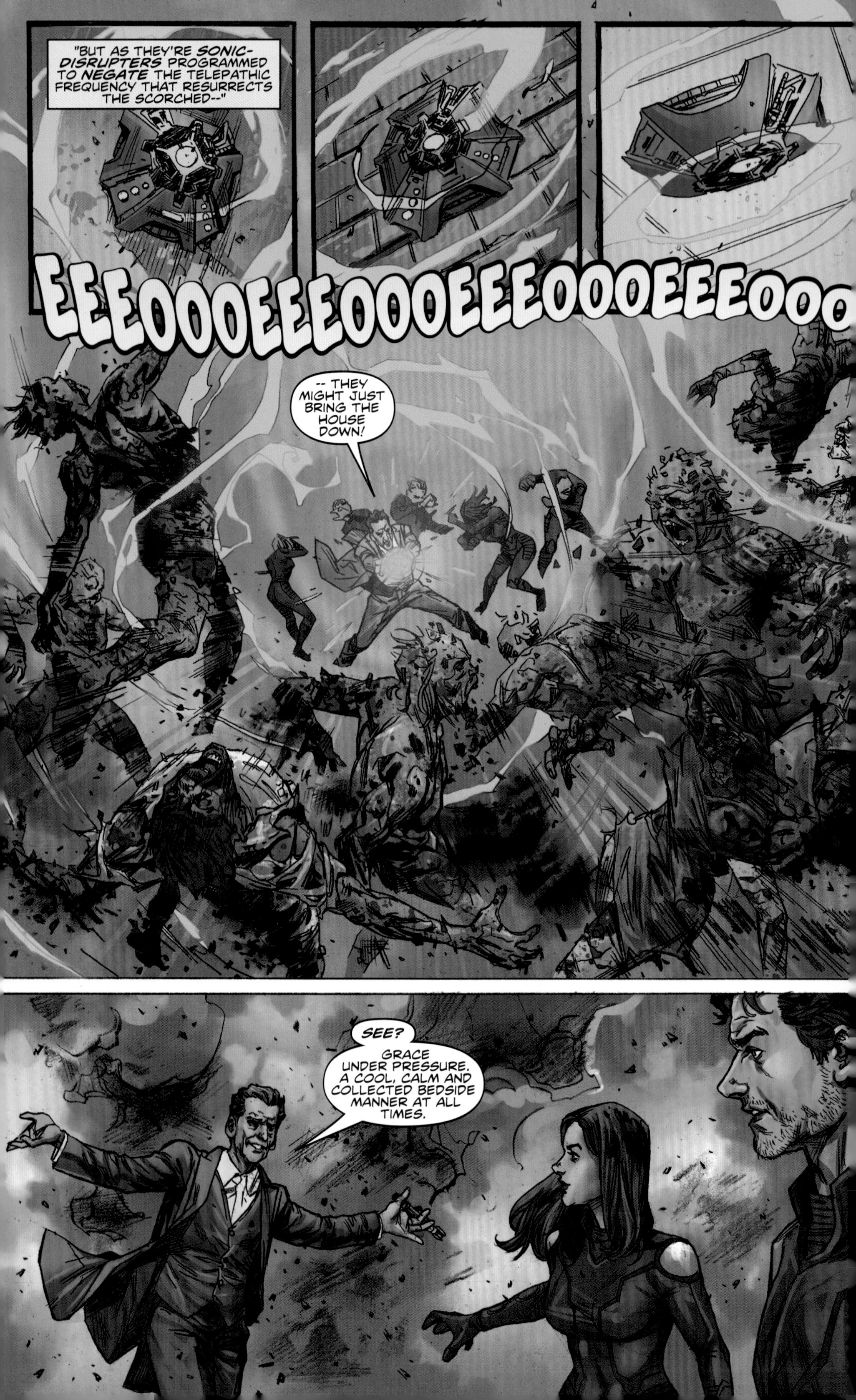
"BUT AS THEY'RE *SONIC-DISRUPTERS* PROGRAMMED TO *NEGATE* THE TELEPATHIC FREQUENCY THAT RESURRECTS THE SCORCHED--"
EEEOOOEEEOOOEEEOOOEEEOOO
-- THEY MIGHT JUST BRING THE HOUSE DOWN!
SEE?
GRACE UNDER PRESSURE. A COOL, CALM AND COLLECTED BEDSIDE MANNER AT ALL TIMES.

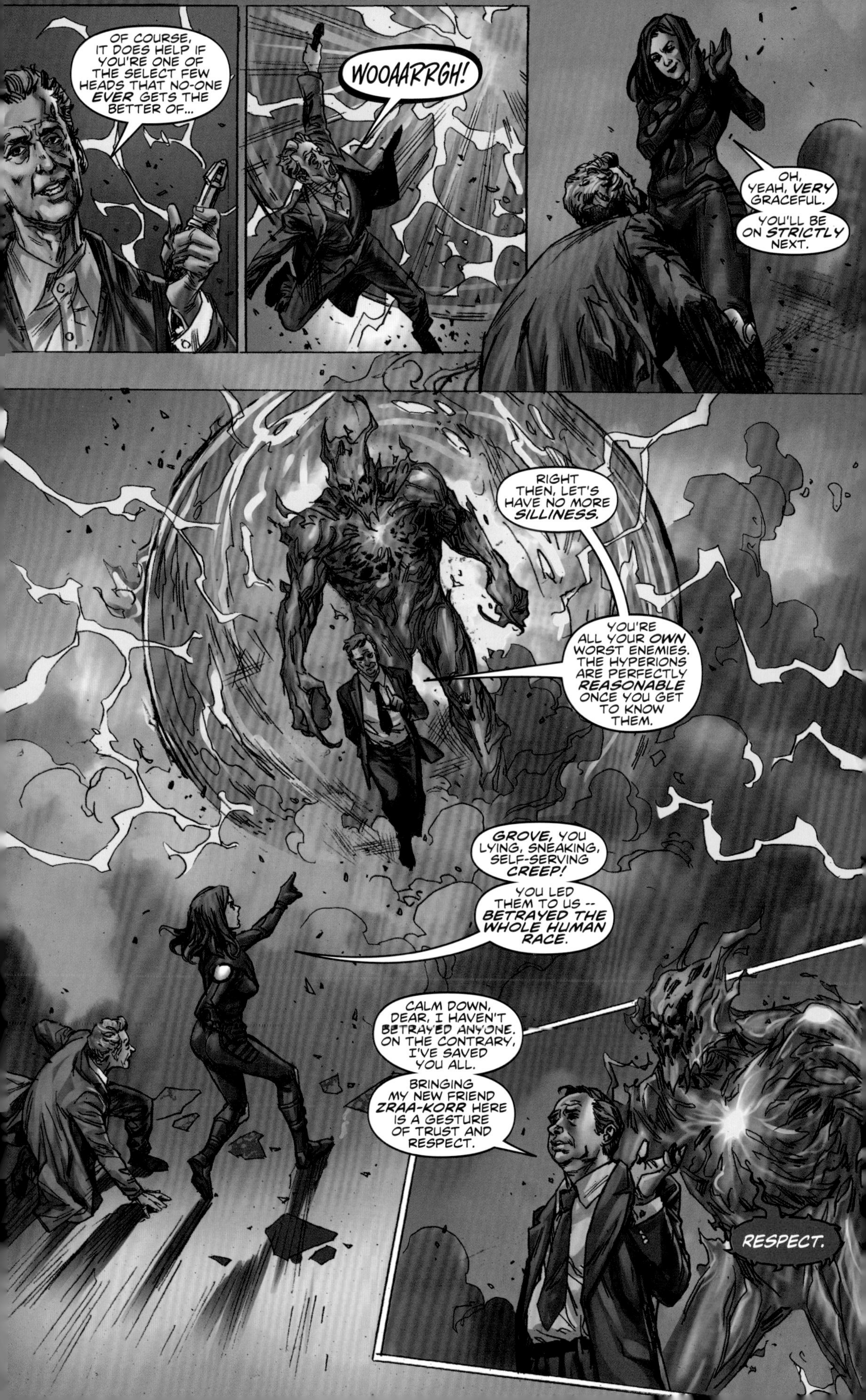
OF COURSE, IT DOES HELP IF YOU'RE ONE OF THE SELECT FEW HEADS THAT NO-ONE EVER GETS THE BETTER OF...
WOOAARRGH!
OH, YEAH, VERY GRACEFUL.
YOU'LL BE ON STRICTLY NEXT.
RIGHT THEN, LET'S HAVE NO MORE SILLINESS.
YOU'RE ALL YOUR OWN WORST ENEMIES. THE HYPERIONS ARE PERFECTLY REASONABLE ONCE YOU GET TO KNOW THEM.
GROVE, YOU LYING, SNEAKING, SELF-SERVING CREEP!
YOU LED THEM TO US -- BETRAYED THE WHOLE HUMAN RACE.
CALM DOWN, DEAR, I HAVEN'T BETRAYED ANYONE. ON THE CONTRARY, I'VE SAVED YOU ALL.
BRINGING MY NEW FRIEND ZRAA-KORR HERE IS A GESTURE OF TRUST AND RESPECT.
RESPECT.

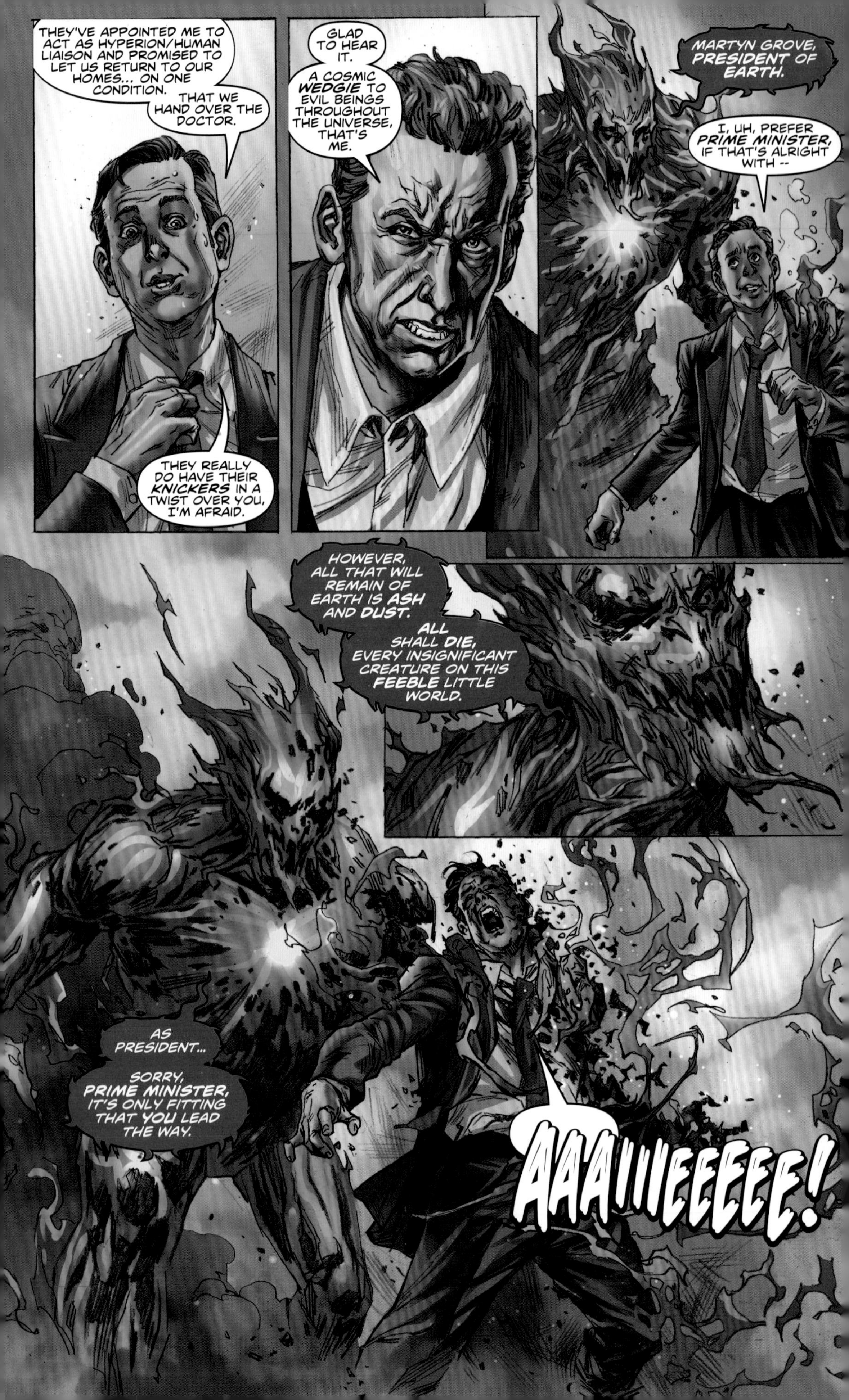
THEY'VE APPOINTED ME TO ACT AS HYPERION/HUMAN LIAISON AND PROMISED TO LET US RETURN TO OUR HOMES... ON ONE CONDITION.
THAT WE HAND OVER THE DOCTOR.
THEY REALLY DO HAVE THEIR KNICKERS IN A TWIST OVER YOU, I'M AFRAID.
GLAD TO HEAR IT.
A COSMIC WEDGIE TO EVIL BEINGS THROUGHOUT THE UNIVERSE, THAT'S ME.
MARTYN GROVE, PRESIDENT OF EARTH.
I, UH, PREFER PRIME MINISTER, IF THAT'S ALRIGHT WITH --
HOWEVER, ALL THAT WILL REMAIN OF EARTH IS ASH AND DUST.
ALL SHALL DIE, EVERY INSIGNIFICANT CREATURE ON THIS FEEBLE LITTLE WORLD.
AS PRESIDENT...
SORRY, PRIME MINISTER, IT'S ONLY FITTING THAT YOU LEAD THE WAY.
AAAIIIEEEEEE!

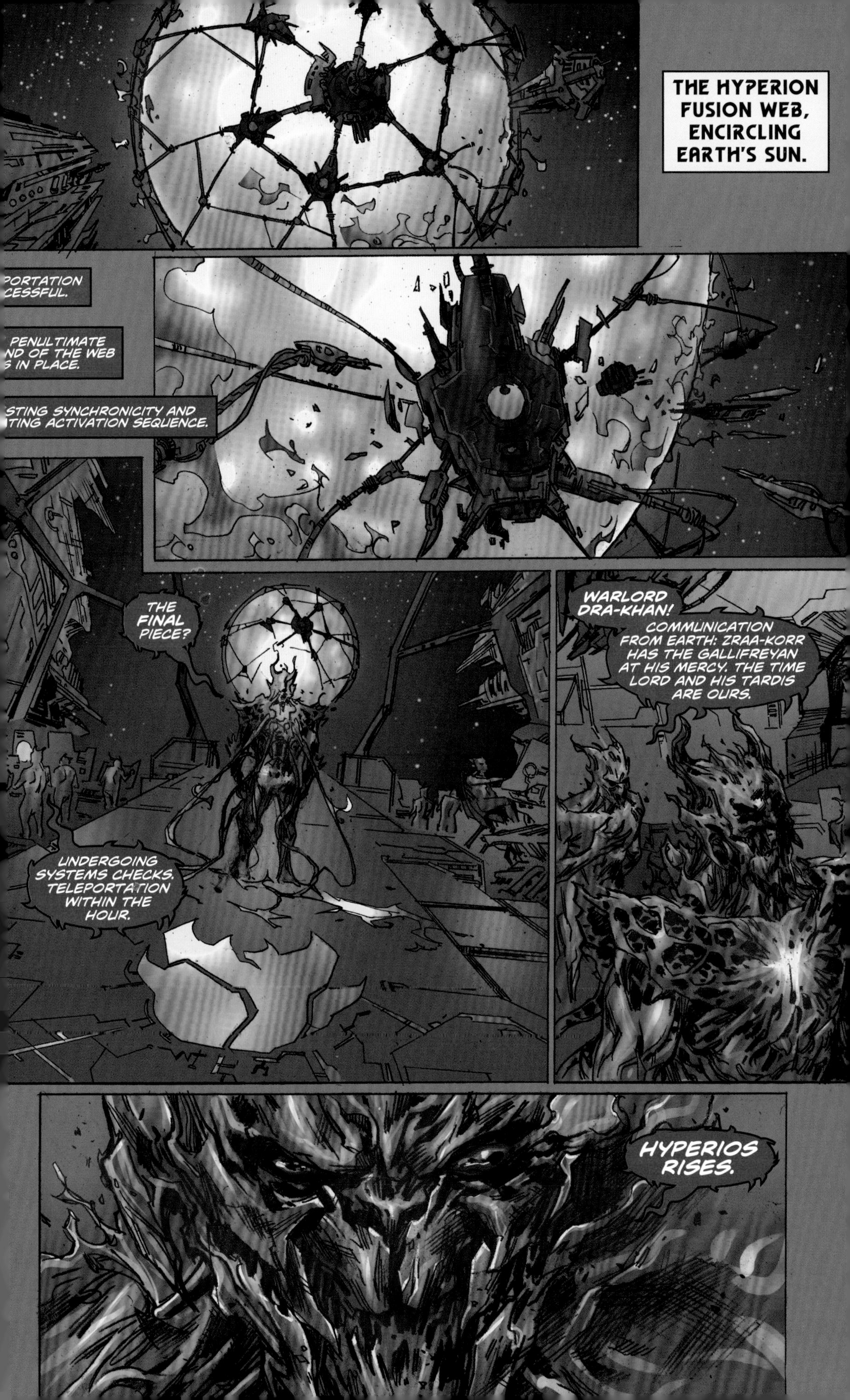
THE HYPERION FUSION WEB, ENCIRCLING EARTH'S SUN.
PORTATION CESSFUL.
PENULTIMATE ND OF THE WEB S IN PLACE.
STING SYNCHRONICITY AND TING ACTIVATION SEQUENCE.
THE FINAL PIECE?
UNDERGOING SYSTEMS CHECKS. TELEPORTATION WITHIN THE HOUR.
WARLORD DRA-KHAN!
COMMUNICATION FROM EARTH: ZRAA-KORR HAS THE GALLIFREYAN AT HIS MERCY. THE TIME LORD AND HIS TARDIS ARE OURS.
HYPERIOS RISES.

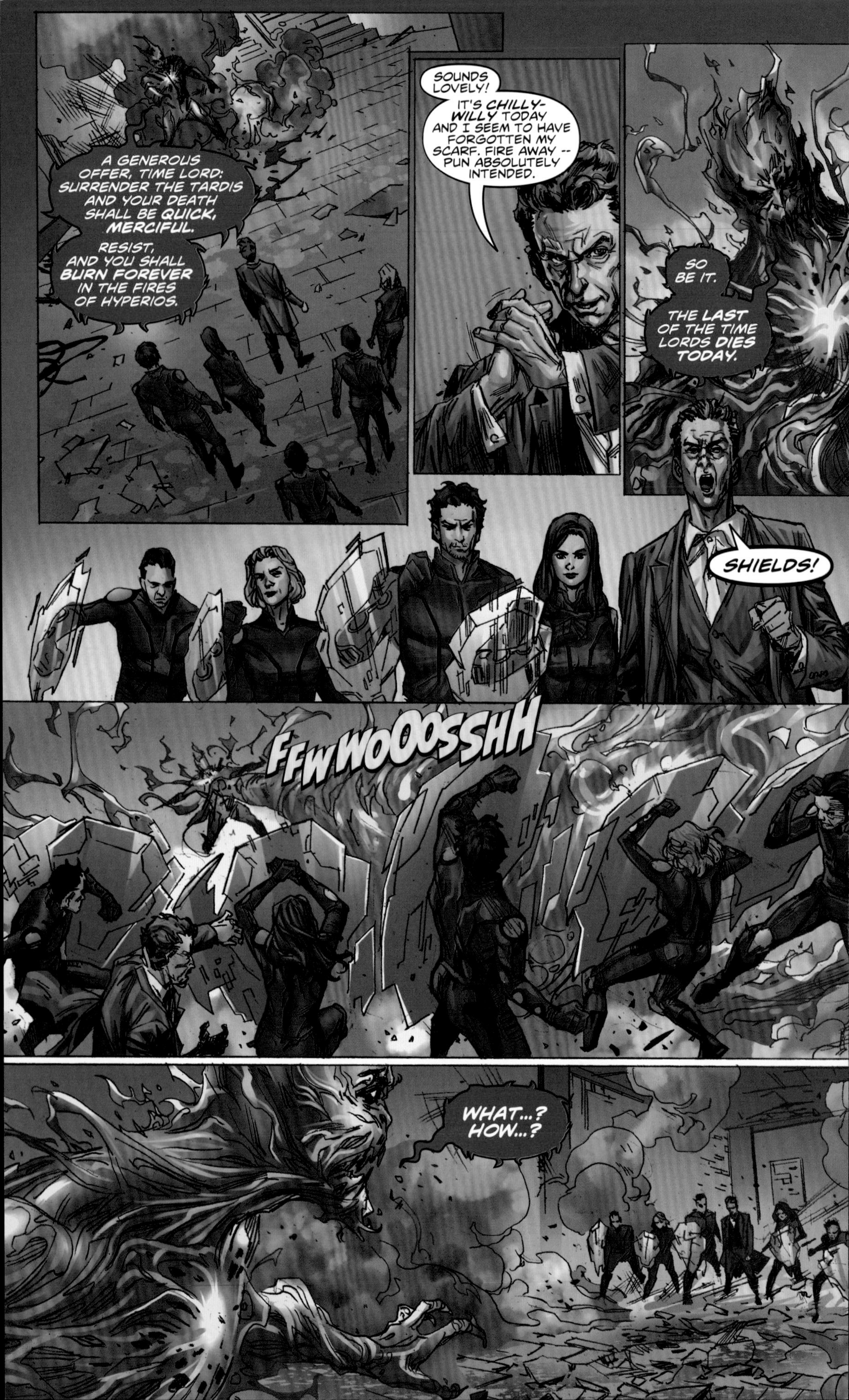
A GENEROUS OFFER, TIME LORD: SURRENDER THE TARDIS AND YOUR DEATH SHALL BE QUICK, MERCIFUL.
RESIST, AND YOU SHALL BURN FOREVER IN THE FIRES OF HYPERIOS.
SOUNDS LOVELY!
IT'S CHILLY-WILLY TODAY AND I SEEM TO HAVE FORGOTTEN MY SCARF. FIRE AWAY -- PUN ABSOLUTELY INTENDED.
SO BE IT.
THE LAST OF THE TIME LORDS DIES TODAY.
SHIELDS!
FFWWOOOSSHH
WHAT...? HOW...?

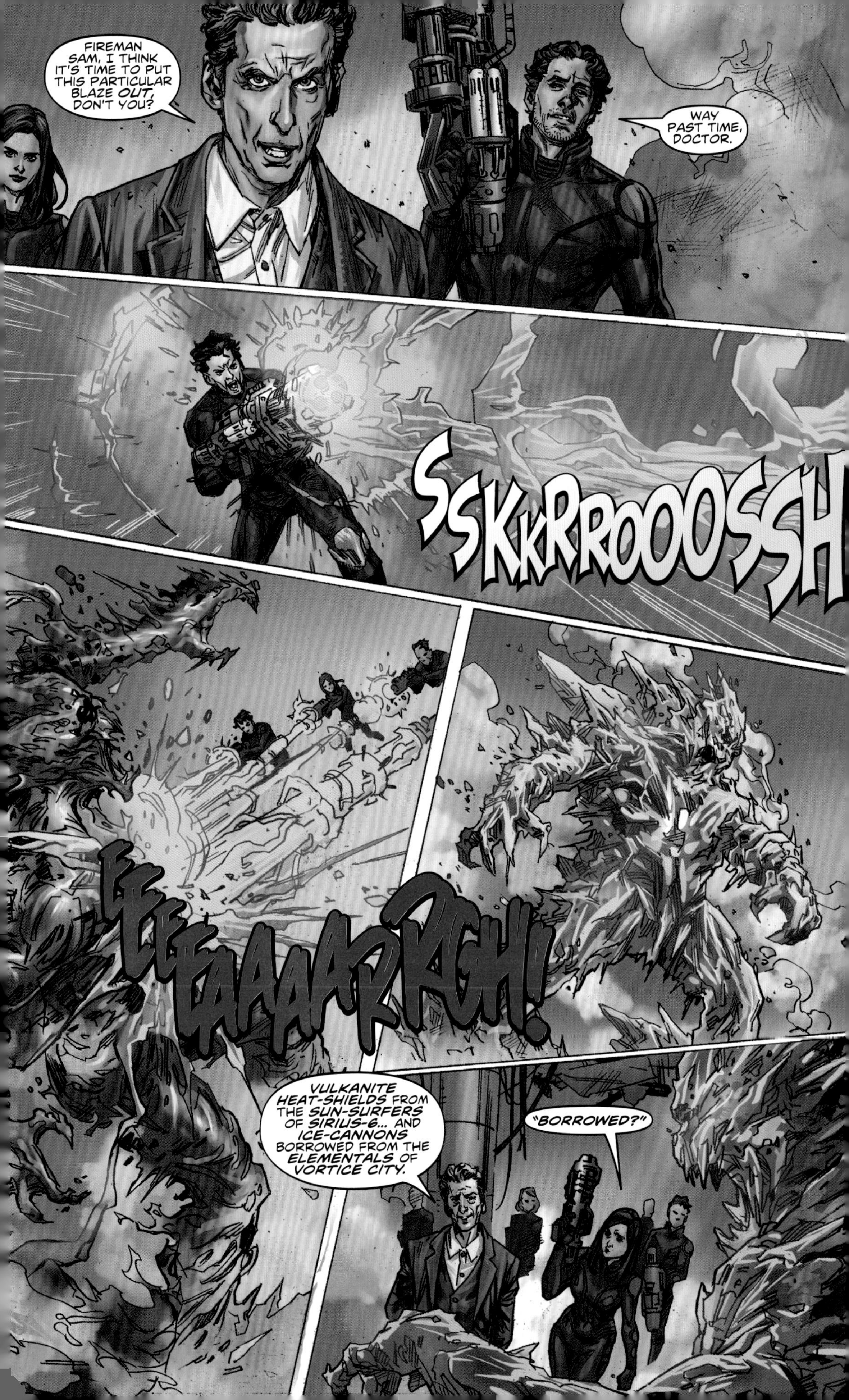
FIREMAN SAM, I THINK IT'S TIME TO PUT THIS PARTICULAR BLAZE OUT, DON'T YOU?
WAY PAST TIME, DOCTOR.
SSKKRROOOSSH
EEEEAAAARRGH!
VULKANITE HEAT-SHIELDS FROM THE SUN-SURFERS OF SIRIUS-6... AND ICE-CANNONS BORROWED FROM THE ELEMENTALS OF VORTICE CITY.
"BORROWED?"

HMM, YES. REMIND ME TO RETURN THEM BEFORE ANYONE REALIZES THEY'VE GONE *MISSING*.

THEY DON'T PLAY WELL, THE ELEMENTALS. NEVER QUITE GRASPED THE CONCEPT OF *SHARING*.

THEY'RE NOT THE ONLY ONES, MR. PRESIDENT. THAT'S WHY WE LOCKED YOU UP LAST TIME.

I TAKE IT YOU *DO* INTEND TO EXPLAIN THE PURPOSE OF THAT ALIEN SHOPPING SPREE?

OF COURSE, COMMANDER, HOW CAN I HIDE ANYTHING FROM YOU, ONE OF THE FINEST SCIENTIFIC MINDS IN THE GALAXY?

ONCE WE'V SECURED TH SAFE EVACUAT OF CIVILIANS I'LL REVEAL EVERYTHING

CROSS M HEART.

CAPTAIN HARRIS!

GET THOSE PEOPLE MOVING OFF THE PLATFORMS AND INTO THE --

VWOORRR VWOORRR

VWOORRRP VWOORRRP

DOCTOR!

YOU *LIED* TO HER, DOCTOR. *AGAIN*.

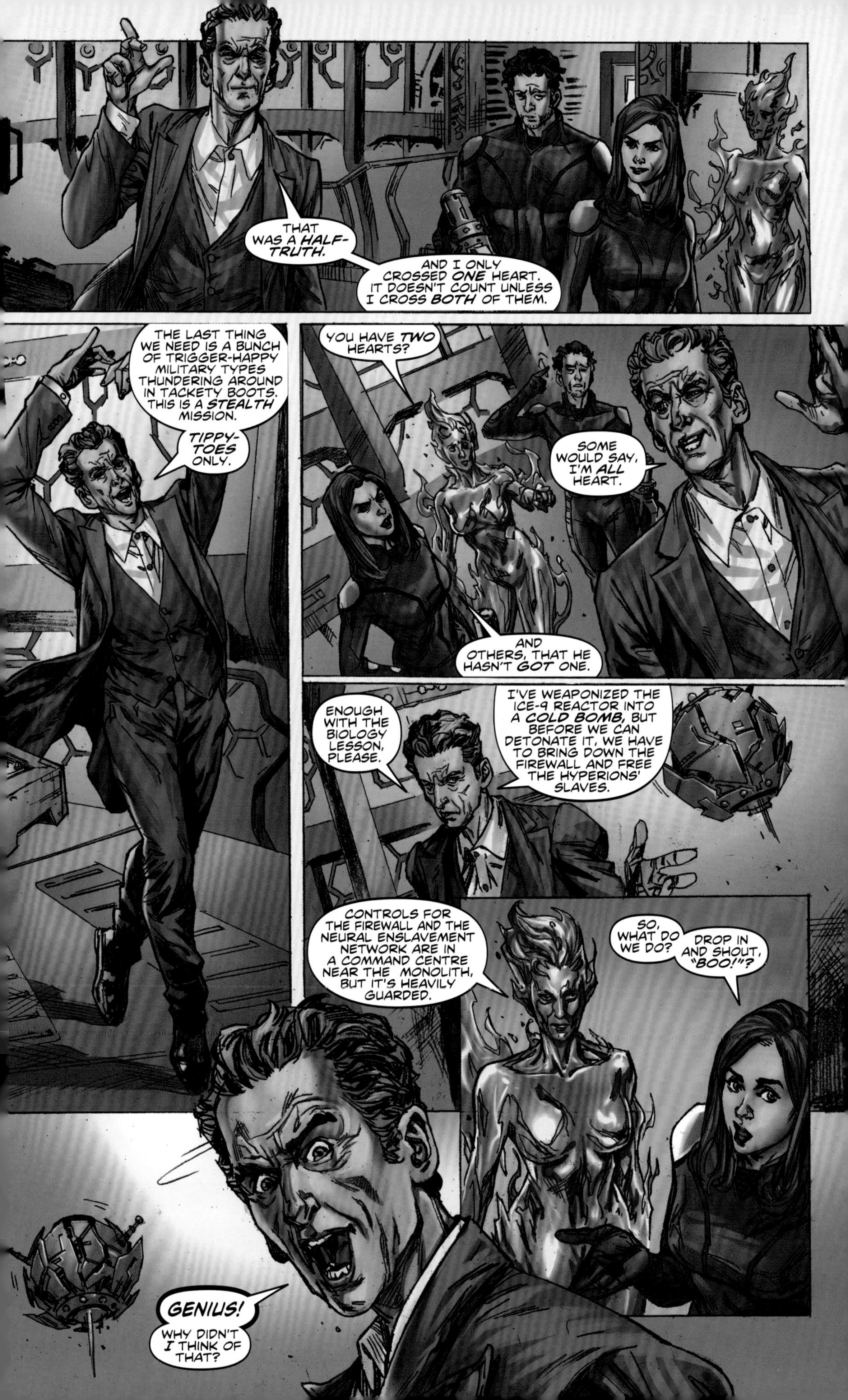
THAT WAS A HALF-TRUTH.
AND I ONLY CROSSED ONE HEART. IT DOESN'T COUNT UNLESS I CROSS BOTH OF THEM.
THE LAST THING WE NEED IS A BUNCH OF TRIGGER-HAPPY MILITARY TYPES THUNDERING AROUND IN TACKETY BOOTS. THIS IS A STEALTH MISSION.
TIPPY-TOES ONLY.
YOU HAVE TWO HEARTS?
SOME WOULD SAY, I'M ALL HEART.
AND OTHERS, THAT HE HASN'T GOT ONE.
ENOUGH WITH THE BIOLOGY LESSON, PLEASE.
I'VE WEAPONIZED THE ICE-9 REACTOR INTO A COLD BOMB, BUT BEFORE WE CAN DETONATE IT, WE HAVE TO BRING DOWN THE FIREWALL AND FREE THE HYPERIONS' SLAVES.
CONTROLS FOR THE FIREWALL AND THE NEURAL ENSLAVEMENT NETWORK ARE IN A COMMAND CENTRE NEAR THE MONOLITH, BUT IT'S HEAVILY GUARDED.
SO, WHAT DO WE DO?
DROP IN AND SHOUT, "BOO!"?
GENIUS!
WHY DIDN'T I THINK OF THAT?

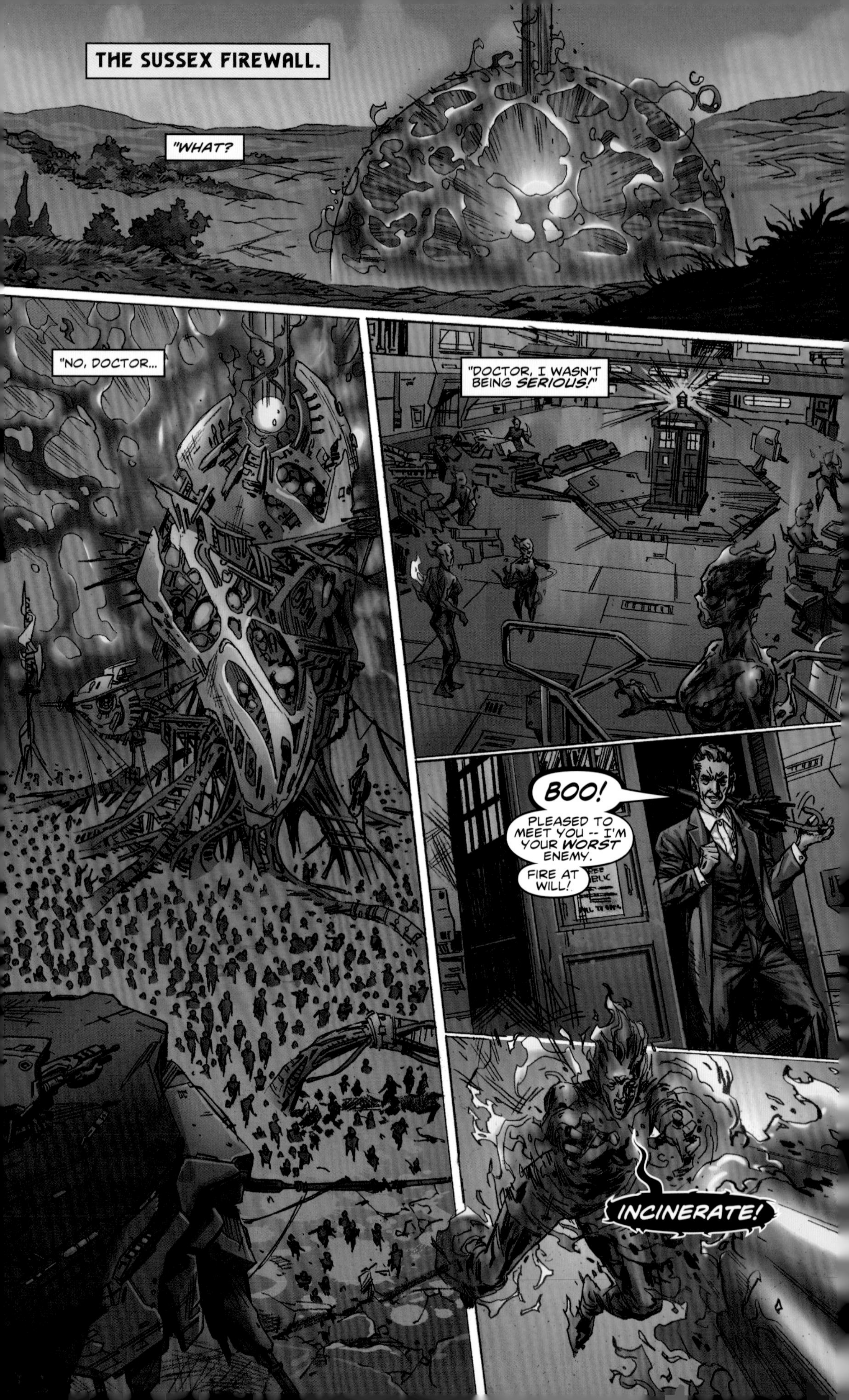
THE SUSSEX FIREWALL.
"WHAT?
"NO, DOCTOR...
"DOCTOR, I WASN'T BEING SERIOUS!"
BOO!
PLEASED TO MEET YOU -- I'M YOUR WORST ENEMY.
FIRE AT WILL!
INCINERATE!

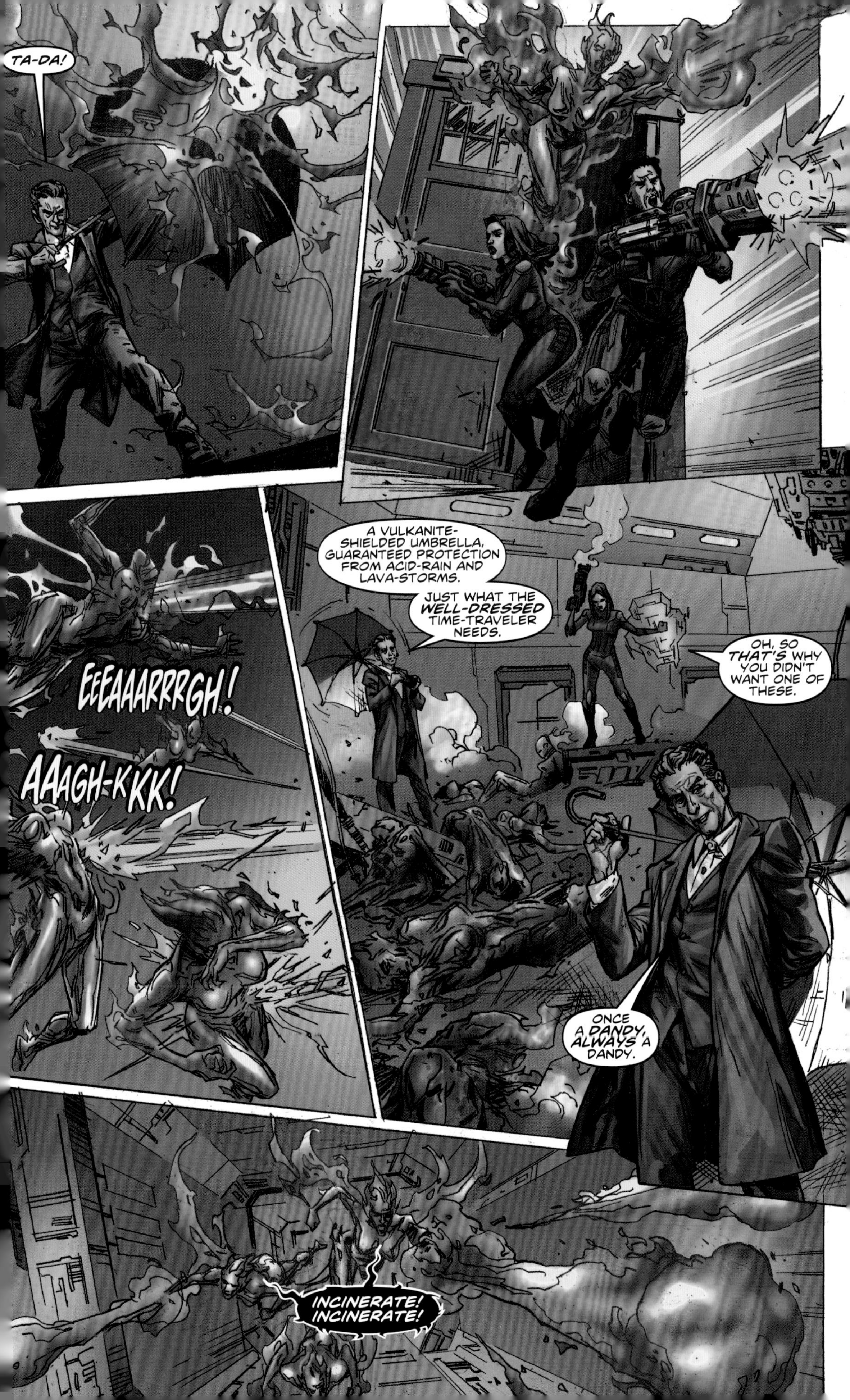
TA-DA!
EEEAAARRRGH!
AAAGH-KKK!
A VULKANITE-SHIELDED UMBRELLA, GUARANTEED PROTECTION FROM ACID-RAIN AND LAVA-STORMS.
JUST WHAT THE WELL-DRESSED TIME-TRAVELER NEEDS.
OH, SO THAT'S WHY YOU DIDN'T WANT ONE OF THESE.
ONCE A DANDY, ALWAYS A DANDY.
INCINERATE! INCINERATE!

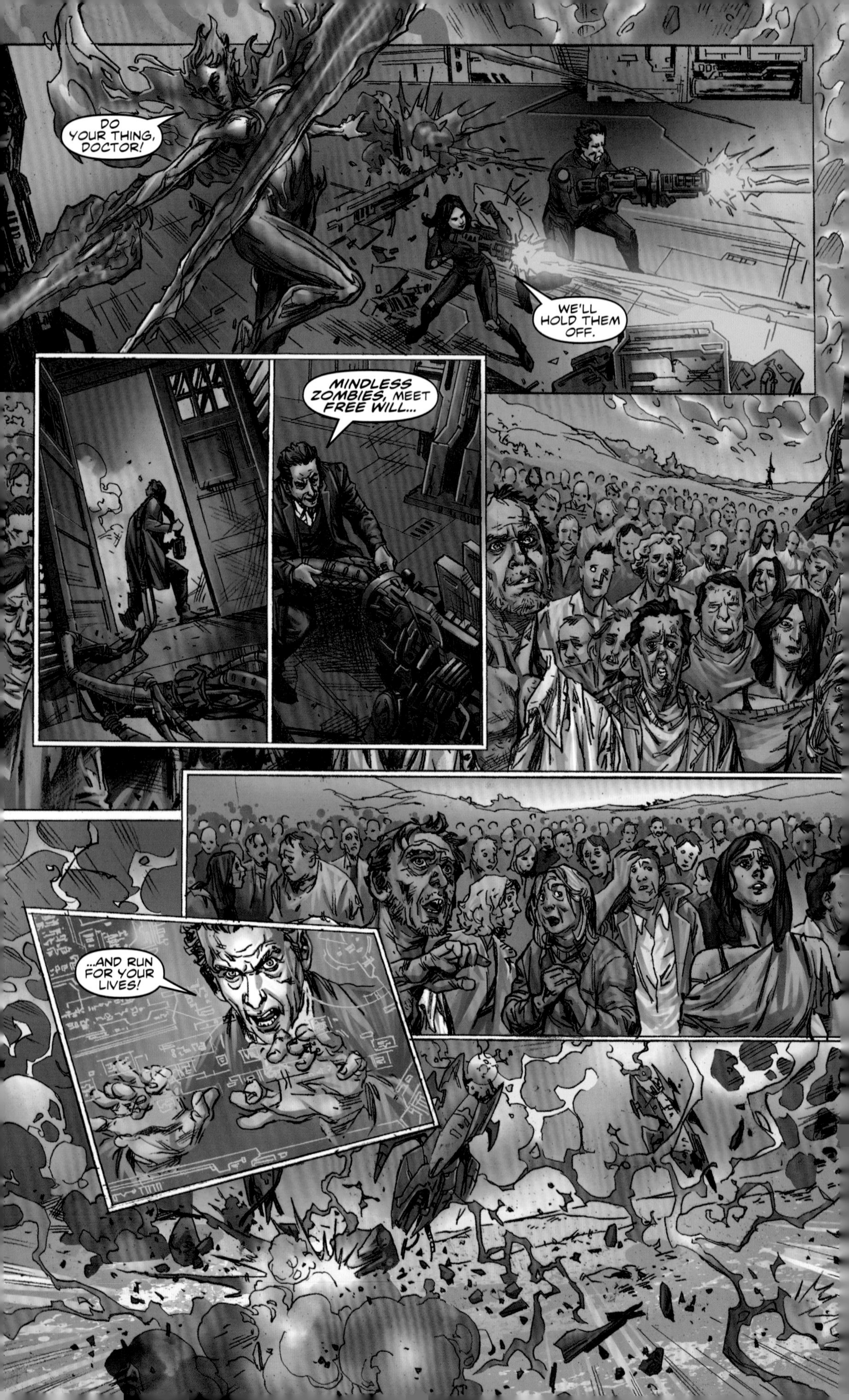
DO YOUR THING, DOCTOR!
WE'LL HOLD THEM OFF.
MINDLESS ZOMBIES, MEET FREE WILL...
...AND RUN FOR YOUR LIVES!

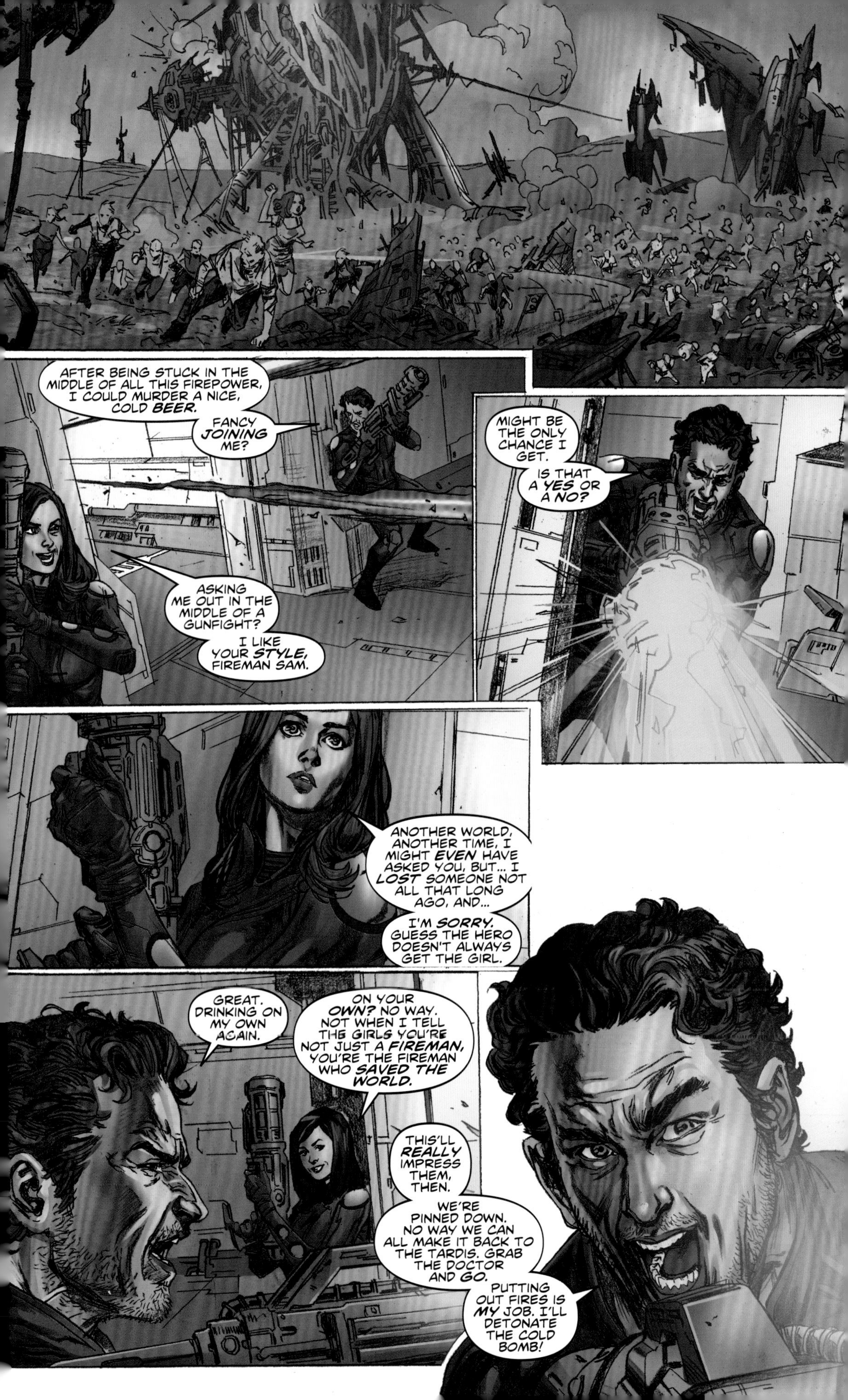
AFTER BEING STUCK IN THE MIDDLE OF ALL THIS FIREPOWER, I COULD MURDER A NICE, COLD BEER.
FANCY JOINING ME?
MIGHT BE THE ONLY CHANCE I GET.
IS THAT A YES OR A NO?
ASKING ME OUT IN THE MIDDLE OF A GUNFIGHT?
I LIKE YOUR STYLE, FIREMAN SAM.
ANOTHER WORLD, ANOTHER TIME, I MIGHT EVEN HAVE ASKED YOU, BUT... I LOST SOMEONE NOT ALL THAT LONG AGO, AND...
I'M SORRY. GUESS THE HERO DOESN'T ALWAYS GET THE GIRL.
GREAT. DRINKING ON MY OWN AGAIN.
ON YOUR OWN? NO WAY. NOT WHEN I TELL THE GIRLS YOU'RE NOT JUST A FIREMAN, YOU'RE THE FIREMAN WHO SAVED THE WORLD.
THIS'LL REALLY IMPRESS THEM, THEN.
WE'RE PINNED DOWN. NO WAY WE CAN ALL MAKE IT BACK TO THE TARDIS. GRAB THE DOCTOR AND GO.
PUTTING OUT FIRES IS MY JOB. I'LL DETONATE THE COLD BOMB!

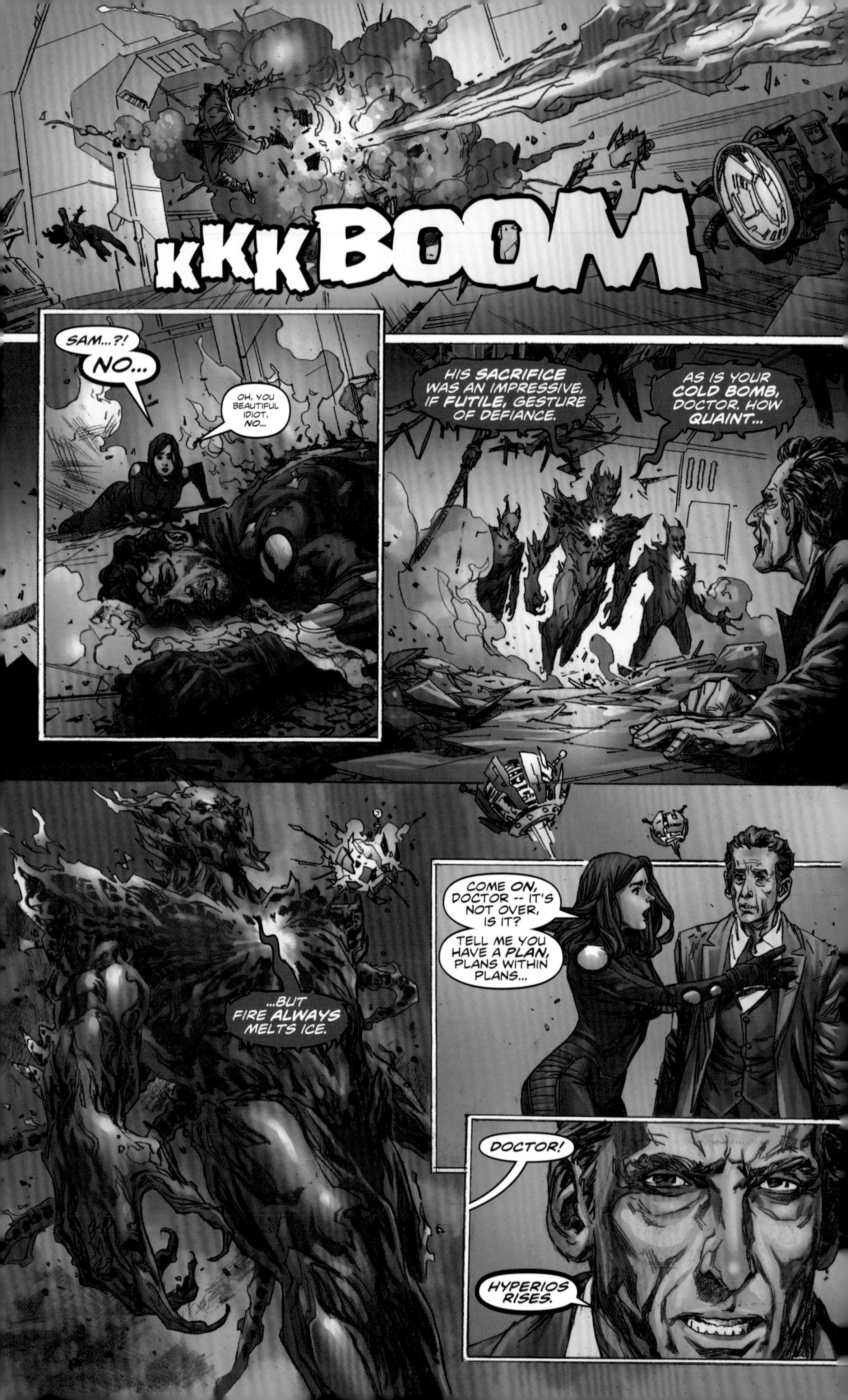
kKKBOOM
SAM...?! NO...
OH, YOU BEAUTIFUL IDIOT, NO...
HIS SACRIFICE WAS AN IMPRESSIVE, IF FUTILE, GESTURE OF DEFIANCE.
AS IS YOUR COLD BOMB, DOCTOR. HOW QUAINT...
...BUT FIRE ALWAYS MELTS ICE.
COME ON, DOCTOR -- IT'S NOT OVER, IS IT?
TELL ME YOU HAVE A PLAN, PLANS WITHIN PLANS...
DOCTOR!
HYPERIOS RISES.

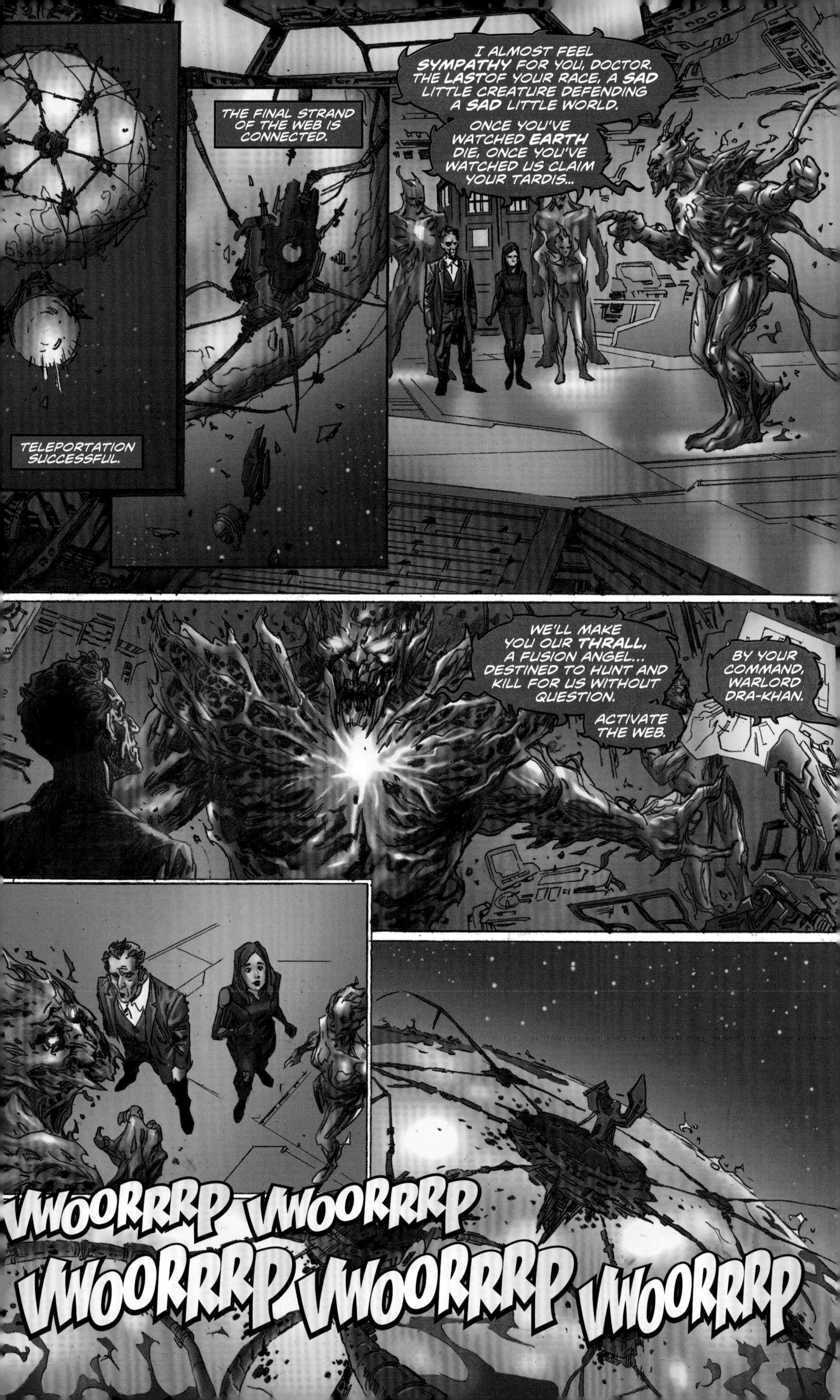

TELEPORTATION SUCCESSFUL.
THE FINAL STRAND OF THE WEB IS CONNECTED.
I ALMOST FEEL SYMPATHY FOR YOU, DOCTOR. THE LAST OF YOUR RACE, A SAD LITTLE CREATURE DEFENDING A SAD LITTLE WORLD.
ONCE YOU'VE WATCHED EARTH DIE, ONCE YOU'VE WATCHED US CLAIM YOUR TARDIS...
WE'LL MAKE YOU OUR THRALL, A FUSION ANGEL... DESTINED TO HUNT AND KILL FOR US WITHOUT QUESTION.
ACTIVATE THE WEB.
BY YOUR COMMAND, WARLORD DRA-KHAN.
VWOORRRP VWOORRRP
VWOORRRP VWOORRRP VWOORRRP

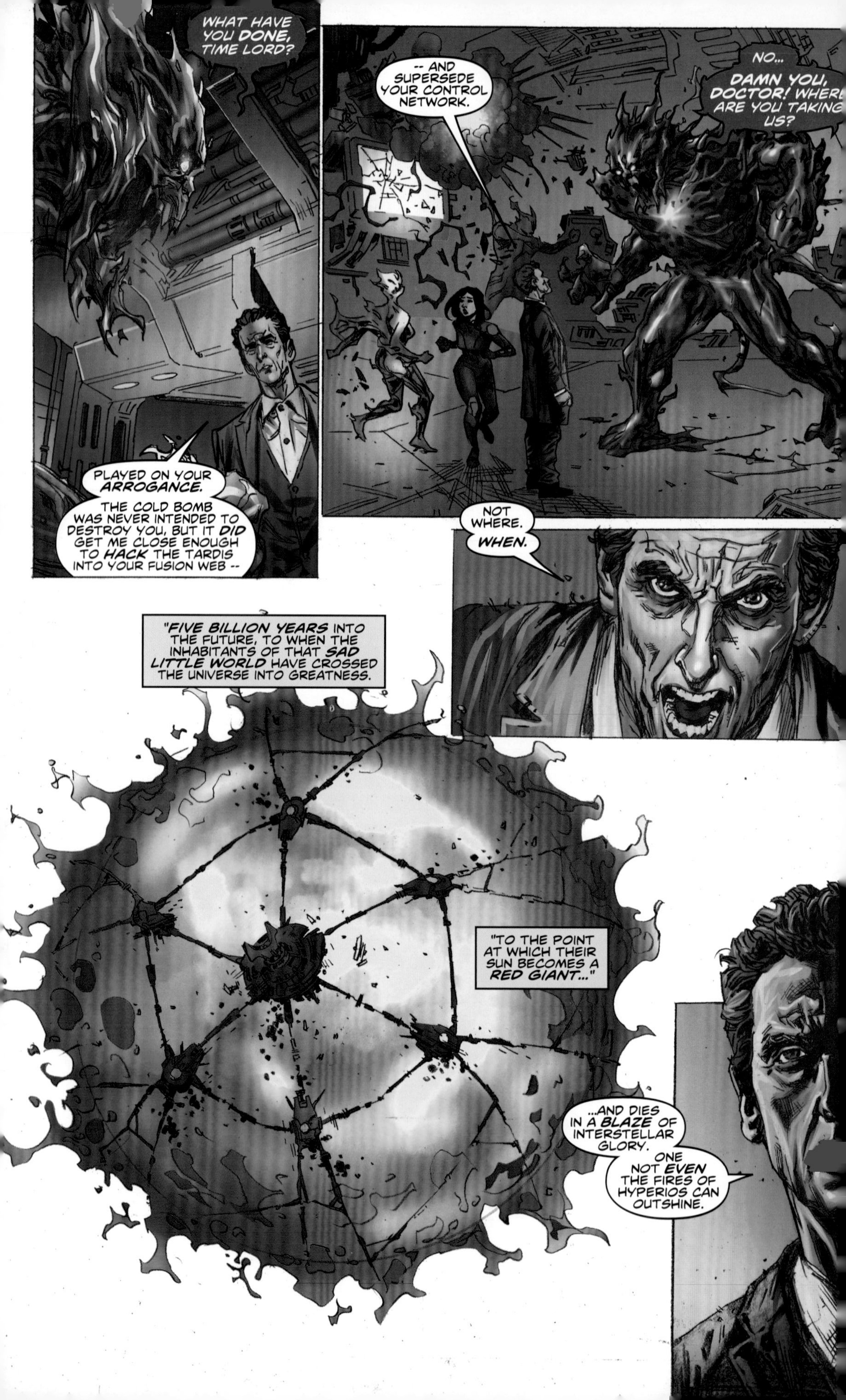
WHAT HAVE YOU DONE, TIME LORD?
PLAYED ON YOUR ARROGANCE.
THE COLD BOMB WAS NEVER INTENDED TO DESTROY YOU, BUT IT DID GET ME CLOSE ENOUGH TO HACK THE TARDIS INTO YOUR FUSION WEB --
-- AND SUPERSEDE YOUR CONTROL NETWORK.
NO...
DAMN YOU, DOCTOR! WHERE ARE YOU TAKING US?
NOT WHERE.
WHEN.
"FIVE BILLION YEARS INTO THE FUTURE, TO WHEN THE INHABITANTS OF THAT SAD LITTLE WORLD HAVE CROSSED THE UNIVERSE INTO GREATNESS.
"TO THE POINT AT WHICH THEIR SUN BECOMES A RED GIANT..."
...AND DIES IN A BLAZE OF INTERSTELLAR GLORY.
ONE NOT EVEN THE FIRES OF HYPERIOS CAN OUTSHINE.

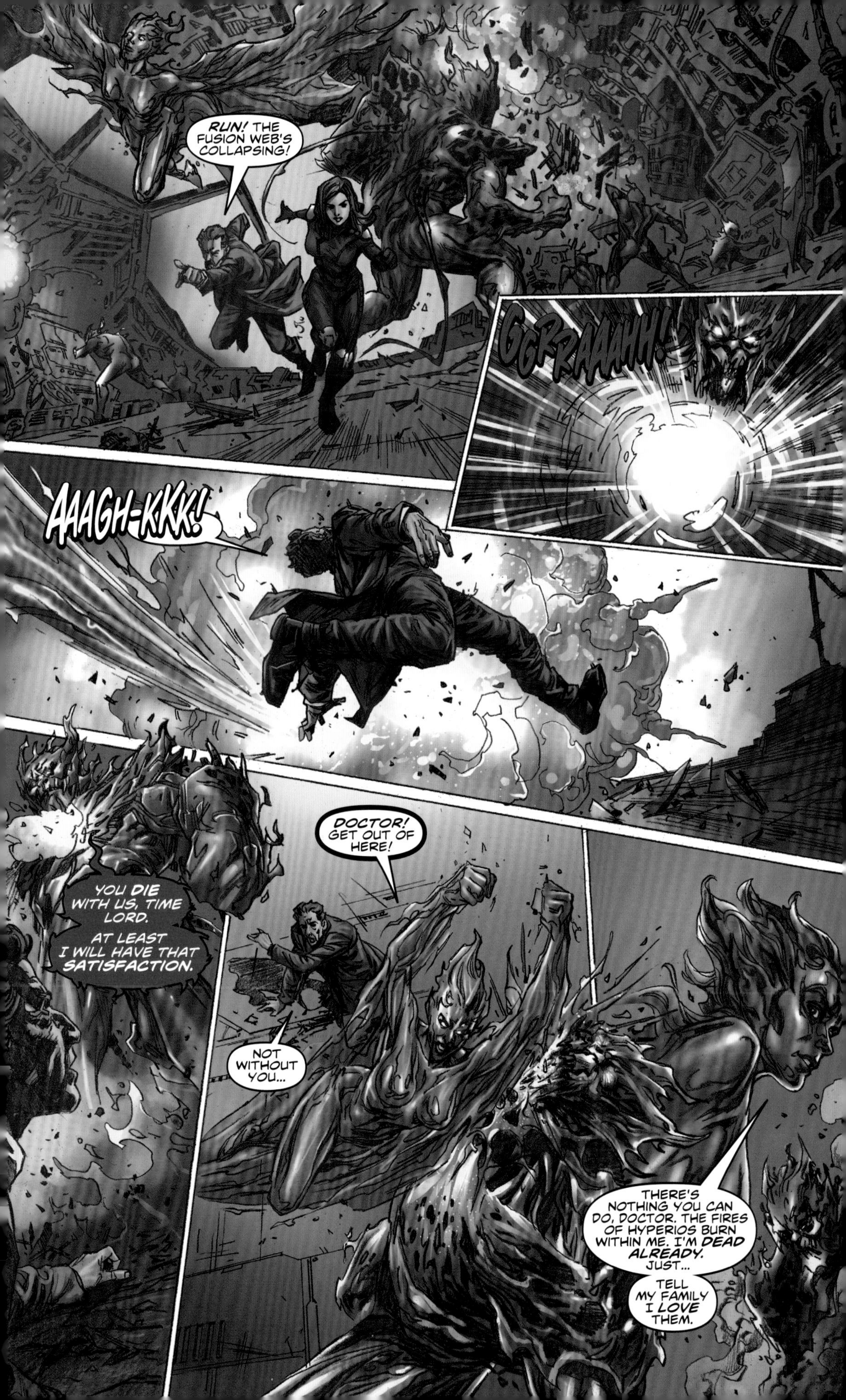
RUN! THE FUSION WEB'S COLLAPSING!
GGRRAAAHH!
AAAGH-KKK!
YOU DIE WITH US, TIME LORD.
AT LEAST I WILL HAVE THAT SATISFACTION.
DOCTOR! GET OUT OF HERE!
NOT WITHOUT YOU...
THERE'S NOTHING YOU CAN DO, DOCTOR. THE FIRES OF HYPERIOS BURN WITHIN ME. I'M DEAD ALREADY. JUST...
TELL MY FAMILY I LOVE THEM.

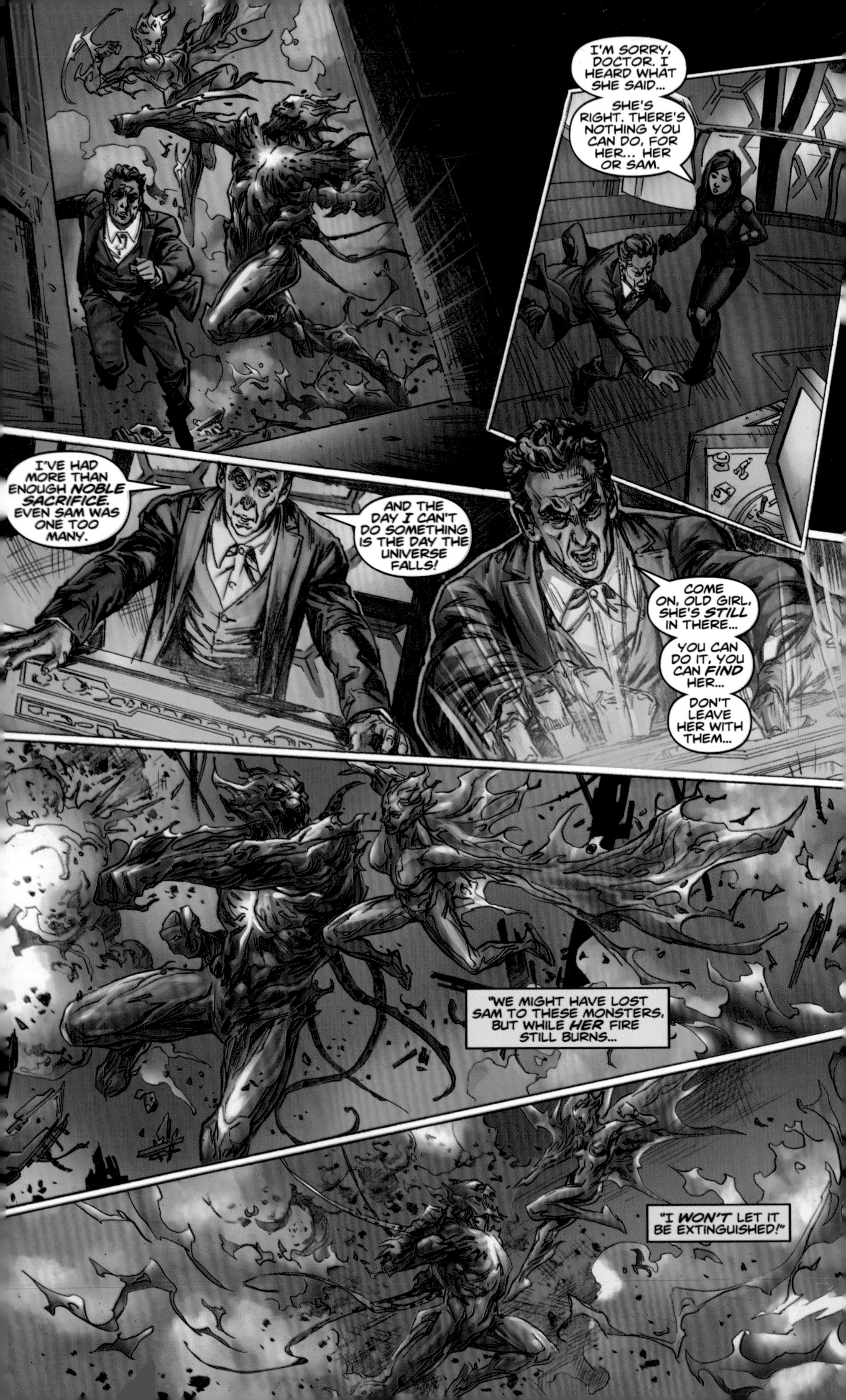
I'M SORRY, DOCTOR. I HEARD WHAT SHE SAID...
SHE'S RIGHT. THERE'S NOTHING YOU CAN DO, FOR HER... HER OR SAM.
I'VE HAD MORE THAN ENOUGH NOBLE SACRIFICE. EVEN SAM WAS ONE TOO MANY.
AND THE DAY I CAN'T DO SOMETHING IS THE DAY THE UNIVERSE FALLS!
COME ON, OLD GIRL, SHE'S STILL IN THERE...
YOU CAN DO IT, YOU CAN FIND HER...
DON'T LEAVE HER WITH THEM...
"WE MIGHT HAVE LOST SAM TO THESE MONSTERS, BUT WHILE HER FIRE STILL BURNS...
"I WON'T LET IT BE EXTINGUISHED!"

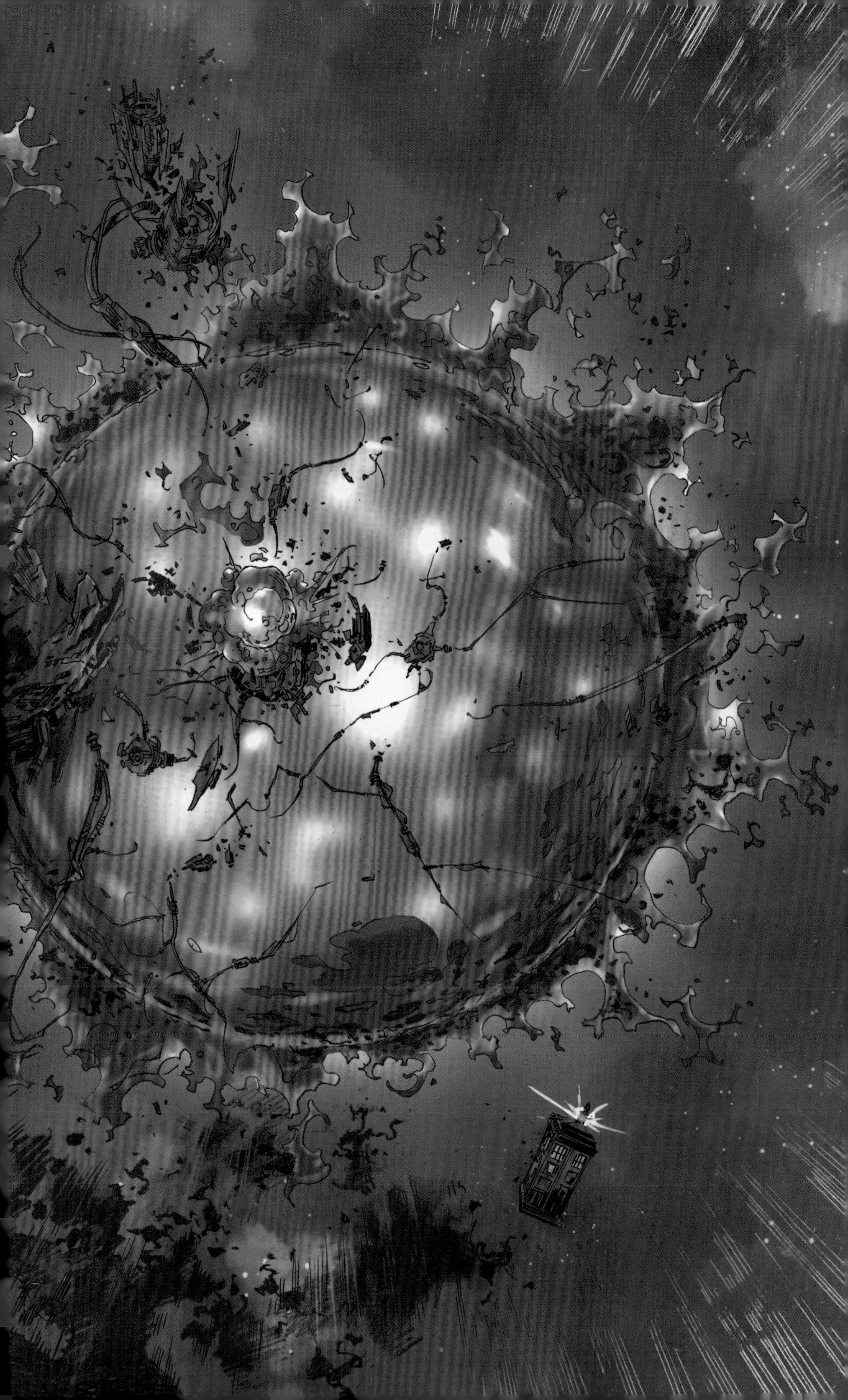

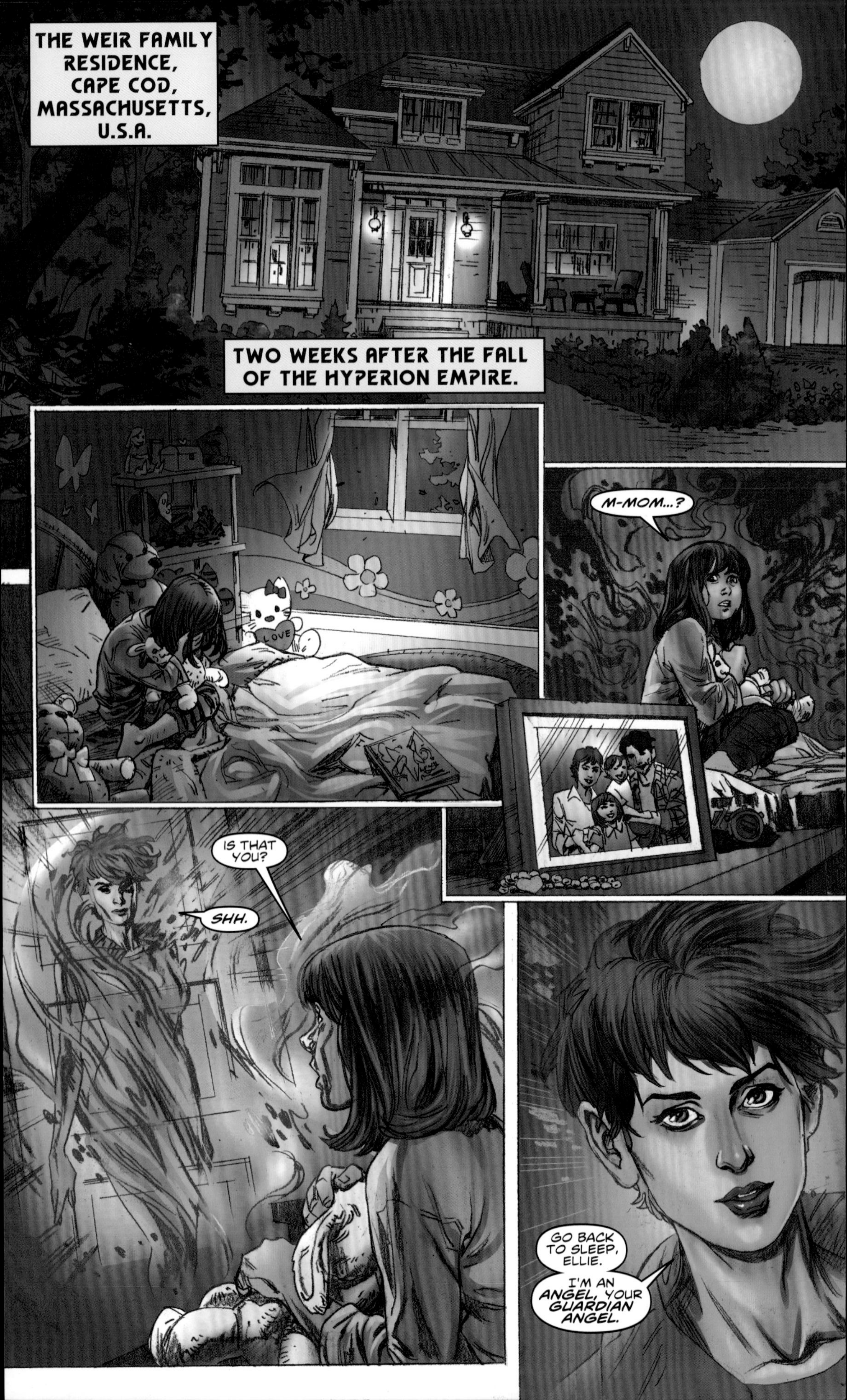
THE WEIR FAMILY RESIDENCE, CAPE COD, MASSACHUSETTS, U.S.A.
TWO WEEKS AFTER THE FALL OF THE HYPERION EMPIRE.
LOVE
M-MOM...?
IS THAT YOU?
SHH.
GO BACK TO SLEEP, ELLIE.
I'M AN ANGEL, YOUR GUARDIAN ANGEL.

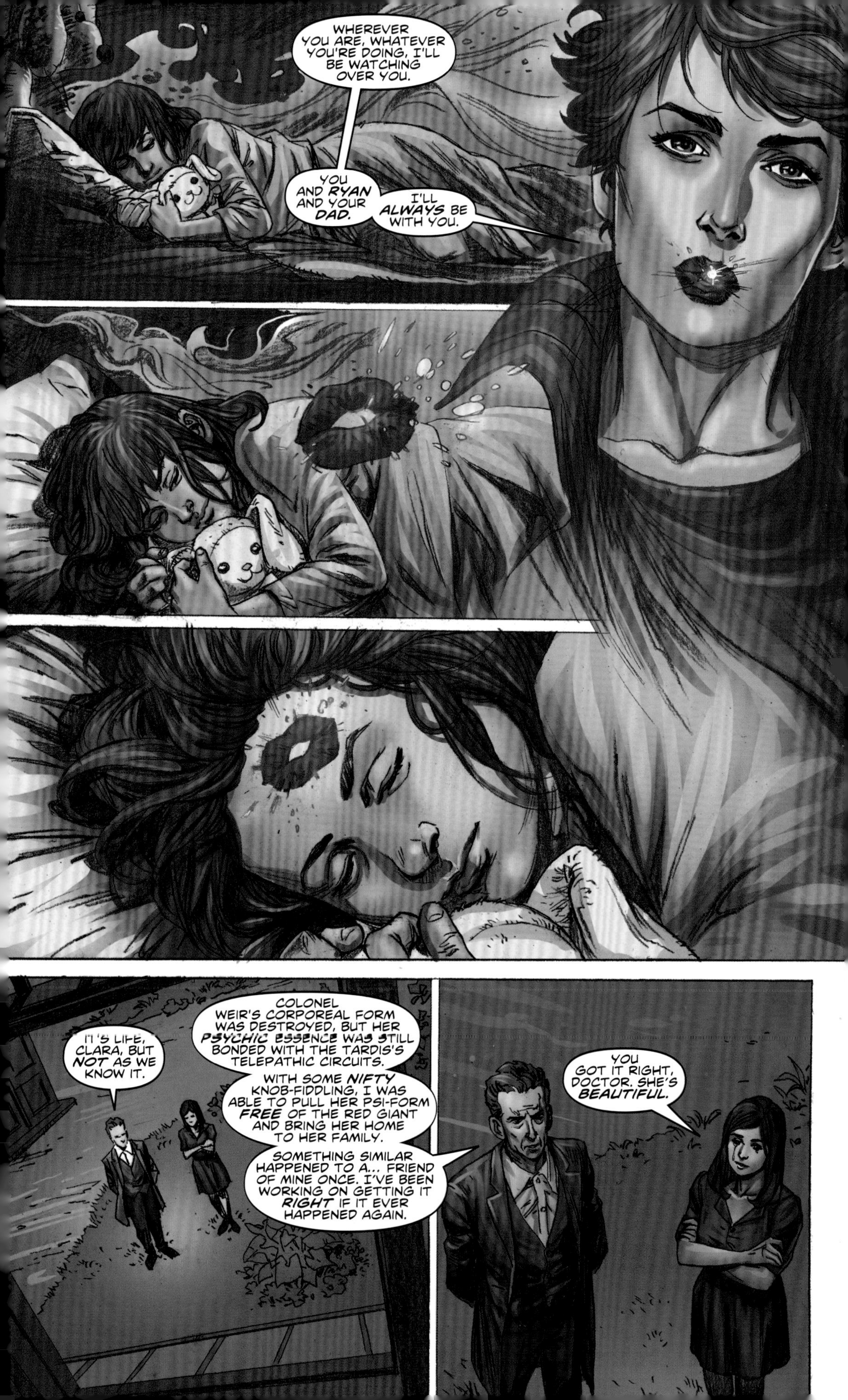
WHEREVER YOU ARE, WHATEVER YOU'RE DOING, I'LL BE WATCHING OVER YOU.
YOU AND RYAN AND YOUR DAD.
I'LL ALWAYS BE WITH YOU.
IT'S LIFE, CLARA, BUT NOT AS WE KNOW IT.
COLONEL WEIR'S CORPOREAL FORM WAS DESTROYED, BUT HER PSYCHIC ESSENCE WAS STILL BONDED WITH THE TARDIS'S TELEPATHIC CIRCUITS.
WITH SOME NIFTY KNOB-FIDDLING, I WAS ABLE TO PULL HER PSI-FORM FREE OF THE RED GIANT AND BRING HER HOME TO HER FAMILY.
SOMETHING SIMILAR HAPPENED TO A... FRIEND OF MINE ONCE. I'VE BEEN WORKING ON GETTING IT RIGHT IF IT EVER HAPPENED AGAIN.
YOU GOT IT RIGHT, DOCTOR. SHE'S BEAUTIFUL.

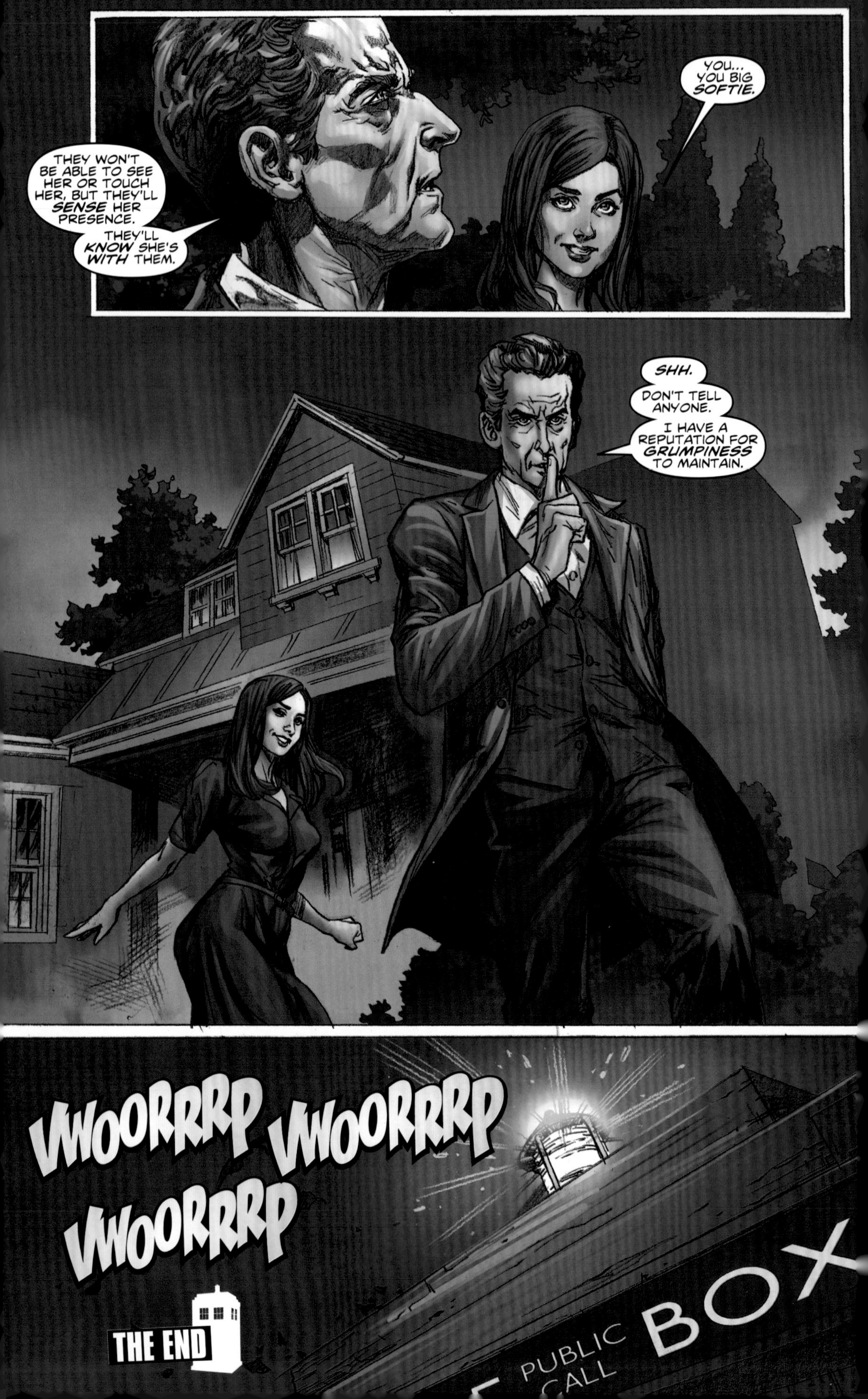
THEY WON'T BE ABLE TO SEE HER OR TOUCH HER, BUT THEY'LL SENSE HER PRESENCE.
THEY'LL KNOW SHE'S WITH THEM.
YOU... YOU BIG SOFTIE.
SHH.
DON'T TELL ANYONE.
I HAVE A REPUTATION FOR GRUMPINESS TO MAINTAIN.
VWOORRRP VWOORRRP VWOORRRP
PUBLIC CALL BOX
THE END

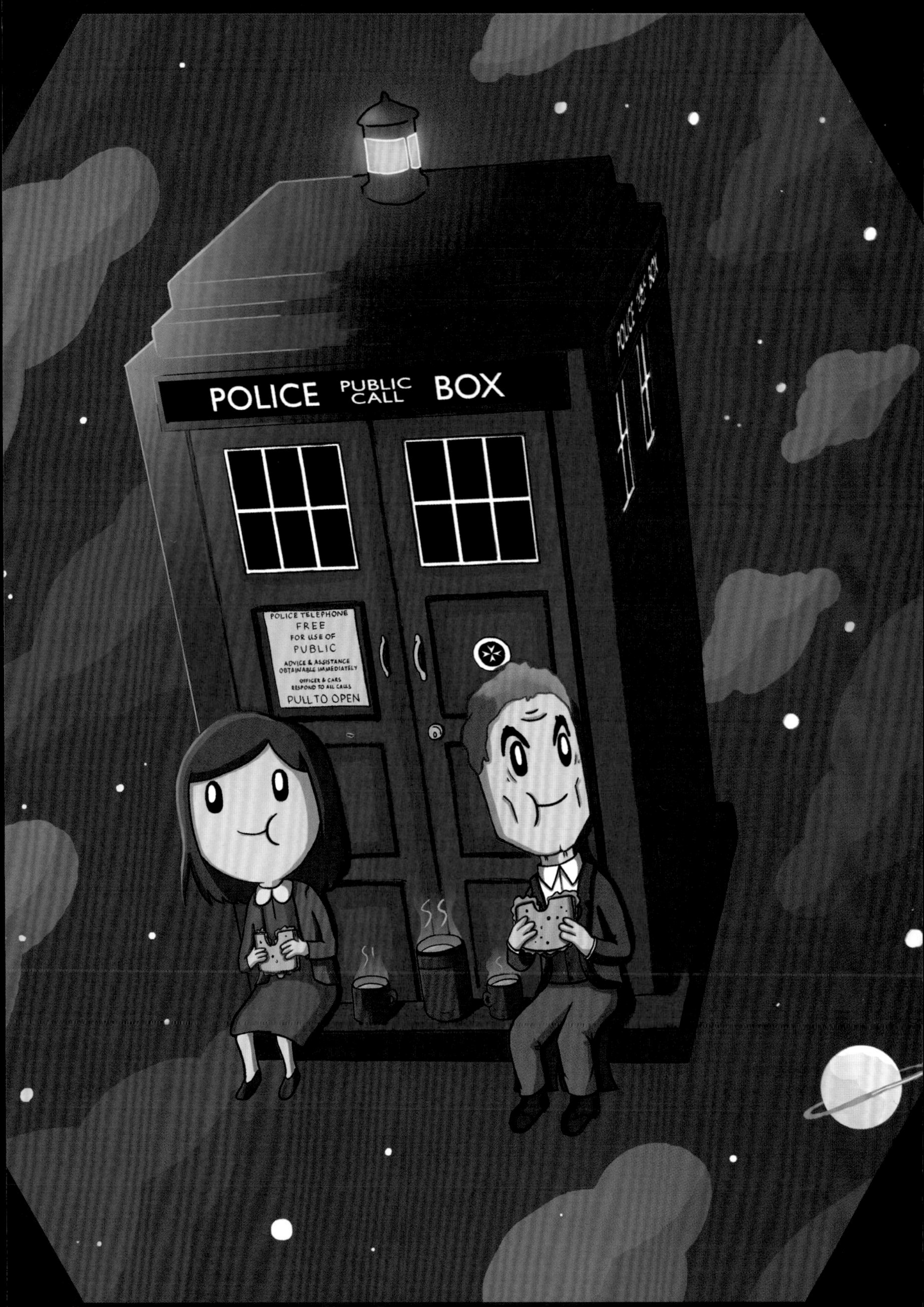
POLICE PUBLIC CALL BOX
POLICE TELEPHONE
FREE
FOR USE OF
PUBLIC
ADVICE & ASSISTANCE OBTAINABLE IMMEDIATELY
OFFICER & CARS RESPOND TO ALL CALLS
PULL TO OPEN

12D #15 Cover Art by NEIL SLORANCE

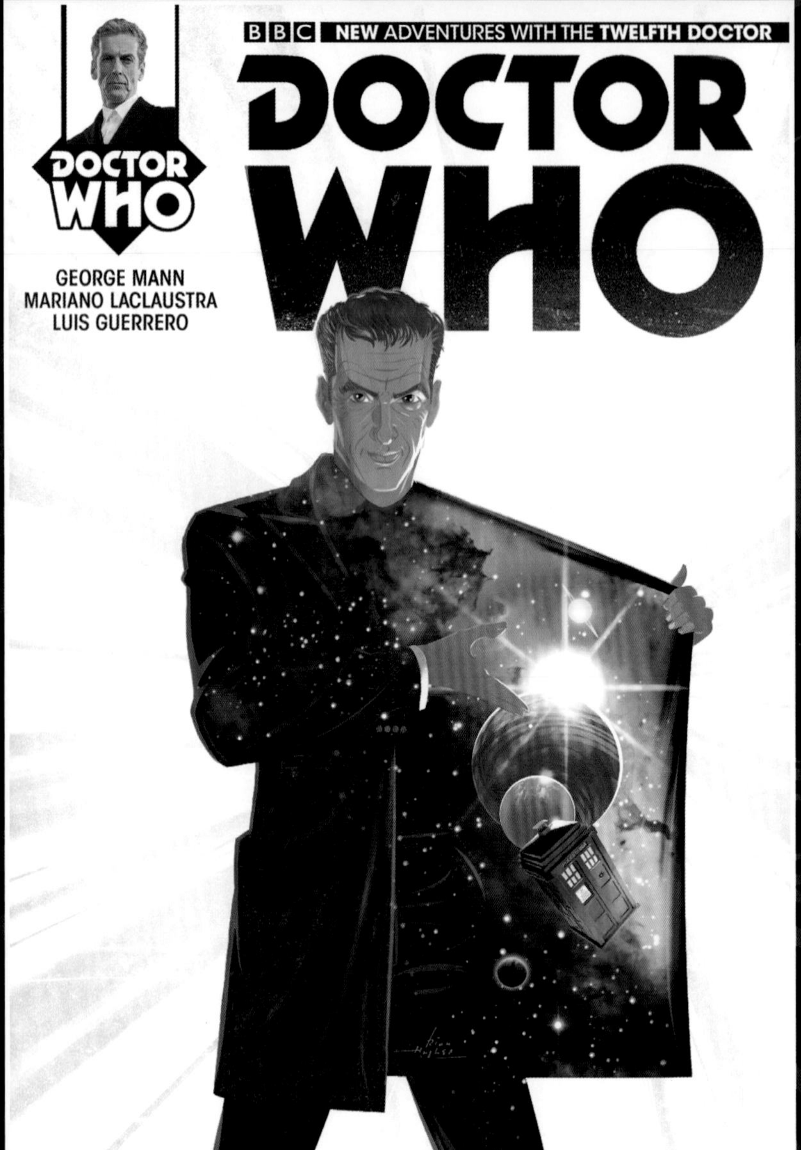
BBC
NEW ADVENTURES WITH THE TWELFTH DOCTOR
DOCTOR WHO
DOCTOR WHO
GEORGE MANN
MARIANO LACLAUSTRA
LUIS GUERRERO

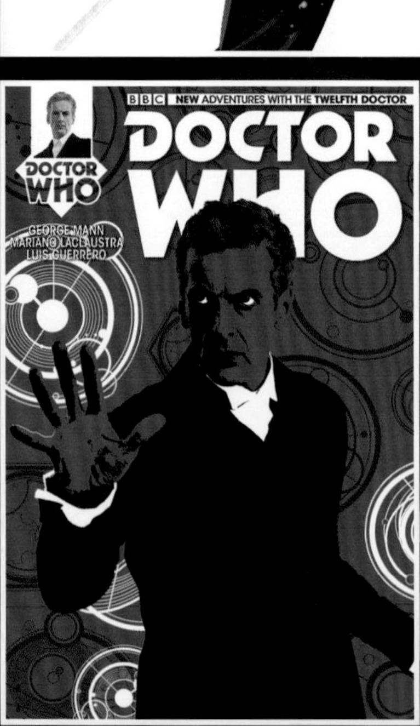
BBC
NEW ADVENTURES WITH THE TWELFTH DOCTOR
DOCTOR WHO
DOCTOR WHO
GEORGE MANN
MARIANO LACLAUSTRA
LUIS GUERRERO

11B

#11 A: RIAN HUGHES
#11 B: PHOTO AJ

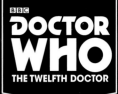

BBC DOCTOR WHO THE TWELFTH DOCTOR

COVER GALLERY

A

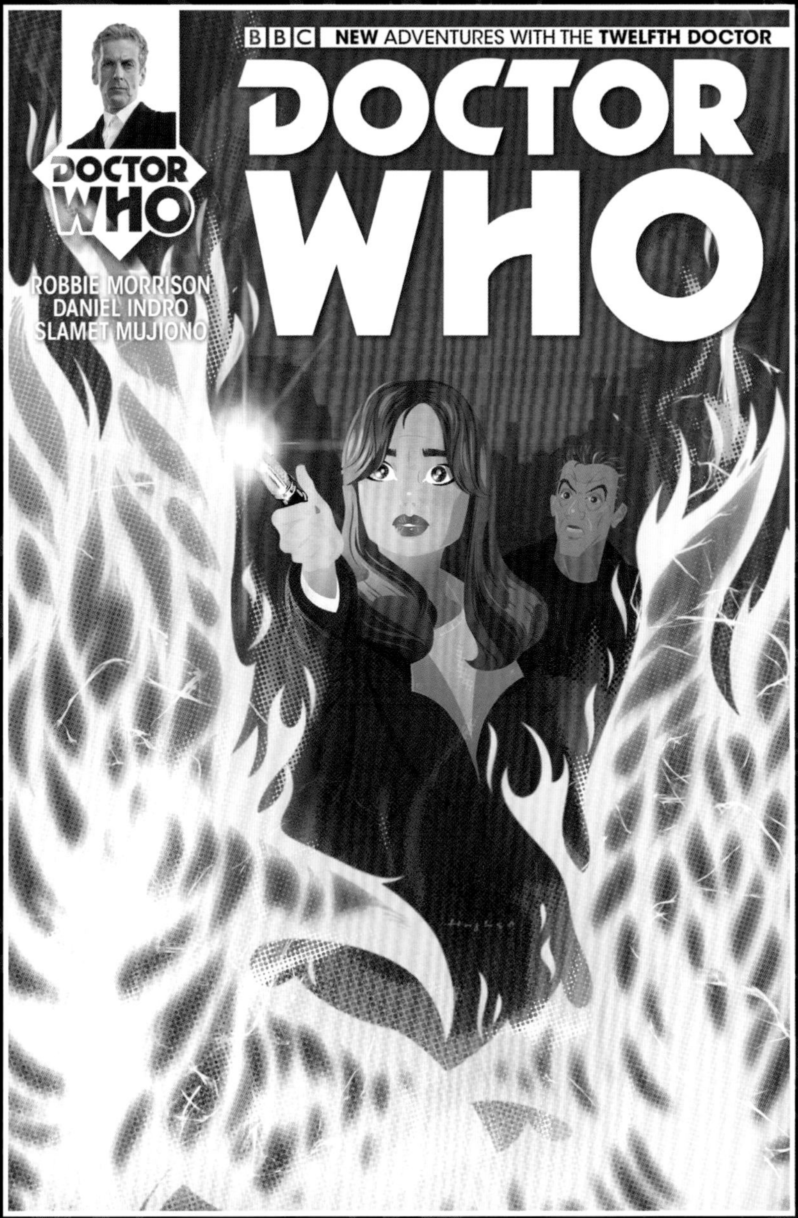
BBC NEW ADVENTURES WITH THE TWELFTH DOCTOR
DOCTOR WHO
DOCTOR WHO
ROBBIE MORRISON
DANIEL INDRO
SLAMET MUJIONO

12B

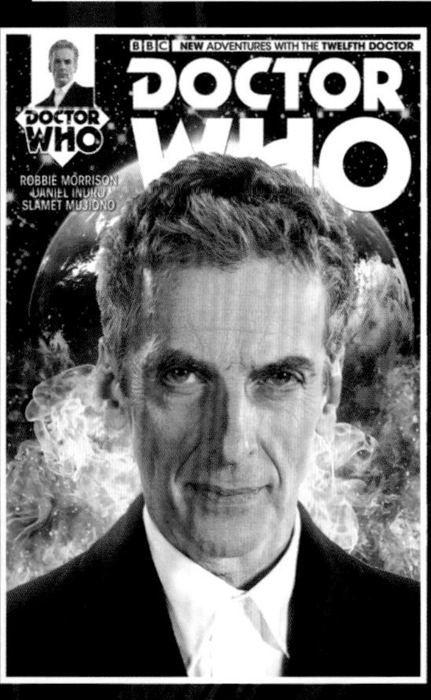
BBC NEW ADVENTURES WITH THE TWELFTH DOCTOR
DOCTOR WHO
DOCTOR WHO
ROBBIE MORRISON
DANIEL INDRO
SLAMET MUJIONO

12C

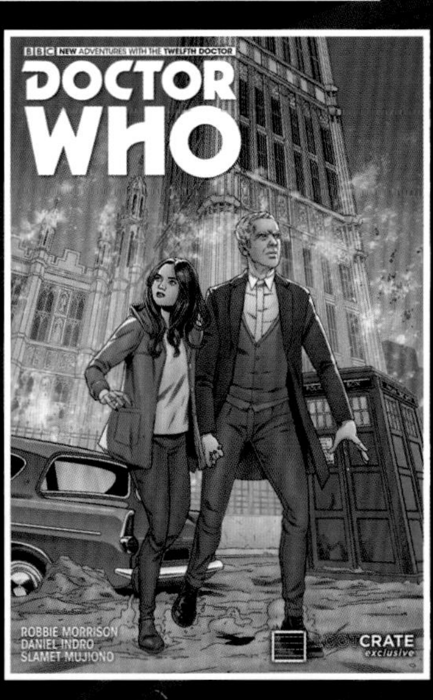
BBC NEW ADVENTURES WITH THE TWELFTH DOCTOR
DOCTOR WHO
ROBBIE MORRISON
DANIEL INDRO
SLAMET MUJIONO
CRATE exclusive

#12 A: RIAN HUGHES

#12 B: PHOTO A.J.

#12 C: RACHAEL STOTT/HI-FI

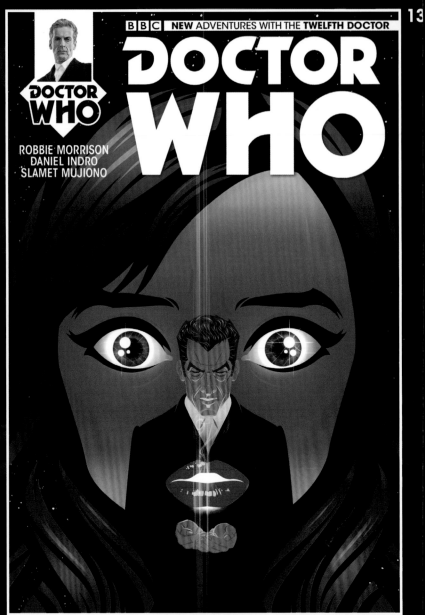

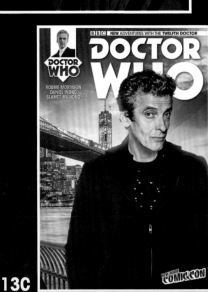

#13 A: RIAN HUGHES   #13 B: PHOTO AJ   #13 C: NYCC PHOTO AJ

BBC DOCTOR WHO THE TWELFTH DOCTOR

COVER GALLERY

4A

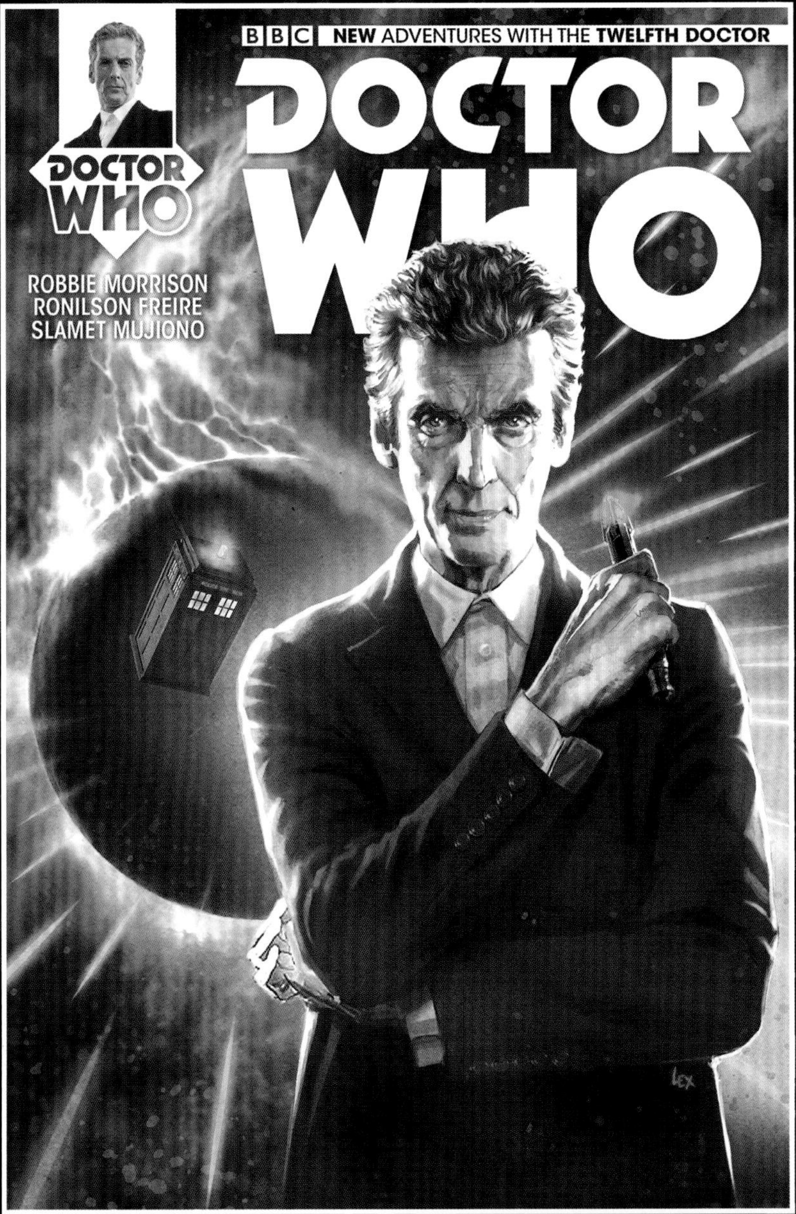
BBC NEW ADVENTURES WITH THE TWELFTH DOCTOR
DOCTOR WHO
DOCTOR WHO
ROBBIE MORRISON
RONILSON FREIRE
SLAMET MUJIONO
LEX

14B

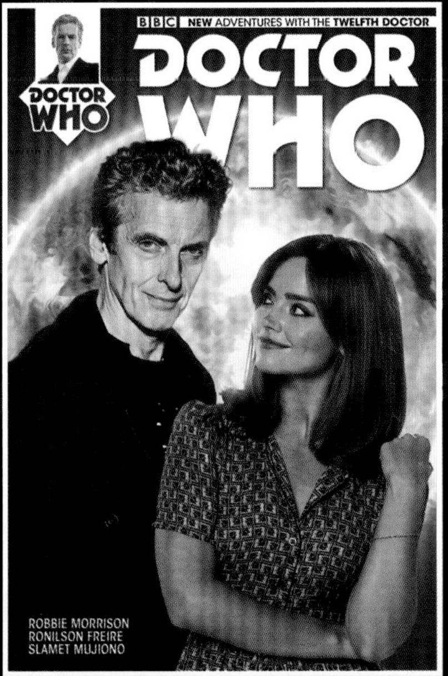
BBC NEW ADVENTURES WITH THE TWELFTH DOCTOR
DOCTOR WHO
DOCTOR WHO
ROBBIE MORRISON
RONILSON FREIRE
SLAMET MUJIONO

#14 A: ALEX RONALD
#14 B: PHOTO AJ

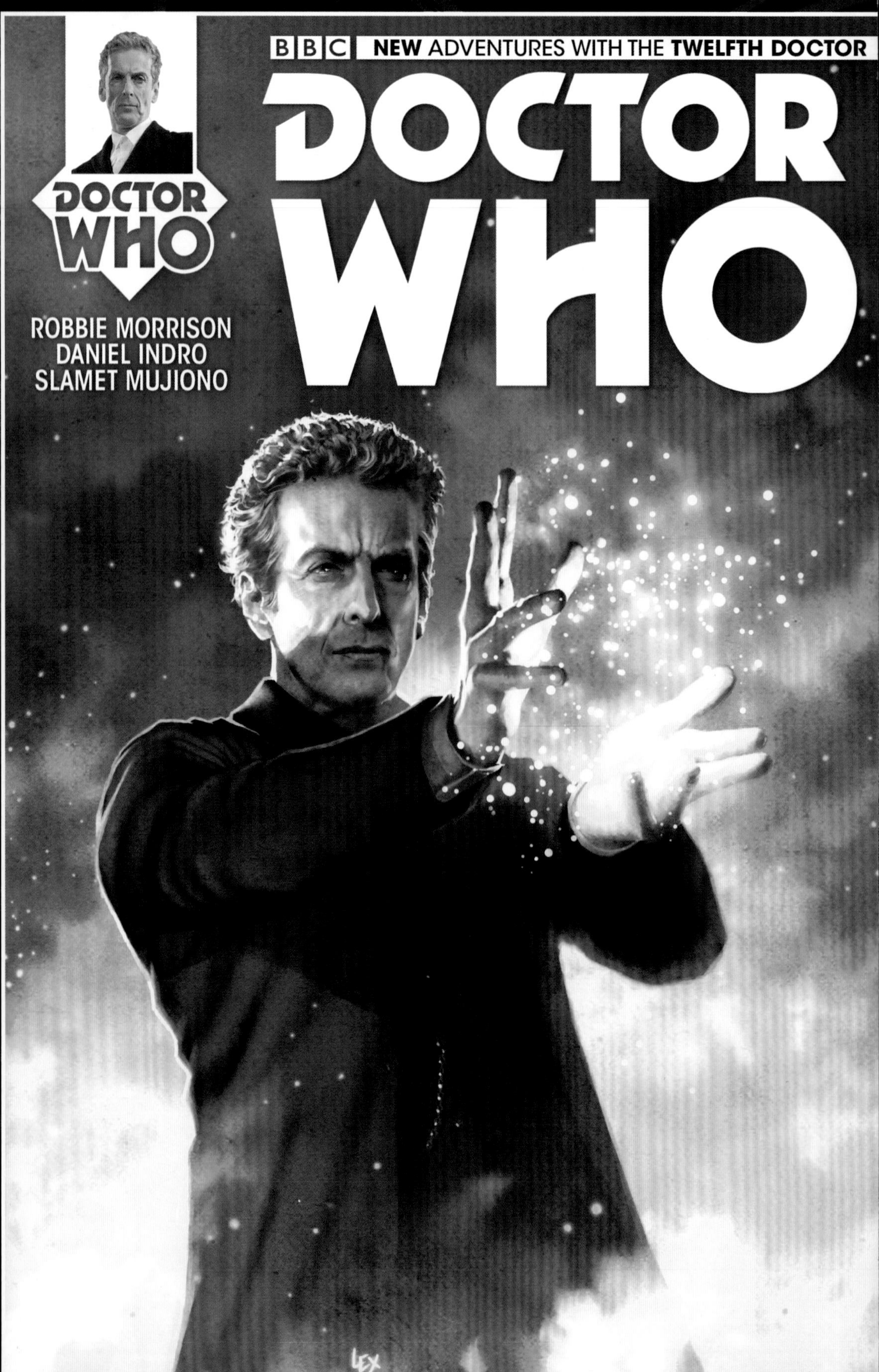
BBC
NEW ADVENTURES WITH THE TWELFTH DOCTOR
DOCTOR WHO
DOCTOR WHO
ROBBIE MORRISON
DANIEL INDRO
SLAMET MUJIONO
LEX

#15 A: ALEX RONALD

COVER GALLERY

5B

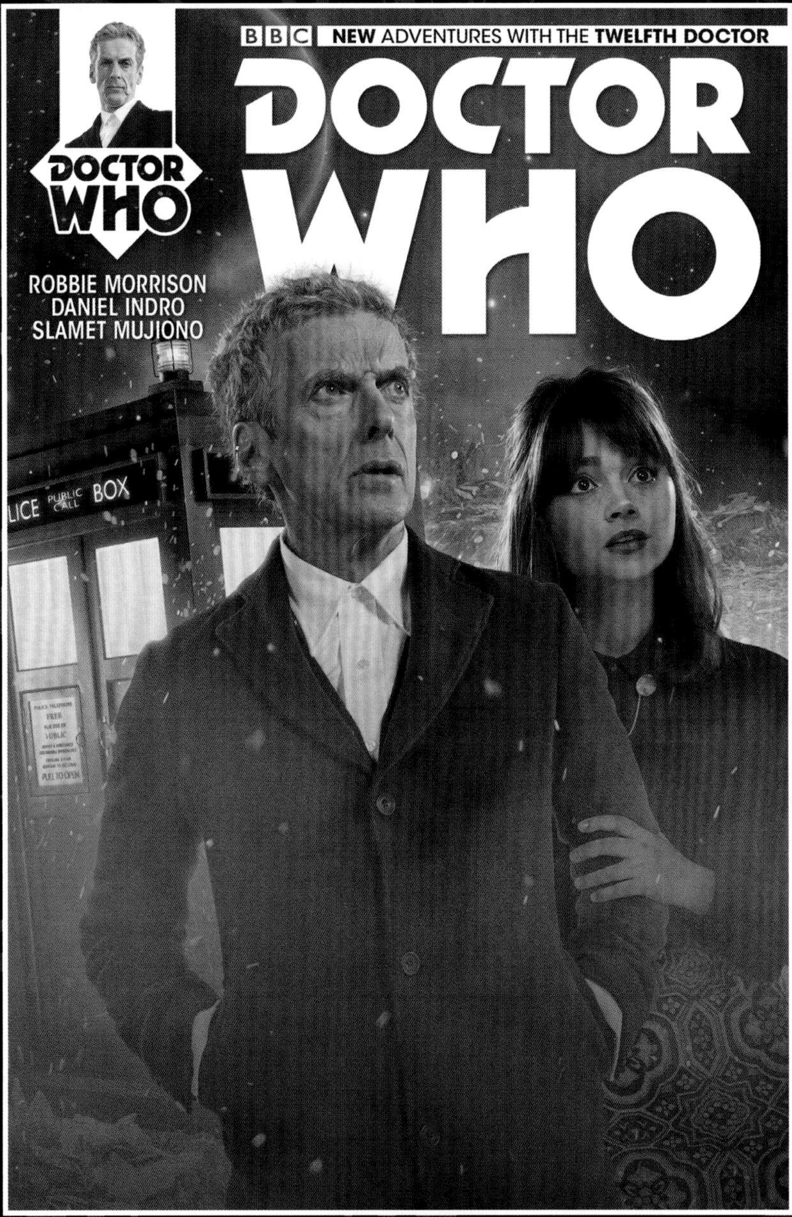
BBC
NEW ADVENTURES WITH THE TWELFTH DOCTOR
DOCTOR WHO
ROBBIE MORRISON
DANIEL INDRO
SLAMET MUJIONO
BOX

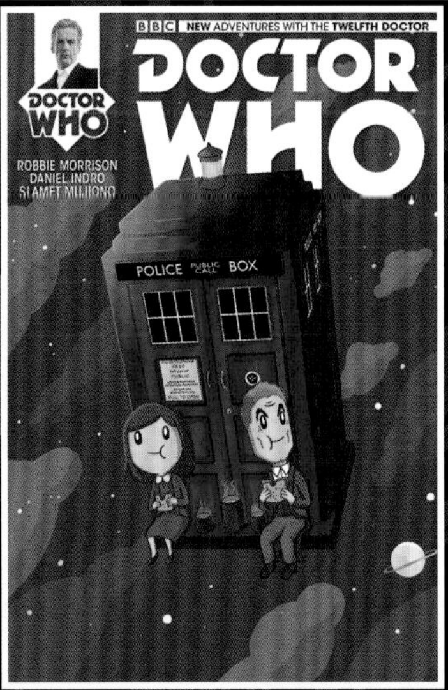
BBC
NEW ADVENTURES WITH THE TWELFTH DOCTOR
DOCTOR WHO
ROBBIE MORRISON
DANIEL INDRO
SLAMET MUJIONO
POLICE PUBLIC CALL BOX

15C

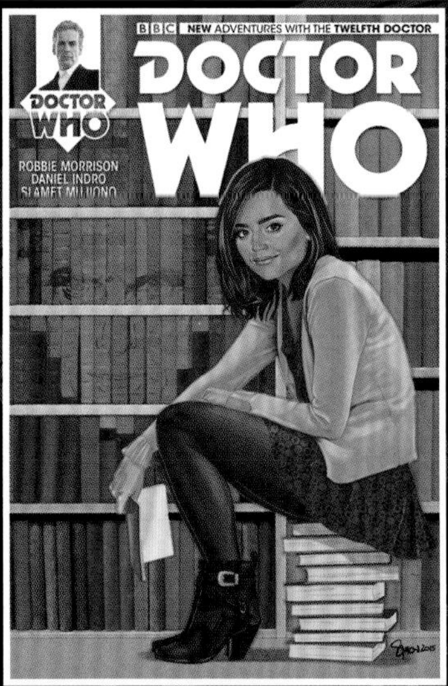
BBC
NEW ADVENTURES WITH THE TWELFTH DOCTOR
DOCTOR WHO
ROBBIE MORRISON
DANIEL INDRO
SLAMET MUJIONO

15D

#15 B: PHOTO WILL BROOKS

#15 C: NEIL SLORANCE

#15 D: SIMON MYERS

FOLLOW YOUR FAVORITE INCARNATIONS ACROSS THESE FANTASTIC COLLECTIONS!

**DOCTOR WHO: THE TENTH DOCTOR
VOL. 1: REVOLUTIONS OF TERROR**

BBC NEW ADVENTURES WITH THE TENTH DOCTOR
DOCTOR WHO
REVOLUTIONS OF TERROR
NICK ABADZIS • ELENA CASAGRANDE • ARIANNA FLOREAN

ISBN: 9781782761747
ON SALE NOW - $19.99 / $22.95 CAN / £10.99
(UK EDITION ISBN: 9781782763840)

**DOCTOR WHO: THE TENTH DOCTOR
VOL. 2: THE WEEPING ANGELS OF MONS**

BBC NEW ADVENTURES WITH THE TENTH DOCTOR
DOCTOR WHO
THE WEEPING ANGELS OF MONS
ROBBIE MORRISON • DANIEL INDRO • SLAMET MUJIONO

ISBN: 9781782761754
ON SALE NOW - $19.99 / $25.99 CAN / £10.99
(UK EDITION ISBN: 9781782766575)

**DOCTOR WHO: THE TENTH DOCTOR
VOL. 3: THE FOUNTAINS OF FOREVER**

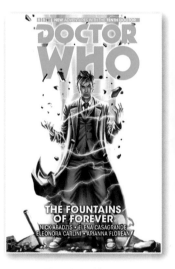

NEW ADVENTURES WITH THE TENTH DOCTOR
DOCTOR WHO
THE FOUNTAINS OF FOREVER
NICK ABADZIS • ELENA CASAGRANDE
ELEONORA CARLINI • ARIANNA FLOREAN

ISBN: 9781782763024
COMING SOON - $19.99 / $25.99 CAN / £10.9
(UK EDITION ISBN: 9781782767404)

**DOCTOR WHO: THE ELEVENTH DOCTOR
VOL. 1: AFTER LIFE**

BBC NEW ADVENTURES WITH THE ELEVENTH DOCTOR
DOCTOR WHO
AFTER LIFE
AL EWING • ROB WILLIAMS • SIMON FRASER • BOO COOK
GARY CALDWELL • HI-FI

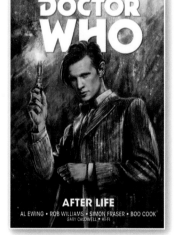

ISBN: 9781782761730
ON SALE NOW - $19.99 / $22.95 CAN / £10.99
(UK EDITION ISBN: 9781782763857)

**DOCTOR WHO: THE ELEVENTH DOCTOR
VOL. 2: SERVE YOU**

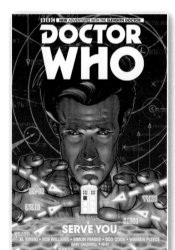

BBC NEW ADVENTURES WITH THE ELEVENTH DOCTOR
DOCTOR WHO
SERVE YOU
AL EWING • ROB WILLIAMS • SIMON FRASER • BOO COOK • WARREN PLEECE
GARY CALDWELL • HI-FI

ISBN: 9781782761754
ON SALE NOW - $19.99 / $22.95 CAN / £10.99
(UK EDITION ISBN: 9781782766582)

**DOCTOR WHO: THE ELEVENTH DOCTO
VOL. 3: CONVERSION**

BBC NEW ADVENTURES WITH THE ELEVENTH DOCTOR
DOCTOR WHO
CONVERSION
AL EWING • ROB WILLIAMS • SIMON FRASER • BOO COOK • WARREN PLEECE
GARY CALDWELL • HI-FI

ISBN: 9781782763024
COMING SOON - $19.99 / $25.99 CAN / £10.9
(UK EDITION ISBN: 9781782767435)

TITAN COMICS

For information on how to subscribe to our great Doctor Who titles, or to purchase them digitally, visit:

WWW.TITAN-COMICS.COM

COMPLETE YOUR COLLECTION!

DOCTOR WHO: THE TWELFTH DOCTOR
VOL. 1: TERRORFORMER

ISBN: 9781782761778
ON SALE NOW - $19.99 / $22.95 CAN / £10.99
(UK EDITION ISBN: 9781782763864)

DOCTOR WHO: THE TWELFTH DOCTOR
VOL. 2: FRACTURES

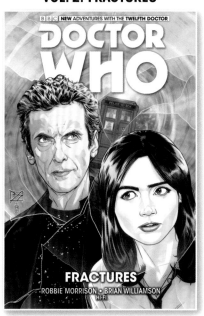

ISBN: 9781782763017
ON SALE NOW - $19.99 / $25.99 CAN / £10.99
(UK EDITION ISBN: 9781782766599)

DOCTOR WHO: THE NINTH DOCTOR
VOL. 1: WEAPONS OF PAST DESTRUCTION

ISBN: 9781782763369
COMING SOON - $19.99 / $25.99 CAN / £10.99
(UK EDITION ISBN: 9781782761056)

DOCTOR WHO EVENT 2015
FOUR DOCTORS

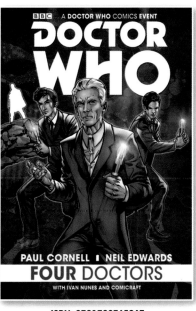

ISBN: 9781782765967
ON SALE NOW - $19.99 / $25.99 CAN / £10.99
(UK EDITION ISBN: 9781785851063)

AVAILABLE FROM ALL GOOD COMIC STORES,
BOOK STORES, AND DIGITAL PROVIDERS!

BIOGRAPHIES

Robbie Morrison is a Scottish comics writer living in England, who has written popular titles such as *Drowntown*, *Spider-Man*, and *The Authority*. He is perhaps best known for his work at 2000 AD, where he co-created the Eagle Award-winning series *Nikolai Dante*, with artist Simon Fraser, and *Shimura*, with Frank Quitely, along with stints on *Judge Dredd*.

George Mann is an author and editor, primarily of science-fiction. He has written several *Doctor Who* novels, comics and audiobooks, as well as being the author of *Sherlock Holmes: The Will of the Dead*, and his own series, *Newbury and Hobbes*. He works and lives in Nottinghamshire, England.

Daniel Indro is a tremendous emerging talent. Best known for *The Tenth Doctor: The Weeping Angels of Mons* and several *Sherlock Holmes* comic series, he lives in Indonesia with his wife and two young daughters.

Ronilson Freire is an acclaimed artist, best known for his work on *Green Hornet*. He has also had his work published by many magazines in his native Brazil, as well as the famous *Heavy Metal*.

Slamet Mujiono specialises in digital coloring and has worked on titles such as *Robyn Hood*, *Red Sonja* and *Doctor Who*. He lives in Indonesia with his family.

Mariano Laclaustra is a fast-rising talent with a background in the Fine Arts. A freelance artist based in Argentina, he has worked with publishers across Europe and the United States, including for *Dark Horse Presents*. In between drawing and coloring comics, he teaches oil painting.

Luis Guerrero is a Mexican artist and colorist. He has produced work for *Rivers of London*, *Man Plus* and *The Troop*.

POLICE PUBLIC CALL BOX
POLICE PUBLIC CALL BOX

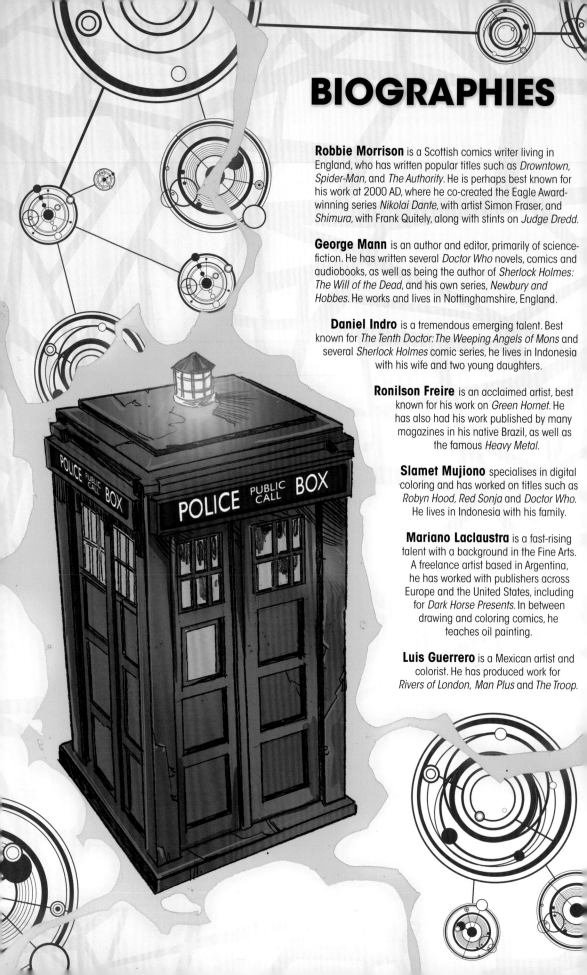